THE PHILOSOPHY
OF PLOTINUS

THE GIFFORD LECTURES AT ST. ANDREWS, 1917-1918

BY

WILLIAM RALPH INGE, K.C.V.O., D.D.

IN TWO VOLUMES

VOL. II

GREENWOOD PRESS, PUBLISHERS
NEW YORK   1968

Originally printed in 1929 by,
and reprinted with the permission of
Longmans, Green and Co. Ltd.

First Greenwood reprinting, 1968

LIBRARY OF CONGRESS catalogue card number: 68-8740

PRINTED IN THE UNITED STATES OF AMERICA

Thou art the unanswered question ;
    Couldst see thy proper eye,
Alway it asketh, asketh,
    And each answer is a lie.
So take thy quest through nature ;
    It through thousand natures ply ;
Ask on, thou clothed eternity ;
    Time is the false reply.
                        EMERSON.

To vision profounder
    Man's spirit must dive ;
His aye rolling orb
    At no goal will arrive ;
The heavens that now draw him
    With sweetness untold
Once found, for new heavens
    He spurneth the old.
                        EMERSON.

SYLLABUS OF LECTURES

LECTURES XII, XIII

THE IMMORTALITY OF THE SOUL

The philosophical and religious belief in immortality came to the Greeks from the mystical tradition associated with the worship of Dionysus. These orgiastic cults produced flashes of intuition that man is immortal. But the belief was slow in taking root, as the literature shows. Pythagoreanism, an intellectualised Orphism, taught the immortality of the Soul, its migration to other bodies, and the doctrine of cosmic cycles. Plato argues in favour of immortality, but we cannot find any fixed and definite views on the subject in his writings. Aristotle seems to have disbelieved in what we should call personal immortality. The eschatology of the Stoics was vague and uncertain ; the Epicureans denied a future life altogether. Plutarch is a believer, and narrates visions of judgment not unlike those of Dante.

Christian eschatology was by no means consistent in the second and third centuries. Tertullian is strangely materialistic : his real belief seems to have been that the soul dies with the body, to be raised again at the last day by a miracle. Widely different views were held about the intermediate state. Clement and Origen accept, with some reservations, the Greek conception of immortality ; the resurrection of the body, though not denied, is tacitly shelved. Origen is notable as teaching a succession of world-orders, with sustained upward progress.

For Plotinus, the Soul neither comes into existence nor perishes ; it is the indestructible principle of life. He has no room for bodily resurrection ; and rejects the popular notion of spiritual bodies in a semi-gaseous condition. The distinctions of individuals are not lost in the eternal world ; but Spirits are completely transparent to one another ; all that separates us here will have disappeared. Souls which have lived unrighteously are reincarnated in bodies of a lower order, and are sometimes chastised by their dæmon or guardian angel. But only the lower soul can thus fall ; the higher part is sinless.

The problem is how to maintain the true view of eternity, as supratemporal existence, without either sundering the eternal and temporal from each other, or reducing the world of time to a vain shadow. We know under the form of eternity whatever we know as sharing in Goodness, Truth, and Beauty. Eternity is the kingdom of Divine Ideas or absolute values.

The doctrine of reincarnation offers us chains of personalities linked together by impersonal transitions. Nothing survives except the bare being of the Soul, and its liabilities. The doctrine has found strong support in modern times, e.g. in Krause, Swedenborg, Lavater, Ibsen, Maeterlinck, McTaggart, Hume, Goethe, and Lessing speak of it with respect.

LECTURES XIV–XVI

THE SPIRITUAL WORLD

'Spirit' is the best word for Nous. Reality consists in the Trinity in Unity of *Nous, Noēsis,* and *Noēta,* in which the whole nature of the Absolute is manifested. Spirit and the spiritual world involve each other and cannot be separated. Plotinus is not an idealist or mentalist, in the modern sense.

The doctrine of Ideas in Plato and Plotinus. The view of Plotinus is that so far as every thought in Spirit is also an eternal form of being, all the thoughts of Spirit are Ideas. Each Idea is Spirit, and Spirit is the totality of the Ideas. The kingdom of the Ideas is the true reality.

The categories of the Spiritual World. The category of Being is unsatisfactory ; Thought and its Object are not a pair of the same kind as Identity and Difference, Change and Permanence. The whole theory of categories is open to criticism. Proclus supports my contention that Plotinus would have done better to discard the Platonic and Aristotelian lists, and to make Goodness, Truth, and Beauty the attributes of Spirit and its world. It would then be clear that the Spiritual World is a Kingdom of Values, Values of truly existing Reality. Goodness, Truth, and Beauty are in our experience ultimates. They cannot be fused, or wholly harmonised, but they have the characteristic of mutual inclusion which belongs to the Spiritual World.

The individual Spirit is the same life as the individual Soul, only raised above itself and transfigured into the Divine image. Blessed Spirits are fully known to each other ; in heaven the whole is in every part. And they enjoy unbroken communion with the Great Spirit, who is really the God of the Neoplatonic religion. Individuality is not lost, but there is distinction without separation.

Eternal life is not 'the future life.' The Platonic doctrine of immortality is very different from the wish for survival in time. The kind of immortality which physical research endeavours to establish would be the negation of the only immortality which the Platonist desires or believes in.

Eternity is an experience and a conception partly latent and partly patent in all human life. It is life amid truths which are neither born nor die. The Christian schoolmen intercalated *aevum* between time and eternity. 'Spiritual creatures, as regards their affections and intellections, are measured by time ; as regards their natural being, by *aevum ;* as regards their vision of glory, they participate in eternity' (Aquinas). *Aevum* seems to be perpetual duration, and as such a symbol or sacrament of eternity. We cannot dispense with modes of envisaging eternity which depend on spatial and temporal imagery ; but popular religion has impoverished the idea of eternal life by insisting on its pictures of a material fairyland.

LECTURES XVII–XIX

THE ABSOLUTE

The paths of Goodness, Truth, and Beauty all lead up the hill of the Lord. Plotinus shows us all three.

Dialectic is the study of first principles, which leads to intuitive wisdom. It shows us that the common source of Goodness, Truth, and Beauty must be beyond existence and beyond knowledge. The duality in unity of Spirit and the Spiritual World points to an absolute unity behind them. This unity is beyond knowledge and existence, and is revealed only in the mystical experience. In considering this train of reasoning, we must remember that (1) the nature of the Godhead is certainly unknown to us ; (2) we are not cut off from the highest form of life ; (3) we have in the mystical state an experience of formless intuition. The doctrine goes back to a famous passage in the *Republic* and has had a long history. Augustine says that God is *essentia*, not *substantia*. Dionysius describes God the Father as ' super-essential indetermination ' ; and Erigena is not afraid to say, ' Deus per excellentiam non immerito Nihilum vocatur.' For Plotinus, the One is ' beyond οὐσία and beyond Spirit.' It is what it willed to be, but it wills nothing not yet present. It is all necessity, and the giver of freedom. It does not think, but abides in ' a state of wakefulness beyond Being.' It is infinite, in the sense that its centre is every-where, its circumference nowhere. It is the First Cause and Final Cause of all. Plotinus does not profess to explain how plurality can emanate from unity : the problem is equally insoluble for natural science. His hypothesis is that of Creation. ' The One could not be alone.' It creates a ' second nature,' without passing out of itself in doing so. The activity of the Absolute is one-sided. The manner of creation is incomprehensible by us, because it can never fall within our experience; the path back to the One can be trodden in experi-ence. The Plotinian Absolute is different from the Hegelian, in that for Plotinus the world is not an essential factor in the Being of the Absolute. We cannot deny the possibility of this one-sided creative activity without surrendering the transcendence of God, an essential doctrine of theism.

'Plotinus does not call the One the Beautiful ; but he really puts Goodness, Truth, and Beauty on the same level. ' The One is the beginning and end of Beauty.' ' The First Beautiful, and Beauty, are formless.'

' The Good ' means the Perfect. The Good makes things what they are ' good for,' and we must not take this in a narrowly ethical sense. The Good is unity as the goal of desire. The longing for self-completion and self-transcendence is universal ; our whole life is a striving towards its proper goal. ' Virtue is not the Good, but a good.' All things aspire to the Good. The ' Spirit in love ' yearns for the source of all perfection.

The character of the Plotinian mysticism is best illustrated by his own descriptions. They are based on personal experience, and closely resemble the visions of God described by other mystics. The ' method of abstraction,' or *via negativa*, which is often blamed as a progressive emptying of the personality, ending in a blank trance, is really only intense concentration on what are believed to be the essentials of the quest. Plotinus never despises the rich world of concrete experience, still less the fullness of life in the Kingdom of the eternal Ideas. Nor is there (as some have alleged) any contradiction between his philosophy and his personal religion.

In some particulars the mysticism of Plotinus differs from the prevailing type in Catholic Christianity. (1) There is no occultism or thaumaturgy in it, and no lore of Divine favours and supernatural visitations. There are no ' bodily showings ' and no revelations imparted during ecstasy. (2) There is in Plotinus no trace of the experience of dereliction, ' the dark night of the Soul.' The absence of this experience characterises philosophical as opposed to emotional mysticism ; but it is also connected with the comparatively slight consciousness of sin and alienation from God in the Neoplatonists. (3) The ecstatic state is for the Neoplatonist a very rare experience, and is reserved for those who have climbed the heights of Divine wisdom. The mystics of the cloister, on the other hand, found it by no means uncommon, and tended to regard it as an encouragement often vouchsafed to beginners. Here much must be attributed to expectation and tradition, and something to the greater strain of monastic discipline. The mystical state always follows intense mental concentration, and is not confined to religious contemplation. Poets and musicians have described similar experiences.

The importance of ecstasy in Neoplatonism has often been much exaggerated, as has that of *Nirvana* in Buddhism. The mystic does not crave for absorption or annihilation, but for deliverance from the fetters of *separate* existence : he longs to know that there is ' nothing between ' himself and God. There is and must be an element of illusion in the vision ; the mind which thinks that it contemplates the One really visualises symbols of the unlimited. But the *idea* of the One is capable of inspiring love and devotion for the source of all goodness, truth, and beauty.

The object of this love is never personalised, as in Christianity. But the Christian mystic also transmutes the objects of his veneration into Ideas, and knows them, and his fellows, ' no more after the flesh.' *Conversio fit ad Dominum ut Spiritum.* Christian Platonism invests Christ with the attributes of the Neoplatonic.

LECTURES XX, XXI

ETHICS, RELIGION, AND ÆSTHETICS

The connexion of Ethics with Metaphysics became closer all through the course of Greek philosophy, and at its latest stage the fusion is almost complete. For Plotinus, the course of moral progress begins with the *political virtues*, which include all the duties of a good citizen ; but Plotinus shows no interest in the State as a moral entity. After the political virtues comes *purification*. The Soul is to put off its lower nature, and to cleanse itself from external stains : that which remains when this is done will be the image of Spirit. Neoplatonism enjoins an ascetic life, but no harsh self-mortification. The conflict with evil is a journey through darkness to light, rather than a struggle with hostile spiritual powers. Repentance is not emphasised. The desire to be invulnerable underlies all Greek philosophy, and in consequence the need of deep human sympathy is undervalued. The philosopher is not to be perturbed by public or private calamities. Purification leads to the next stage—*enlightenment.* Plotinus puts

the philosophic life above active philanthropy, though contemplation
for him is incomplete unless it issues in creative activity. ' We *are*
the activity of Spirit.' His disparagement of mere action which is not
based on spiritual enlightenment is quite defensible. Free will means
spiritual activity ; we are not free until our highest selves are liberated,
Freedom does not belong to our desires or passions, nor can we control
the general order of the world. But our true selves are not cogs in a
machine ; we are the machine itself and the mind which directs it.
' Exaggerated determinism ' destroys the idea of causation. Each
Soul is a little ' first cause,' and the Universal Soul is above the antithesis
of freedom and necessity. ' Necessity includes freedom.' The highest
stage—*unification*—hardly belongs to ethics ; but the noble doctrine
that ' there is progress even yonder,' depends on the doctrine of the
One. Love, the activity of the Soul desiring the Good, is never transcended. In spite of this, the moral isolation of the sage may be regarded
as a defect in Neoplatonic ethics.

The Religion of Plotinus is really independent of the Pagan Gods
and their cultus. He allegorises the myths in the most arbitrary
manner. But he believes in the *dæmons*, who rule the intermediate
sphere between earth and heaven. This was a current belief of the
time, which has no inner connexion with his philosophy. Similarly,
magic and sorcery, though he dislikes and minimises them, could not
be repudiated. Theurgy is no integral part of Neoplatonism ; but the
school fell into it later, and even helped to elevate superstition into a
dogma, Prayer, especially the ' prayer of quiet,' was the life of religion
for the Neoplatonist. ' All things pray except the One.' The main-
spring of religion is experimental ; faith begins as an experiment
and ends as an experience. God is at first an ideal, and at last an
atmosphere. Man may worship either the Universal Soul, or the
Great Spirit, or the ineffable One. The difference between Neoplatonism and Christianity has often been exaggerated. Augustine finds
all Christianity in the Platonists, except the Incarnation. His criticism
remains the most penetrating comparison of the two creeds. The
Incarnation and Passion of the Son of God, with the acceptance of
suffering for others which those doctrines imply, do not refute the
philosophy of Plotinus ; they complete it. But the attempt of some
Christian Platonists to equate the three Divine hypostases of Neoplatonism with the Trinity was not successful.

' The *Beautiful* ' includes, for Platonists, all that is worthy of love
and admiration. It is thus impossible to separate æsthetics from
ethics and religion. The beauty of the Soul is to be made like to
God. Plotinus makes an advance in æsthetic theory in refusing to
make symmetry the essence of the beautiful. The forms of beauty
are the mode in which the Universal Soul stamps the image of itself
on Matter. The Soul in contemplating beauty identifies itself with
the formative activity of its own higher principle. Art does not copy
nature ; it creates, like nature, after the model of the spiritual world.
His identification of ugliness with absence of form is less happy. Ugliness is false form. But Plotinus is again valuable when he finds in
art the recognition of hidden sympathies in nature, which enable us
to *translate* beauty into another medium. Most modern writers on
æsthetics are indebted to Plotinus.

LECTURE XXII

CONCLUDING REFLECTIONS

There are disquieting resemblances between the period which ushered in the downfall of ancient civilisation and the present world-calamity. But we must remember the Greek conviction that the nature of anything is its highest development, and find comfort in the spiritual heights often attained by individuals, which may be an earnest of the achievements of humanity in the far future. The educated classes must prepare to practise an austerity of life like that of the ancient philosophers in the grievous time that probably awaits them. The whole heritage of the past is at stake together ; we have a sacred tradition to preserve. Christianity, Platonism, and Civilisation must stand or fall together. Christianity and Platonism agree in maintaining that values are absolute and eternal, and that spiritual things must be spiritually discerned. The Platonist can reconcile this with reverence for reason and science. The too facile optimism of Plotinus in dealing with evil must be corrected by the Christian doctrine of vicarious suffering. In our day we have most need to remember that suffering is a warning symptom, not the disease itself. Our altruistic hedonism has thrown our whole view of life out of perspective. We need to examine the conditions of real happiness and unhappiness, which have very little to do with external goods. Our false view of life presents civilisation to us in such an ugly aspect that we dare not face the facts or obey the laws of science, but fly to sentimentalism, ultimately the most cruel of all moods. We can help our fellows best by purging our own spiritual vision The problems of civil government seem to be at present insoluble. The only deliverance is to correct our standard of values, and to set our hearts on the ' indivisible goods ' which are not lost by being shared. To preach this is the duty of religion and philosophy, and not to be the jackal of any political party. The Neoplatonic mystic must be prepared to outgrow many early enthusiasms, and to break every mould in which his thought threatens to crystallise. The danger of arrested development is always present. Life is a *schola animarum ;* and we must be learners to the end.

THE PHILOSOPHY OF PLOTINUS

LECTURES XII, XIII

IMMORTALITY OF THE SOUL [1]

THE Greeks, like the Jews, soon outgrew the barbarous notions about survival which are almost
universal among savages. Both peoples, and especially
the Jews, for a long period attached very little importance to the life after death ; and when they came at last
to make the belief in immortality a part of their religion,
this belief was not even historically continuous with the
ideas of primitive soul-cultus, which had their centre in
the performance of pious duties to the departed spirit.
This belief in a shadowy survival could lead to no doctrine
of real immortality. The ruling idea in all Greek thought
about life and death was that deathlessness is a preroga-
tive of the gods. The gods, and the gods alone, are the
immortals. In the national Greek religion, before it was
influenced by the beliefs of other nations, there was no
tendency to break down the barrier between the human
nature and the Divine. Greek ethics were largely based on
the maxim that man must know his place. There had no
doubt been instances, so it was believed, when the souls

[1] The great importance of this subject has seemed to me to justify
a more lengthy excursus, or introduction, dealing with the growth and
varieties of the belief among Greek thinkers, than a strict attention
to proportion would have allowed.

of heroes had been admitted into the company of the gods and allowed to share their immortality ; but these were exceptional and miraculous favours, which in no way affected the doom of ordinary men. The popular belief was that after death we have nothing to look forward to except the unsubstantial and unenviable condition of ghosts, ' phantoms of mortal men outworn ' (βροτῶν εἴδωλα καμόντων).

The philosophical and religious belief in immortality came to the Greeks not from the Olympian religion, but from the mystical religion associated with the worship of Dionysus. It was perhaps the fundamental sanity and self-restraint of the Greek genius which led them to view with superstitious awe and amazement the manifestations of religious excitement with which they came in contact among other peoples. Even more than other nations, they were disposed to attribute the wild ebullitions of Oriental and semi-barbarous tribes to a ' Divine madness ' (θεία μανία) or ' possession by a god ' (ἐνθουσιασμός). It was especially Dionysus, the Thracian god, who ' makes men mad.'[1] He was probably the god of religious ecstasy—of dancing dervishes—before he became the god of wine, which produces similar effects. For our present purpose the important thing to note is that religious excitement produced an inner conviction or experience of the Divine origin and destiny of the human soul. The author of the *Contemplative Life*, in a remarkable sentence, says that ' the bacchanals and corybants continue their raptures *until they see what they desire.*'[2] That ecstasy is a form of madness was fully admitted. Galen defines it as ' brief madness,' as madness is ' chronic

---

[1] ὃς μαίνεσθαι ἐνάγει ἀνθρώπους, Herodotus, 4. 79. But even Homer knew of ' Maenads ' : μεγάροιο διέσσυτο μαινάδι ἴση, παλλομένη κραδίην. The deep impression which this orgiastic worship made on the Greek mind is apparent throughout the literature.
[2] *De Vit. Cont.* 2, p. 473, οἱ βακχευόμενοι καὶ κορυβαντιῶντες ἐνθουσιάζουσι μέχρις ἂν τὸ ποθούμενον ἴδωσιν. If this work, which was issued under the name of Philo, is a third-century forgery, as Lucius and others have argued, its value as evidence is not great ; but the words quoted are true of the genesis of orgiastic attempts to induce th mystical state at all times. Conybeare in 1895 argued that the traditional attribution to Philo should be upheld.

ecstasy.' But this did not prevent the belief that a man who was temporarily 'out of his mind' might be the organ of some higher intelligence, and that in particular the gift of prophecy is thus imparted. Thus ecstasy helped to break down the barrier between men and gods, and orgiastic worship gave an empirical support to the philosophic mysticism which taught that there is no impassable cleft between the human and the Divine Spirit. The weakening of the idea of personality which followed from its apparent diremption in ecstasy promoted the belief in reincarnation and the transmigration of souls, which Euripides connects with Thrace and Dionysus.[1] On the whole, we may say that the chief attraction of this worship was that it led up to flashes of intuition that man is immortal, like the gods. *Sentimus et experimur nos aeternos esse*, as Spinoza says. The Greeks attributed the warlike courage of the Thracians to the teaching of their religion, that death is a transition to a happier state.

It cannot be said that this mystical faith in human immortality has left many traces on Greek literature. Pindar, whose poetry as a whole does not suggest deep spirituality, professes to believe in it, and Euripides has a more genuine sympathy with Orphic ideas. The Greek mind remained, throughout its great flowering-time, positivist and humanistic. Even in Plato's *Republic* Glaucon, who is an ordinary young Athenian, answers the question, ' Have you not heard that our soul is immortal ? ' ' No, really I have not.'[2]

Of the philosophers, Thales is vaguely reported to have taught that souls are immortal.[3] But neither he nor his immediate successors can be supposed to have believed in the immortality of particular souls as such. This doctrine belongs to the Orphic tradition.[4] In Heracleitus

---

[1] Euripides, *Hecuba*, 1243.
[2] Plato, *Republic*, 608. Livingstone, *The Greek Genius*, p. 201.
[3] Diogenes Laertius, I. 24. Rohde, *Psyche*, Vol. 2, p. 144.
[4] Cornford, p. 179, emphasises the difference here between the ' Dionysiac ' and the ' Orphic ' view of immortality.

and Parmenides we find the two doctrines of immortality
which are implicit in mysticism, separated out for the first
time. Heracleitus is the champion of the Dionysiac view
that life and death follow each other in an unending
cycle ; Parmenides, under Orphic influence, teaches that
the Soul has fallen from the realm of light and reality to
the dark and unreal world of bodily existence. This,
however, is for Parmenides only ' the way of opinion ' ;
he feels, it would seem, that the substantiality of the
world of common experience is not so easily got rid of.
But he will not give up the unchanging stability of
eternal substance. The most interesting fragment of
Parmenides is that in which he seems to enunciate, for
the first time in Greek thought, the mystical doctrine of
eternity as a timeless Now, as opposed to the popular
notion of unending succession. ' There remains then
only to give an account of one way—that real Being
exists. Many signs there are upon it, showing that it is
unborn, indestructible, entire, unique,[1] unshakable, and
unending. It never was, and it never will be, since it is
all together present in the Now, one and indivisible.'[2]
Empedocles vehemently repudiates the philosophy of
Parmenides, probably on the ground that he reduces
the world of time and change to nullity, and thus leaves
no pathway from appearance to reality. His doctrine
of the soul's exile and wanderings is expounded in a
famous fragment. ' There is a decree of Necessity, an
old ordinance of the gods, everlasting, sealed with broad
oaths, that whenever one of the dæmons, whose portion
is length of days, has sinfully stained his hands with
murder, or followed strife and committed perjury, he

---

[1] οὖλον, μουνογενές. Burnet says that μουνογενές is an anachronism,
and comes from the *Timaeus*. He proposes μοῦνόν τ' οὐλομενές ' alone,
complete.' *Early Greek Philosophy*, p. 185.

[2] μοῦνος δ' ἔτι μῦθος ὁδοῖο
λείπεται, ὡς ἔστιν· ταύτῃ δ' ἔπι σήματ' ἔασι
πολλὰ μάλ', ὡς ἀγένητον ἐὸν καὶ ἀνώλεθρόν ἐστιν
οὖλον μουνογενές τε καὶ ἀτρεμὲς ἠδ' ἀτέλεστον.
οὐδέποτ' ἦν οὐδ' ἔσται, ἐπεὶ νῦν ἔστιν ὁμοῦ πᾶν,
ἕν, συνεχές.

must wander away from the blessed gods for thirty thousand seasons, being born throughout that time in all manner of mortal forms, passing from one to another of the painful paths of life. For the power of the upper air drives him toward the sea, and the sea spews him out upon dry land ; earth throws him into the rays of the burning sun, and the sun into the eddies of the air. One receives him from another, and all loathe him. Of these I myself am now one, an exile from God and a wanderer, because I put my trust in raging strife.'[1] This is the pure Orphic doctrine, which Pindar also gives us in the second Olympian Ode. The Soul sins by separating itself from God, and after many adventures finds its way home again to Him. The fall from God is a fall from love and a choice of 'strife' in the place of harmony. The immortal Soul is said to consist of love and strife blended ; the body, with its senses, is only an 'alien garment,' and perishes at death. When Empedocles describes the Soul as a ratio, or harmony, he means that the complex of discordant factors ('strife') which it contains is bound together by the principle of unity ('love'). As regards Parmenides, it may be true that he rejects the Pythagorean doctrines which he describes, and finds truth in static materialism.

Mr. Cornford says very well that Orpheus, the ideal of the Orphic brotherhood, is 'a Dionysus tamed and clothed and in his right mind.' In the Orphic legend, it

---

[1] ἔστιν ἀνάγκης ῥῆμα, θεῶν ψήφισμα παλαιὸν,
ἀίδιον, πλατέεσσι κατεσφρηγισμένον ὅρκοις.
εὖτέ τις ἀμπλακίῃσι φόνῳ φίλα γυῖα μιήνῃ,
< νείκεΐ θ > ὅς κ' ἐπίορκον ἁμαρτήσας ἐπομόσσῃ,
δαίμονες οἵτε μακραίωνος λελάχασι βίοιο,
τρίς μιν μυρίας ὥρας ἀπὸ μακάρων ἀλάλησθαι,
φυομένους παντοῖα διὰ χρόνου εἴδεα θνητῶν,
ἀργαλέας βιότοιο μεταλλάσσοντα κελεύθους,
αἰθέριον μὲν γάρ σφε μένος πόντονδε διώκει,
πόντος δ' ἐς χθονὸς οὖδας ἀπέπτυσε, γαῖα δ' ἐς αὐγὰς
ἠελίου φαέθοντος, ὁ δ' αἰθέρος ἔμβαλε δίναις,
ἄλλος δ' ἐξ ἄλλου δέχεται, στυγέουσι δέ πάντες.
τῶν καὶ ἐγὼ νῦν εἰμι, φυγὰς θεόθεν καὶ ἀλήτης,
νείκεΐ μαινομένῳ πίσυνος.

[1] In the first line I adopt the emendation of Bernays ῥῆμα for χρῆμα.

was the Maenads who tore Orpheus, the friend of the Muses, to pieces. The Greek spirit could not be content with orgiastic mysticism ; the affinity between human and divine must be realised in a calmer temper, and must be made the basis not only of a cult, but of a philosophy. But the Pythagorean philosophy, like most philosophies which are also religions, attempted to combine logically incompatible ideas. Pythagoreanism is an intellectualised Orphism, in which such questions as the following press for an answer. Is the descent of the Soul part of a cosmic pulsation, a circulation of the life-blood of the spiritual world, as Heracleitus taught, or is it a thing which ought not to have occurred, and which must be remedied by the discipline which leads to deliverance ? Is the Soul a part of nature, or is it radically alien from nature, so that we must live our lives here as prisoners in a hostile country, or at best as pilgrims escaping from the city of destruction to the far-off city of God ? Is the individual Soul a mere mode of a universal life, or is it an eternal and indestructible substance ? And is the Universal Soul a group-soul, of which individual Souls are integral parts, or is it a transcendent substance, from which individual Souls are derived, but from which they remain essentially distinct ? How Pythagoras himself was thought to have combined some of the earlier answers to these questions is best shown by the summary of his doctrines preserved by Dicæarchus. He taught ' first, that Soul is immortal, then, that it is transformed into other kinds of living beings ; further, that whatever comes into existence is born again in the revolutions of a certain cycle, and that nothing is absolutely new, and that all living things should be treated as akin to each other.'[1] But the emphasis is laid on the fortunes of the individual Soul and its purification or deliverance by suffering, both here and hereafter. The Pythagoreans are in Europe the inventors of purgatory. Pythagoreanism was a mystical philosophy of immortality by death unto

[1] Dicæarchus in Porphyry's *Life of Pythagoras*, 18, 19.

sin and new birth unto righteousness.[1] An important question is whether the Pythagoreans conceived of heaven as a timeless state, as we have seen that Parmenides did. Baron von Hügel[2] has rightly insisted that 'all states of trance, or indeed of rapt attention, notoriously appear to the experiencing soul, in proportion to their concentration, as timeless; i.e. as non-successive, simultaneous, hence as eternal. And hence the eternity of the soul is not here a conclusion drawn from the apparent God-likeness, in other respects, of the soul when in this condition, but the eternity, on the contrary, is the very centre of the experience itself, and is the chief inducement to the soul for holding itself to be Divine. The soul's immortality cannot be experienced in advance of death, whilst its eternity, in the sense indicated, is or seems to be experienced in such this-life states; hence the belief in immortality is here derivative, that in eternity is primary.' But though the Orphic-Pythagorean aspiration to escape from the 'weary wheel' of rebirths seems to resemble the Buddhist longing for the timelessness of Nirvana, it is certain that the Pythagoreans did not envisage the future life as unconscious. In the Orphic Tablets, the Soul, when it arrives in the other world, is forbidden to approach a certain spring, which must be the water of Lethe, and is bidden to draw near another, 'by the lake of Memory.' The beatified Soul, then, remembers its past. Here the influence of popular religion may be traced. The question as to the timelessness of the Pythagorean heaven does not admit of an answer, any more than the same question about the Christian heaven. All religious eschatology is a mass of contradictions.

Although Plato has always and justly been regarded as the great champion of human immortality, it is impossible to find any fixed and definite conviction on the subject in his writings. His views of immortality, or at

---

[1] Plato, *Phaedo*, 64, οὐδὲν ἄλλο ἐπιτηδεύουσιν ἢ ἀποθνήσκειν τε καὶ τεθνάναι.

[2] *Eternal Life*, p. 27.

any rate of the arguments by which it may be established, passed through several phases. In the *Phaedo*, the whole argument is that the theory of Ideas and the doctrine of the immortality or divinity of the Soul stand or fall together.[1] This position is rather startlingly different from the agnosticism of the *Apology*, in which Socrates says that no one knows what happens after death, but there is a considerable hope that the good man may find himself in more congenial company than he has met with on earth. It may be that if the speech was actually delivered by Socrates it does not contain those deeper convictions which he reserved for his friends. There is a hint at the beginning of the *Phaedo* that Socrates has ' more convincing arguments ' than those which he used when addressing his judges ; and it is likely enough that he would not make confession of his mystical faith to a mixed and mainly hostile audience. In the *Meno*, an early dialogue, immortality is treated as a beautiful tale of priests and poets ; but he also says that if the truth of real being (τὰ ὄντα) is in the Soul, it must be immortal. In the *Phaedo* the first argument calls in the doctrine of reminiscence, which is used to establish pre-existence. It is inferred that the Soul remains unchanged through successive incarnations. But this is only an indication of survival for a time, not a proof of immortality. Then, finding his hearers not satisfied, the Platonic Socrates argues that the *idea* of Soul is the idea of an entity unchangeable and imperishable. Or, assuming the doctrine of Ideas, we may argue that since the Ideas are simple and indiscerptible, the Soul which knows them must be so too. Lastly, after disposing of the notion that the Soul is a harmony of the body, he argues that the Soul is the idea of life, and is therefore alien to death. This seems to be a fallacy ;[2] the proper inference would only be that the Soul, as far as it exists, is alive and not dead.

---

[1] Plato, *Phaedo*, 76, ἴση ἀνάγκη ταῦτά (sc. τὰ εἴδη) τε εἶναι καὶ τὰς ἡμετέρας ψυχὰς πρὶν καὶ ἡμᾶς γεγονέναι, καὶ εἰ μὴ ταῦτα οὐδὲ τάδε.

[2] It is the familiar fallacy of the old ' ontological proof.'

The argument ends with the well-known ' myth ' about the condition of Souls hereafter, of which Socrates feels sure that ' something like it must be true.'

In the *Republic* and *Phaedrus* he argues no longer that the Soul is immortal because it partakes in the idea of life, but that it has life, indestructible life, in its own right. ' It is not difficult,' he says in the *Republic*,[1] ' to prove immortality, because Soul is substance, and substance is indestructible. Nothing can be destroyed except by that which corrupts its own nature ; and Soul, which cannot be destroyed even by its own evil—injustice or ignorance (' a murderer is very much alive and wide awake ') can still less be destroyed by any physical agency. This argument, he adds, applies to the Soul as it really is, not to the Soul contaminated by its association with flesh ; this latter is like the sea-god Glaucus, who is so encrusted with limpets and sea-weed that he is hardly recognisable. In the *Phaedrus* he argues that the cause of life is a self-moving principle, which cannot perish. Every self-moving principle is Soul. By ' movement ' he means any form of activity. ' Soul ' is the self-determining principle in nature ; and that which is self-determined can be affected by external things only indirectly, through its own will. If it is in a fallen state here, that must be because it has chosen to make for itself an unworthy environment, suited to its own disposition. ' God is not in fault ; the fault is in the chooser.' ' It is impossible to believe that the union of the immortal Soul with the corruptible body,' which only takes place because the Soul has lost its wings, ' is immortal.' If Plato had stopped here, his position would have been not unlike that of some modern philosophers, who hold that the world of reality is constituted by a plurality of independent spirits, each existing in its own right, very much as he at one time thought of the Ideas as distinct and independent spiritual entities. In fact, the Ideas and the Souls would then threaten to coalesce. But this

---

[1] Plato, *Republic*, pp. 608–611.

kind of pluralism could never satisfy Plato or any other
Greek thinker. The Ideas are not the Souls of individuals,
but half-hypostatised Divine attributes, in which individual Souls 'participate,' a word which signifies a
spiritual and non-quantitative relation. Moreover, the
Ideas, as Plato came to see, are not independent of each
other. They are brought together by their common condition of dependence upon 'the Idea of the Good.' Just
so individual Souls derive their being from their Creator,
God. Thus a new argument for immortality appears in
the *Timaeus*. The higher part of Souls, at any rate, is
the direct work of the Divine intelligence which created
them. God cannot wish to destroy His own work, and
nothing else can destroy it. Individual Souls, then, are
not immortal in their own right. They are immortal
because they are made by God in His own image. And
it is only the higher part of the Soul of which this can be
said. We are therefore left in some doubt how much of
what we consider our Souls is really immortal. There
is no abstract ego about which the blunt question 'to
be or not to be' can be asked.

Aristotle's doctrine of immortality depends on his
characteristic view of activity (ἐνέργεια). Instead of the
conception of substance as the unchanging substratum
of change, he holds that perfect activity transcends change
and motion. Activity is the actual functioning of a substance, the nature of which is only so revealed. So far
from activity being a kind of movement (κίνησις), he
says that movement is imperfect activity.[1] Activity
does not necessarily imply motion or change ; in the
frictionless activity of God, which constitutes his happiness, there is neither. 'Change is sweet to us because
of a certain defect.' The happiness of God is derived
from an activity which transcends movement. For Time
is the creature of movement ; it is the 'number of movement' (κινήσεως ἀριθμός). The perfecting of the time-
consciousness carries us into eternity, where there is no

----

[1] Cf. Plotinus, 2. 5. 3.

time and no movement. ' God is an eternal perfect
Being, so that life, and continuous and eternal duration,
belong to God, for God is all this.'[1] As regards the
immortality of the individual, Aristotle has always
been considered to give very dubious support to the
hopes of mankind. In fact his treatment of the subject
in the *De Anima* makes it fairly clear that it is only
(what we should call) the 'impersonal' Nous which is
immortal.

The eschatology of the Stoics is vague and uncertain.
In a sense, the Soul must be immortal, because nothing
ever really perishes. Forms change, but the substance
persists. The destiny of the Soul, as of everything else,
is to be reabsorbed into the primal essence, which the
Stoics, following Heracleitus, identified with, or sym-
bolised by, fire. But they were not agreed whether this
absorption takes place immediately after death ; nor
whether the individual continues to keep his individuality
till the great conflagration ; nor whether he falls by
degrees into the Divine essence, through a course of
gradual purification.[2] Marcus Aurelius is quite agnostic
on the subject. ' Thou hast embarked ; thou hast made
thy voyage ; thou hast come to port ; leave the ship.
If there is another life, there are gods there, as here. If
thou passest to a state without sensation, thou wilt
be delivered from the bonds of pleasure and pain.'[3]
Further, Cleanthes held that the Souls of all men live
on till the conflagration, Chrysippus that only the Souls
of the wise live after death. In a new cycle, they taught,
Souls return to earth, and the successive lives of Socrates
the First and Socrates the Second will resemble each
other, though (in opposition to Plato) there is no reminiscence of former lives. But in some of the later Stoics,[4]
when the prejudice against Platonism had disappeared,

[1] Aristotle, *Metaphysics*, 11. 1072.
[2] Davidson, *The Stoic Creed*, p. 96.
[3] Marcus Aurelius, 3. 3.
[4] Panaetius, an eclectic and independent thinker, stands apart as
a declared disbeliever in individual immortality.

a real belief in personal immortality was not discouraged. Seneca believes in a heaven very like that of the Christian religion. He is able to say of death, ' That day which you dread as your last is your birthday into eternity.' [1] Seneca is known to have been influenced by Pythagorean doctrine; [2] but he is on Stoical ground when he adduces ' common consent ' as an argument for immortality.

The Epicureans, as is well known, denied a future life altogether ; but the influence of this school was declining in the generations before ˙ Plotinus. Educated men probably in most cases believed vaguely in some sort of survival, and sometimes filled in their pictures of a future life with such a jumble of eschatologies as is found in the sixth Æneid of Virgil, which doubtless affected Roman beliefs as much as *Paradise Lost* has affected those of Englishmen. The common people, and religiously-minded conservatives, continued to pay respect to the *Manes* of the dead, and believed that their spirits haunt the neighbourhood of their tombs. Etruria had contributed a less pleasant kind of spiritualism, that which maintained the old festival of the maleficent Lemures in May.[3] Belief in survival was supported by numerous ghost-stories of the familiar type, such as are ridiculed by Lucian in his *Philopseudes*. In this dialogue all the chief philosophical schools, except the Epicureans, are represented as joining in the tales of apparitions. The younger Pliny believes in haunted houses. For the age of the Antonines Galen is as good a witness as any. He believes firmly in Providence, but sees difficulties in all the theories of a future life.

The Platonists of this period, with Plutarch and Maxi-

---

[1] Seneca, *Ep.* 102. ' Dies iste quem tamquam extremum reformidas aeterni natalis est.'

[2] Through his teacher Sotion, who induced him to be a vegetarian.

[3] Ovid thinks that the occurrence of this festival in May is the reason why marriages in that month are supposed to be unlucky. I found this precious superstition very rife in my fashionable West End parish, but those who held it had not read Ovid, and did not observe the Lemuralia.

mus at their head, were the great champions of immortality.[1] Plutarch bases his belief, as so many do in our day, mainly on the justice of God and the rationality of the world-order. He points out that even the most sombre beliefs about the torments of the damned are more welcome to the majority of mankind than the prospect of annihilation. The Epicureans deprive mankind of their highest hopes, while seeking to rescue them from their fears. In two of his works[2] Plutarch recounts myths like those of the *Phaedo* and *Republic*, visions of judgment which, he would have us believe, are probably not very far from the truth. But the two pictures of the world of spirits are not alike. In the first, Thespesius, a bad man, who had apparently been killed by an accident, revives on the third day, and tells his experiences. He has found an Inferno and a Purgatorio, and a third form of punishment, unknown to Dante, in which carnal souls are sent to inhabit the bodies of animals. The penalties are rather ingenious. The hypocrites are turned inside out ; the miser is plunged into a lake of boiling gold ; the soul of the cruel man is blood-red, that of the envious is blue. In the other myth, Timarchus descends into the cave of Trophonius and sees a revelation of the spirit-world. An unseen guide explains to him that it has four divisions. The highest sphere is that of the invisible One. Next comes the region of pure Spirit, ruled over by the sun. The moon is queen of the third kingdom, that of Soul. Below, on the other side of Styx, is the world of Matter. After death—'the first death'—the Soul wanders between the realms of the moon and earth. ' The second death ' finally liberates the Spirit from its association with this muddy vesture of decay. All Souls have a spark of the Divine nature in them, but in some it is clogged and swamped by the baser elements. Some Souls, when released from the body, fly straight upwards, others wander through the middle air, others fall back

[1] Dill, *Roman Society from Nero to Marcus Aurelius*, p. 520.
[2] Plutarch, *De Sera Numinis Vindicta* and *De Genio Socratis*.

again to earth. Even the dæmons may incur this last fate. These and similar myths express in poetical and imaginative form the kind of theodicy which the religious mind of the Greek was at this time prepared to accept. They have an obvious resemblance to some Christian pictures of judgment ; but it was not till theology came under the rigid discipline of the Roman Church that these visions of the invisible became authoritative maps of the undiscovered country and prophecies of future events.

Philo believes that 'immortal life will receive the pious dead, but eternal death the impious living.'[1] The Soul is in its nature immortal ; it cannot perish with the decaying body. But God, who 'renders everything by balance and weight,' ordains that every Soul shall reap what it has sown. The just punishment of sin is not physical torture, but the inward furies of passion and guiltiness. The true hell is the life of the wicked man. This doctrine was especially taught by the Epicureans, and is a commonplace in classical literature. But Philo holds that the punishment of living death—the state of uttermost grief, terror, and despair, is continued and increased after death. There are some for whom there is no forgiveness.[2] Philo says nothing of the resurrection of the body, nor of the last judgment, nor of the Messianic hopes of his people.

The discussion of the Christian doctrine or doctrines of immortality does not fall within the scope of this book. But the writings of the Alexandrian school of Christian theology throw a good deal of light on Neoplatonism, and they are perhaps especially useful in relation to the problems of human immortality. Clement and Origen represent not so much Christian tradition as the atmosphere of learned and educated thought at Alexandria in the half century before Plotinus migrated to Rome. They were loyal and, in intention at least, orthodox

---

[1] Philo, *Post. Cain.* 11.
[2] See references in Drummond, *Philo Judaeus*, Vol. 2, 322–324.

Christians; but there was at Alexandria none of that antipathy to secular culture which at other times and places has erected a barrier between sacred and profane studies. Origen in particular is a valuable help towards the understanding of Plotinus, both when they agree and when they differ.

The future life had from the first a far greater importance in Christian teaching than it has in Philo or any other Jewish writer. The destruction of the world by fire, the resurrection of the dead with their bodies, the great assize, the eternal reward of the good and the eternal punishment of the bad, were in the first age of the Church dogmas accepted without being subjected to philosophical analysis. While the Messianic hope lasted, the 'end of the age' seemed so near that small interest was taken in the questions whether the Soul is essentially immortal, and what will be its condition between the day of death and the general resurrection. It was only when educated Gentiles, and Jews of the Dispersion, who had never been ardent Messianists, became interested in Christianity, that the philosophical doctrine of the immortality of the Soul had to be set by the side of the religious prophecy of the resurrection of the body.

Christian teaching was unanimous in insisting that in some way or other the whole man, and not merely his ghost, is immortal. The doctrine of St. Paul had been that though flesh and blood cannot inherit the kingdom of God, a 'spiritual body,' on the nature of which he does not speculate, is prepared for everyone, or for all the redeemed. The bodies of those who happen to be alive at the end of the existing order will be 'changed' into this spiritual essence. Great confusion prevailed in the early church on the whole subject. Some Christian thinkers were strangely and frankly materialistic. Tertullian says that the Soul is 'nothing if it is not body.'[1] Souls are 'kept in the lower regions till the day of the Lord,' a vague phrase which is meant to cover his real

---

[1] Tertullian, *De Anima*, 7: ' nihil si non corpus.'

conviction that the Soul dies with the body, and that
both are raised again by miracle at the last day.[1]   This,
however, he could not openly admit ; and so he speaks
of the Soul as remaining in a deep slumber till the
day of judgment.   Justin condemns as unchristian the
doctrine that the Soul is taken to heaven at the death
of the body ; such a view does away with the necessity
of a resurrection.   Theophilus will not answer the question whether the Soul is mortal or immortal by nature ;
' it is naturally neither, but is capable of becoming either
one or the other.' [2]   A common view seems to have been
that Souls are by nature both material and mortal, but
that those who receive the Spirit ($\pi\nu\epsilon\hat{\upsilon}\mu a$) live for ever.
Athenagoras has the curious argument that it would be
unjust for the Soul alone to suffer for sins which the body
incited it to commit.   Theology was in an awkward
dilemma, especially about the ' intermediate state.'
Either the souls of the saints and martyrs have perished,
and must wait for their resuscitation till the last day,
which was receding into a very dim future, or the Soul
must be capable of living apart from the body, as a
superior and deathless principle subsisting in its own
right, which was precisely the point at issue between
Platonism and Christianity.

Such was the problem which the Christian school of
Alexandria endeavoured to solve.   With some reservations, they adopt the Greek conception of immortality,
as a natural endowment of the Soul.   The spirits in prison,
to whom Christ preached, could accept His message more
easily because they were delivered from the burden of the
flesh.   After death, souls are sent to purgatory, where
God, who hates no one and inflicts no vindictive punish-

[1] What other conclusion can we draw from such words as the
following : ' Mors, si non semel tota est, non est.   Si quid animae re-
manserit, vita est ; non vitae magis miscebitur mors quam diei nox.
. . . Anima indivisibilis, ut immortalis, etiam indivisibilem mortem
exigit credi, non quasi mortali, sed quasi indivisibili animae indivisibili-
ter accidentem.'   *De Anima*, 51.

[2] Theophilus, *Ad Ant.* 2. 24.

ments, chastises them till they repent. The Logos is the Saviour of all. Our life in time is essentially an education, and our education does not cease when we die. It is continued till we are fit to enjoy the beatific vision. It would be possible to quote statements of Clement which do not agree with these views. He admits frankly that he does not write down all that he thinks ; there is an esoteric Christianity which is not for everybody. But it is plain that he leans towards the doctrines which Origen develops more boldly. The resurrection of the body is an otiose dogma in his creed. The body of Christ, all Christians were bound to believe, was resuscitated ; but the Alexandrians did not believe that His body was like ours.

Origen takes the step which to every Greek seemed the logical corollary of belief in immortality—he taught the pre-existence of Souls. The Soul is immaterial, and *therefore* has neither beginning of days nor end of life. Further, it must be immortal because it can think Divine thoughts and contemplate Divine truths ; its love of God and desire for Him are also signs that it belongs to the eternal world. So convincing is this Platonic faith to him, that he cannot restrain his impatience at the crude beliefs of traditionalists about the last day and the resurrection of the dead. The predictions in the Gospels cannot have been intended literally. How can material bodies be recompounded, every particle of which has passed into many other bodies ? To which body do these molecules belong ? So, he says scornfully, men fall into the lowest depths of absurdity, and take refuge in the pious assurance that ' everything is possible with God.'[1] We shall not need teeth to masticate food in the next world, and we need not suppose that God will provide the wicked with new teeth ' to gnash with.'[2] The Christian doctrines of the destruction of the world by fire and

---

[1] Origen, *in Psalmos*, 533, τίνος οὖν ἔσται σῶμα ἐν τῇ ἀναστάσει ; καὶ οὕτως εἰς βύθον φλυαρίας συμβήσεται ἐμπίπτειν, καὶ μετὰ ταύτας τὰς ἀπορίας ἐπὶ τὸ πάντα δυνατὰ εἶναι τῷ Θεῷ καταφεύγουσι.   [2] *Id.* p. 535.

of the resurrection of the dead are interpreted on the lines not of Platonism but of Stoicism. The Stoics taught that the end of a world-period is brought about by a conflagration (ἐκπύρωσις); and that creation and renovation are the work of the ' seminal Logoi.' These Stoical doctrines in truth are difficult to reconcile either with Platonism or Christianity ; but Origen had a difficult course to steer between the Gnostics, who thought that the Soul can exist without a body, and the simple believers—really the inheritors of the Jewish Messianic tradition—who hoped for such a resurrection as that which Ezekiel saw in the valley of dry bones, in preparation for a new life under quasi-terrestrial conditions. So he adopted the Stoic doctrine of the ' conflagration ' in a manner which we will consider presently, and maintained that in each body there is a ' seminal Logos,' a principle of individuation, which is sown in the earth like a seed, and finally produces another body true to type.[1] But this involves him in great difficulties. Samuel in the Old Testament appears to Saul in the form of an old man ; Moses and Elijah were seen at the Transfiguration in their former shapes. It is plain, then, that the Spirit is clothed with a spiritual body before the resurrection, and the general resurrection is tacitly abandoned. Moreover, though the seminal Logoi are ' forms,' the spiritual body which they create must be totally unlike the forms which we know here. If we were destined to live in the water, we should have to be changed into fish ; since we are to live in the spiritual world, we must have an ethereal body, without organs or limbs which will be useless in that state of existence. Lastly, what part of our personality is the ' seminal Logos ' ? It cannot be Spirit, and it cannot be Body. Is it then the Soul ? But if it is buried in the earth like a grain of wheat, we are

---

[1] Jerome, an unfair critic, no doubt, says that Origen taught ' corporales substantias penitus dilapsuras, aut certe in fine omnium hoc esse futura corpora quod nunc et aether et caelum et si quid aliud corpus sincerius et purius intelligi potest.'

driven back to Stoic materialism. The inherent contradictions of traditional eschatology have never been more forcibly exhibited, precisely because Origen was not the man to glide over difficulties.

As for the ' conflagration ' and the ' end of the age,' Origen, as is well known, follows the Stoics in teaching, quite contrary to the Christian tradition, that there will be a series of world-orders. But whereas Greek philosophy could admit no prospect except a perpetual repetition of the same alternate evolution and involution, a never-ending systole and diastole of the cosmic life, Origen holds that there is a constant upward progress. Each world-order is better than the last, and the whole process is working out a single design of the Creator. The conflagration is really a purifying fire ; though, Origen adds, it would not do to tell this to everybody, since the fear of endless perdition exercises a salutary restraint on many sinners. But the truth is, that as all Spirits were created blameless, all must at last return to their original perfection.[1] The education of Souls is continued in successive worlds.

A comparison of Origen and Plotinus, who resembled each other in their devotion to truth, and in lovableness and nobility of character, cannot fail to be instructive. In treating of the all-important subject with which we are now concerned, Origen is beset by difficulties from which Plotinus is free. He has not only to reconcile, if he can, the conflicting opinions of the great Greek philosophers ; he has to solve, if possible, the most formidable problem of Christian theology—how to make room for the Jewish philosophy of history by the side of the Platonic philosophy of eternal life. He falls into contradictions, as we have seen ; but it is while struggling with these that he strikes out the noble theory of

[1] Even if Origen was harassed into denying the logical consequence of his doctrine (Rufinus, *De Adulteratione Librorum Origenis*), that the devil himself will ultimately be saved, it is plain that no other conclusion can be drawn from his arguments. For Origen's defence against this charge see Denis, pp. 378–388.

a stairway of worlds, superimposed one on another not in space but in time, and leading up, by their ascending grades of perfection, to the consummation in which ' God shall be all in all.' The ascent of the Soul, which Plotinus describes as an inner process of the individual, is in Origen's philosophy writ large in the life-history of the universe itself. It is as if the Universal Soul of the Neoplatonic system were travelling, with all individual Souls, towards the heavenly city. For Plotinus, the Universal Soul can always pray and aspire, but it seems to have no history. Whether Origen's vision of cosmic progress is tenable scientifically is another question. In the history of philosophy his theory holds a place as an interesting attempt to give the world a real history, within the Divine scheme, without at the same time admitting progress or development in God Himself.

The main passage in which Plotinus deals with the immortality of the Soul is the seventh chapter of the Fourth Ennead. There are, he says, three possible answers to the question whether the Souls of individuals are immortal. Either the individual, as such, is immortal ; or he entirely perishes, or part of him perishes and another part lives for ever. Man is not a simple being, but is compounded of Body and Soul. That the body is dissoluble needs no proof. If then the body is an integral part of us, we cannot be entirely immortal. But it is a truer view that the relation of the Soul to the Body is like that of Form to Matter, or of an artificer to his instrument. The Soul is the man himself.

The Soul exists in its own right ; it neither comes into existence nor perishes. It is itself the principle of life, the ' one and simple activity in living,'[1] and as such it is indestructible. Can anyone doubt this, asks Plotinus, who considers the capacity of the Soul to behold and contemplate pure and eternal realities, to see even the world that is illuminated by Spirit, to mount up to God

---

[1] 4. 7. 9-12, ἀρχὴ κινήσεως, ζωὴν τῷ ἐμψύχῳ σώματι διδοῦσα—φύσις τις πάντως ζῶσα—μία καὶ ἁπλῆ ἐνέργεια ἐν τῷ ζῆν.

and gaze on His likeness within itself ? Purification and education bring us to the knowledge of the highest things ; and all these spiritual glories are beheld by Soul, not as things outside itself, but as things in which it shares, as its own inmost nature. The Soul has life and being in itself, and life can never die. Even the lower animals and plants, since they are sharers in Soul, must have an immortal principle in them.

The Soul, when separated from the body, no longer exercises its lower functions, which are not extinguished by death, but survive potentially only.[1] Such faculties as opinion, reasoning, and memory are not used in the spiritual world, not because they need bodily organs, but because they are superfluous under the conditions of eternal life. Disembodied Souls may still act on the world, benefiting mankind by revealing the future in oracles.[2]

As for the resurrection of the body, Greek thought would have been horrified at the idea that the Soul will be swathed to all eternity in what Empedocles called the 'alien garment of flesh.' Resurrection, says Plotinus explicitly, is an awakening from the body, not with the body.[3] Flesh and blood cannot inherit the Kingdom of God, neither can corruption inherit incorruption. But Plotinus does not need the hypothesis of an ethereal 'spiritual body.' He does not help out his notion of the spiritual world by peopling it with creatures in a semi-gaseous condition—an expedient which had been tried by many of the Stoics. His rejection of a bodily resurrection is a necessary consequence of the very doctrine on which he bases the immortality of the Soul. Nothing that has true being can ever perish,[4] nor can it ever come into existence. There are no new

---

[1] 6. 4. 16. Whittaker shows that there was some hesitation among the later Neoplatonists as to the survival of the 'irrational soul.'
[2] 4. 7. 15.   [3] 3. 6. 6.
[4] We may compare Browning's "All that is at all Lasts ever past recall"; and Goethe's "Kein Wesen kann zu nichts zerfallen, Das Ewge regt sich fort in allen."

Souls—all have existed from eternity. But there are new bodies ; therefore bodies have not true οὐσία, and bodies must die. The lower Soul, he says in one place,[1] when it has been illuminated by the higher, may accompany it after it leaves the body ; but the fate of the lower Soul depends on our manner of living.

It is not easy to answer the question how far individuality is maintained Yonder. For Plotinus unity is the source and highest character of true existence, separation the very sign of imperfection and defect of reality. Soul Yonder, he says explicitly, is undifferentiated and undivided.[2] Thus individuality in heaven is hardly a prize to be striven for. And yet Souls are Logoi of Spirits, and each represents a distinct entity in the spiritual world. This distinctness can never be destroyed. But the distinctions of Souls, though not lost, are latent in the world of Spirit.[3] Discarnate Souls are in a sense absorbed into the Universal Soul, and help it to govern the world.[4] Plotinus believes in and ·describes a blessed state in which the Souls of just men made perfect live in joy and felicity ; but the condition and crown of this felicity is precisely their liberation from all that here below shuts them off from the most complete communion with each other.

The question is not whether in a state of blessedness the circumference is indefinitely enlarged, but whether the centre remains. These centres are centres of consciousness ; and consciousness belongs to the world of will ; it comes into being for the purposes of will, when the will has to grapple with new conditions. It is not conterminous with life ; there is a life below consciousness, and there is a life above what we mean by consciousness. The metaphor of a centre of consciousness is purely spatial, and the idea of a continuing state

---

[1] 4.7.14. Contrast the medieval dictum, 'Omnia tendunt naturaliter in non esse.'

[2] 4. 1. 1, ψυχὴ ἐκεῖ ἀδιάκριτος καὶ ἀμέριστος.

[3] 6. 4. 16, οὐκ ἔστιν ἐνεργείᾳ οὐδ᾽ αὖ ἀπόλωλεν.

[4] 4. 8. 4 ; 3. 2. 4.

of consciousness is purely temporal. In the spiritual sphere the problem may be actually meaningless. Spiritual existence has an infinite richness of content ; the eternal world is no ' undifferentiated jelly.' And this rich life implies reciprocal action among Souls. ' They see themselves in each other.' They have then characteristics of their own which are not merged in the unity of all spiritual life. We may further assume that since every life in this world represents a unique purpose in the Divine mind, and since all psychic ends, though striven for in time, have their source and consummation in eternity, this, the inner meaning and reality of each individual life, remains as a distinct fact in the world of Spirit.

' Mysticism,' says Keyserling, ' whether it likes it or not, ends in an impersonal immortality.' But impersonality is a negative conception, like timelessness. What is negated in ' timelessness ' is not the reality of the present, but the unreality of the past and future. Time is only forbidden to devour itself. So impersonality, for the mystic, means simply the liberation of the idea of personality—it is allowed to expand as far as it can. How far that is, we admit that we do not know clearly ; but the expansion is throughout an enrichment, not an impoverishment. When Keyserling adds : ' The instinct of immortality really affirms that the individual is not ultimate,' we entirely agree with him. If this were not true, how could men die for an idea ?

Souls which have lived unrighteously are sent into other bodies as a punishment, and a man's dæmon or guardian angel may chastise his Soul when it is out of the body.[1] Punishments are proportioned by Divine law to offences.[2] But the notion that virtue is hereafter rewarded by pleasure and comfort, while vice is chastised by torments, is repugnant to the later Platonism. Plotinus says severely that if any man desires from a virtuous life anything beyond itself, it is not a virtuous life that he

[1] 3. 4 6; 1. 6. 6.   [2] 4. 3. 24.

desires. This was the opinion of the Alexandrian school generally. Origen speaks with contempt of those Christians who take literally the temporal promises and threats of the Old Testament. He is ashamed to think that the heathen, whose moral sense is more advanced than to accept such inducements to a virtuous life, may hear of the teaching which is commonly given in the churches. Origen will never believe that health, power, riches, or other advantages of the same kind, are the end of virtue ; to say this would be to admit that these vulgar rewards are of greater worth than virtue itself.[1] The bad man, says Plotinus,[2] is doomed to dwell with shadows here and hereafter ; he is punished by being depraved in his Soul and degraded into a lower place in the scale of being.[3] We must, however, remember that for Plotinus, though not for Proclus, it is only the lower part of the Soul that can sin and be punished.[4] This inferior part he sometimes calls 'the image of the Soul.'[5] The higher Soul is sinless.

How far, it may be asked, does this doctrine of the Soul's destiny affect what Christian theology calls salvation ? Can the Soul be lost ? The answer would seem to be that the self which we call ' I ' when we are thinking of our future prospects in time or eternity, may or may not be identical with the higher Soul which has its place indefectibly in the spiritual world. We gain our Souls by identifying our personal interests, our thoughts and actions, our affections and hopes, with this pure and eternal essence, which is ours if we will. The Soul of the bad man may be lost, but not the Soul which he would have called his if he had not been a bad man. The Soul which cannot be lost is that which he calls ' Spirit in Soul ' ($νοῦς ἐν ψυχῇ$). So in Origen the Spirit seems to be an impersonal power which is and is not part of the Soul. ' If the Soul is disobedient to the Spirit, if it

---

[1] Cf. (e.g.) his Commentary on Psalm 4.
[2] I. 6. 8.   [3] 3. 2. 4, 8.   [4] I. I. 12.
[5] I. I. II ; 4. 3. 27.

obstinately rebels against it, the two are separated after the Soul leaves the body.' Similarly, immortality in the vulgar sense, the survival of the empirical ego, is in a sense a goal which we may win or lose, or win imperfectly. So far as we can make ourselves, during our earthly life, instruments for the purposes of God which He intends to realise through our means, we give indestructible value and reality to our life. We are what we love and care about. 'All souls,' says Plotinus,[1] 'are potentially all things. Each of them is characterised by the faculty which it chiefly exercises. One is united to the spiritual world by activity, another by thought, another by desire. The souls, thus contemplating different objects, are and become that which they contemplate.' There are other Souls, however, which contemplate only some vain phantom of time, soon to pass into nothingness. Those who so live are not living the life of Souls in any true sense. For it is *within* our true selves that the world and we as in it are passing away. Otherwise we should not be aware of its passing.

The supreme importance of human immortality, not only for the philosophy which is the subject of this book, but for any philosophy of religion, must be my justification for offering some further reflexions upon it before ending this lecture.

Immortality may be understood in three ways. It may mean unending continuance in time ; or a state which is absolutely timeless ; or a state which transcends time, but for which the time-series has a meaning and importance. The popular notion of eternity is that it is a series of moments snipped off at one end but not at the other. 'This life ' is a similar series snipped off at both ends. The individual comes into being at one point of time, and is 'launched into eternity ' at another. His birth is commonly regarded as a quantitative addition to the sum of existence. This belief hardly belongs to philosophy. It is part of the naïve conception of human

[1] 4. 3. 8.

survival under conditions of time and place, which popular Christian teaching, in fear of losing the elements of strength contributed by the concrete and positive Jewish tradition, has not discouraged. It is well known how long the geographical heaven and hell held their own in popular belief—indeed they have not yet ceased to hold it. There are parts of Christendom in which it is unorthodox to deny the existence of a subterranean torture-house, which in the Middle Ages furnished a plausible explanation of volcanic eruptions. Modern astronomy has destroyed the popular Christian cosmology, and has thereby profoundly modified religious belief; but the parallel doctrine of a temporal eternity still survives, though the difficulties attending it are no less formidable. This doctrine postulates the ultimate reality of time as an unending series of moments, but destroys it again by giving no permanent value to each moment as it passes. The series is never summed and leads to nothing. Further, the popular notion of eternity destroys all essential connexion between our present lives and our future state. We are to be rewarded or punished; but these rewards and punishments are the award of a tribunal, and are only externally connected with the acts of which the tribunal takes cognizance. Nevertheless, Kant admits the idea of an unending process, adding that in the mind of God this process takes the form of a timeless attainment. But an unending process can surely not be the symbol of any attainment whatsoever. If any purpose is involved in it, that purpose must be eternally frustrate.

The idea of eternity as timeless existence is clearly stated by Plato. He says in the *Timaeus* that while the Father was ordering the universe, He made, out of eternity, which abides in unity, an eternal image moving according to number, which we call time. Past and future are relations of time, which we wrongly ascribe to the Divine essence. ' We say that it was and shall be, though we can rightly say only that it is.'[1] How this teaching

[1] Plato, *Timaeus*, 37.

was developed by Plotinus will be seen in the next chapter.

The problem is how to maintain this view of eternity as supratemporal existence, without either sundering the higher and lower worlds entirely from each other, or reducing the world of time and change to a vain shadow. The view of Plotinus is, as we shall see, that eternity is the sphere of the ultimately real, above the forms of space and time, in which all meanings and values, all real distinctions, are preserved, and in which the Divine attributes of beauty, goodness, and truth are fully realised and fully operative. The Soul determines its own rank in the scale of being, for it is what it loves and desires and thinks about. It is its nature to aspire to the eternal world, to endeavour to know the things of time under the form of eternity. ' Our mind, so far as it understands, is an eternal mode of thought.'[1] We should add that so far as it loves the true, and wills the good, and sees the beautiful, it is an eternal mode of life. ' Whatever can be known under the form of eternity is to that extent eternal,' as Spinoza says again. All that participates in the attributes of the eternal world, as they are known to us—namely, goodness, truth, and beauty, can be known under the form of eternity. By participation in goodness I mean a certain disposition of the intellect, will, and feelings. Intellectual goodness is a just appreciation of values, positive and negative. Goodness of the will is a steady desire and purpose to make the positive values actual in the world around and within us, and to suppress the negative. In feeling, goodness is an emotional attraction towards all that is pure and noble and lovely and of good report. By truth or wisdom I mean the correspondence of idea with fact. Intellectual wisdom is the knowledge of the laws, physical, psychical, and spiritual, by which the world is governed. In the will, it is consent to and active co-operation with these laws, which are its own laws, not imposed from outside,

[1] Spinoza.

but created by the Divine wisdom itself. This consent and co-operation constitute the freedom of the will. In feeling, it is the love of God's law. By beauty I mean the expression of a true idea under an appropriate form. As in the two other cases, there is a beauty of thought, of action, and of feeling.

It is by living resolutely (as Goethe said) in the whole, the good, and the beautiful, that the Soul wins its eternal life. As we rise to this sphere, we apprehend more and more significant facts about existence. The lower facts are not lost or forgotten, but they fall into their true place, on a greatly reduced scale. Mere time-succession, as well as local position, becomes relatively unimportant. The date and duration of life are seen to be very insignificant facts. Individuality, as determined by local separation in different bodies, and not on distinctions of character, is seen to be a very small matter. On the other hand, the great unselfish interests, such as science and love of knowledge of all kinds, the love of art and beauty in all its forms, and above all goodness in its purest form—unselfish affection—are seen to be the true life of the Soul. In attaining this life it has in a sense to pass out of the normal soul-life into a higher sphere, not dominated by time : it has passed from death unto life, and enjoys eternal life though in the midst of time. Christ says quite explicitly that we can only save our Souls by losing them ; that is to say, the Soul must sacrifice what seem at the time to be its own interests, in the service of the higher life which it will one day call its own. The Soul thus enters heaven by ' ascending in heart and mind ' to ' the things that are above '— above itself.

The religious faith in immortality is the faith that all true values are valid always and everywhere ; that the order of the universe is just, rational, and beautiful ; and that those principles which exalt us above ourselves and open heaven to us are the attributes of the Creator in whom we live and move and have our being.

Transmigration of Souls (παλιγγενεσία)

I shall not follow the fashion and discuss the survivals of totemism in civilised religions. Researches into the psychology of the savage are interesting to the anthropologist, and would have some importance to the student of comparative religion, if we could have any confidence that European travellers can ever really understand the mentality of primitive races. But the Platonist and Aristotelian can have no sympathy with attempts to poise a pyramid on its apex. For us the nature of religion is what it may grow into ; and our starting-point, if we turn to history, must be the conceptions of early civilised races. In this case we begin with Egypt, from which, according to the tradition of antiquity, Pythagoras derived his doctrine. In Egypt the theory of transmigration united the belief in retribution after death with the old popular notion that human souls can enter into the bodies of lower animals. The Egyptian doctrine differed from the Indian in three ways. It is only the wicked who are doomed by the Egyptian theory to transmigration ; the Soul ultimately returns into human form ; and, though there is no escape from the cycle when once it has started, the Soul may gain deliverance after returning to human form.[1] In India, good and bad alike transmigrate ; and there is no deliverance from rebirths. Hence the Buddhist revolt against the doctrine.[2] Em-

---

[1] Jevons, *Introduction to the History of Religion*, p. 317.
[2] An interesting account of ' Modernist ' Buddhist teaching on Karma will be found in David, *Le Modernisme Bouddhiste* (Paris, 1911). The theory of Karma, which properly means ' action,' is much older than Buddha. In Buddhism its basis is the inexorable law of psychical continuity. Educated Buddhists do not believe in individual retribution—e.g. that an idiot is a man who in a former state misused his intellectual faculties. Buddhism does not believe in permanent psychic individuality. Actions and their consequences are indissolubly linked together, but the notion of individual retribution belongs to the ' illusion of the ego,' which this philosophy seeks to eradicate. What we call a person is only the transient embodiment of past activities. ' It is only in considering the whole of humanity as bound together, like the parts of a universal whole, that we can seize the full signifi-

pedocles, repeating perhaps the teaching of Pythagoras himself, says that the cause of transmigration is sin, that the term of it is 30,000 years, and that finally the Soul will become a god, which indeed it has always been. Pindar, another good witness to early Pythagorean teaching, holds that only the bad are condemned to transmigration, the good being admitted to a state of happiness in a place which was variously described as the sky, the air, Elysium, or Olympus.

The doctrine of transmigration offers us ' chains of personalities linked together by impersonal transitions.'[1] Nothing survives except the bare being of the Soul, and, we may add, its liabilities. But Plato does not hold the doctrine in an uncompromising form : Souls do not all drink enough of the waters of Lethe to forget everything ; the importance of 'recollection' in his writings is well known. Leibnitz thought that ' immortality without recollection is ethically quite useless ' ; and many others profess that such an immortality would have no attractions for them. But others would be satisfied to know that they will live on in the great spiritual interests with which they identified themselves ; they could say with Browning, ' Other tasks in other lives, God willing.' It is not continuity of consciousness which they prize, but perpetuity of life amid the eternal ideas.

The doctrine has found many supporters in modern times. The philosophy of Krause is on this and some other subjects of special value to a Neoplatonist. Pflei-

cance of the doctrine of Karma ' (quoted from Prof. Narasu). ' There are no creators or created, and men are not real beings ' (Kuroda). Nevertheless, liberation from the bonds of the past is possible. ' If the will was free, it would be impossible to change our character by education. Precisely because the will of man obeys motives and depends on causes, he can transform himself by changing his environment and regulating the motives of his will ' (Narasu). Karma, so regarded, is impersonal perpetuity, modifiable by disinterested volition. It is clear that Karma and Heaven-Hell are two alternative theodicies, which cannot be blended without confusion. If we adopt the former, punishment, like sin, is finite, and belief in eternal life is quite independent of any idea of compensation. Attractive as the belief in reincarnation is, it seems to have no *intuitive* sanction.

[1] Bosanquet, *Value and Destiny of the Individual*, p. 267.

derer, who writes most sympathetically about Krause, thus sums up his views about the life of the Soul.[1] ' Man's whole vocation is likeness to God in this life, or the unfolding of his godlike essence in his own distinctive way as an independent active being, according to his three faculties, true knowing, blessed feeling, and holy willing and doing. That man may know himself aright it is first of all necessary that he should distinguish aright what he is as spirit and what he is as body, and how these two are related to each other. As spirit, man knows himself in the light of his knowledge of God to be an eternal, unborn, and immortal rational being, destined to fulfil in infinite time his divine destiny as a finite spirit an infinite number of times in an infinite number of periods or life-centres. The souls of men upon the earth are the spirits living together on the earth with individual bodily natures ; they form a part of the infinite spirit-realm of the universe, which suffers neither increase nor diminution, but lives in and with God as an eternally perfect organism of all the infinite number of spirits. Each separate spirit enters by union with a body upon one of its infinite number of life-periods, develops itself to its maturity, and then declines to the point of returning to its unity in God. But this death of one life-course is at the same time a beginning, a second birth into a new life-course.' The doctrine of reincarnation was taught by the Manicheans and Cathari, by Giordano Bruno and the theosophist Van Helmont. Swedenborg believed that men who lead bestial lives will be reincarnated in the forms of the animals which they resembled in character. Goethe and Lichtenberg dallied with the idea of transmigration more or less seriously ; Hume declared that metempsychosis is the only doctrine of the kind worthy of attention by a philosopher ; Lessing speaks respectfully of it, without being himself a believer ; the friends of Lavater at Copenhagen taught the doctrine, quite in the manner of Pythagoras, but with extrava-

[1] *Philosophy of Religion*, Vol. 2.

gancies of their own. Lavater himself had been King
Josiah, Joseph of Arimathæa, and Zwingli. The apostle
Peter had come to life again as Prince Karl of Hesse.
Schopenhauer says of metempsychosis, 'Never will a
myth be more closely connected with philosophical
truth.' Ibsen and Maeterlinck are more recent supporters of the belief.[1]

Plotinus, as we have seen, says that the true awakening of the Soul is the awakening *from* the body, not with
the body. Successive reincarnations are like one dream
after another, or sleep in different beds.[2] It is a universal law that the Soul after death goes where it has
longed to be ;[3] it 'goes to its own place,'[4] as was said
of Judas. 'Particular Souls are in different conditions.
Soul, as Plato says, wanders over the whole heaven in
various forms. These forms are the sensitive, the rational,
and even the vegetative (φυτικόν). The dominating
part of the Soul fills the function which belongs to it ;
the other parts remain inactive and external. In man
the inferior parts do not rule, but they are present ;
however, it is not always the highest part which rules ;
the lower parts also have their place. All parts work
together, but it is the best part which determines our
Form as man. When the Soul leaves the body, it becomes
that faculty which it has developed most. That is why
we ought to flee to the higher, so as not to fall into the
life of the senses, through association with sense-images,
nor into the vegetative life, through abandoning ourselves to the pleasures of uncleanness and greediness :
we must rise to the Universal Soul, to Spirit, to God.
Those who have exercised their human faculties are born
again as men ; those who have lived only the life of the
senses, as lower animals. The choleric become wild
beasts, with bodies suitable to their character ; the lust-

---

[1] Fourier thought that the souls of planets will be reincarnated,
like those of individuals. Leroux is another Frenchman who has held
the doctrine.
  [2] 3. 6. 6.   [3] 4. 3. 13, 15.
  [4] 4. 3. 24, εἰς τὸν προσήκοντα τόπον.

ful and greedy become lascivious and greedy quadrupeds. The merely stupid become plants ; they have lived like vegetables in this life, and have prepared themselves only to be turned into trees. Those who have been too fond of music, but otherwise have lived pure, become singing birds ; unreasonable tyrants, if they have no other vice, are changed into eagles. Dreamy speculators who occupy themselves with high things above their capacities become high-flying birds. The man who has practised the civic virtues becomes a man again ; or if he has been indifferently successful in this pursuit, he is reborn as a social animal, a bee for instance.[1]

Plotinus is obviously trying his hand at a Platonic myth in this passage, and he seems, for once, to be slightly amused at the picture which he is drawing. In another passage[2] he shows how distributive justice may be exercised among those who are reincarnated as men. Cruel masters become slaves ; those who have misused their wealth become paupers. The murderer is murdered himself ; the ravisher is reborn as a woman and suffers the same fate. As for the Souls which have freed themselves from the contamination of the flesh, they dwell ' where is reality and true being and the divine, in God ; such a Soul as we have described will dwell with these and in God. If you ask where they will be, you must ask where the spiritual world is ; and you will not find it with your eyes.'[3]

It is plain, I think, that Plotinus does not take the doctrine of reincarnation very seriously, as scientific truth. He is inconsistent. Sometimes he speaks of a purgatory for disembodied Souls ;[4] sometimes the bad (as we have seen) are reborn as lower animals, and sometimes retribution in kind falls upon them in their next life as human beings. Porphyry and Iamblichus both refuse to believe that human Souls are ever sent to inhabit the

[1] 3. 4. 2.   [2] 3. 2. 13.   [3] 3. 4. 4.
[4] It is the worst Souls which are punished for their good by their dæmon, 3. 4. 6 ; 4. 8. 5.

bodies of beasts and birds ; and these two do not contradict Plotinus lightly.[1] The fact is that Plotinus is not
vitally interested either in the question of individual
survival in time, or in that of rewards and punishments.
As Dr. McTaggart says[2] of Hegel, 'he never attached
much importance to the question whether Spirit was
eternally manifested in the same persons, or in a succession of different persons.' Dr. McTaggart adds that 'no
philosophy can be justified in treating this question as
insignificant.' But perhaps Plotinus and Hegel would
agree in answering that it is not so much insignificant as
meaningless.

Dr. McTaggart is a strong believer in reincarnation,
and his chapter on ' Human Immortality ' is very instructive. In comparing the philosophy of Lotze with that of
Hegel, he blames the former for making his God ' something higher than the world of plurality, and therefore
something more than the unity of that plurality. . . .
There is no logical equality between the unity which is
Lotze's God and the plurality which is his world. The
plurality is dependent on the unity, but not the unity on
the plurality. The only existence of the world is in God,
but God's only existence is not in the world.' No clearer
statement of the fundamental difference between Hegel
and Plotinus could be made. The view of Plotinus is
precisely that which Dr. McTaggart blames in Lotze.
Dr. McTaggart proceeds to say that on this theory any
demonstration of immortality is quite impossible. That
is to say, unless I am as necessary to God as God is to me,
there can be no guarantee that I have any permanent
place in the scheme of existence. We have already seen
how Plotinus would answer this. Souls have οὐσία—real
being ; but their being is derived, like the light of the

---

[1] Augustine, *De Civ. Dei*, 10. 30. Porphyrio tamen iure displicuit.
Stobaeus, *Ecl.* 1. 1068, οἱ δὲ περὶ Πορφύριον ἄχρι τῶν ἀνθρωπίνων βίων.
Nemesius, *De Nat. Hom.* 2 (about Iamblichus) ; and Æneas of Gaza,
Theophr. p. 61. Proclus (*in Tim.* 5. 329) tries to prove that Plato
never meant that human Souls can inhabit the bodies of beasts.
[2] *Hegelian Cosmology*, p. 6.

moon. They are not constituent factors of God, or of the Absolute, but are created by Him. It is an essential attribute of God that He should create, but His creatures are not parts of His being. Souls are indestructible and immortal because they possess οὐσία ; there is a qualitative difference between creatures that have οὐσία and those that have it not. But the empirical self, about whose survival we are unduly anxious, is a compound which includes perishable elements. And this composite character is found all through nature ; even trees have a share in Soul, in true being, and in immortality. Our immortal part undoubtedly pre-existed, as truly as it will survive ; but the true history of a Soul is not what Aristotle calls an episodic drama, a series of stories disconnected from each other, or only united by ' Karma.' The true life of the Soul is not in time at all. Dr. McTaggart says that ' the relations between selves are the only timeless reality.' Plotinus would certainly not admit that relations can be more real than the things which they relate ; and he would also deny that Souls find themselves only in the interplay with other Souls. On the contrary, it is only in self-transcendence that the individual finds himself ; and he is united to his fellows not directly but through their common relationship to God. Dr. McTaggart asks, ' How could the individual develop in time, if an ultimate element of his nature was destined not to recur in time ? ' But what ground have we for supposing that the destiny of the individual is to ' develop in time,' beyond the span of a single life ? It is a pure assumption, like the unscientific belief in the perpetual progress of the race, so popular in the last century.

But a Neoplatonist might arrive at reincarnation by another road. Since the nature of spiritual beings is always to create, is not the Orphic aspiration to escape from the ' grievous circle ' after all a little impious ? Must not work, which means activity in time, be its eternal destiny ? The active West, on the whole, sympathises with Tennyson's ' Give her the wages of going on and not to die.' Why should not the ' saved ' Soul ' go forth on adventures brave and new ? '[1] The Orphic and Indian doctrine of release seems to be condemned by the Neoplatonic philosophy, when it has the courage to follow its own path. The beatified Soul has its citizenship in heaven ; but it must continue always to produce its like on the stage of time. In what sense these successive products of its activity are continuous or identical with each other is a question which we must leave to those whom it interests. To us their only unity is in the source from which they flow, and in the end to which they aspire.

[1] Sallustius (*De Dis et Mundo*, 20, 21) raises this point, and Proclus (*Comm*. 3, 277-8) says that every soul must descend at least once in every cosmic cycle.

LECTURES XIV–XVI

THE SPIRITUAL WORLD

Νοῦς—νόησις—νοητά

WE have already noticed the peculiar difficulty of finding equivalents for the most important terms in the philosophy of Plotinus. It was unfortunate that we could find no word except 'Matter' for ὕλη, which is above all things immaterial. For λόγος there is no single English word. It is quite different from the Logos of Christian theology, whom the Christian Platonists invested with the attributes of the Plotinian Νοῦς.[1] 'Creative activity' comes near the usual meaning of the word in Plotinus. Ψυχή again is often nearer to 'Life' than 'Soul.' Even more serious is the difficulty of finding a satisfactory equivalent for Νοῦς. Modern writers on Neoplatonism have chosen 'intellect,' 'intelligence,' 'thought,' 'reason,' 'mind,' 'das Denken.' All these are misleading. Plotinus was neither an intellectualist (in the sense in which Hegel has been called an intellectualist or 'panlogist'), nor, in the modern sense, an idealist. He does not exalt the discursive reason (διάνοια or λογισμός) to the highest place. These are the activities proper to Soul, not to the principle higher than Soul.[2] The discursive reason has its function in separating, distributing, and recombining the data of

[1] Cf. (e.g.) Clement, Strom. 7. 2. 8, ἔστιν τὸ ὡς ἀληθῶς ἄρχον τε καὶ ἡγεμονοῦν ὁ θεῖος λόγος . . πρωτουργὸς κινήσεως δύναμις, ἄληπτος αἰσθήσει.
[2] Nemesius (De Nat. Hom. 3. 59) says quite correctly, giving the doctrine of Ammonius: ἡ ψυχὴ ἐν ἑαυτῇ ἐστιν ὅταν λογίζηται, ἐν δὲ τῷ νῷ ὅταν νοῇ.

experience. For this reason, its world is not wholly real. But *Noûs* beholds all things in their true relations without the need of this process.[1] And we shall see in the course of this chapter how far he is from the view of modern idealism, that things are real when and because they appear to a mind which creates and contains them.

By far the best equivalent is *Spirit*. It need not cause any confusion with πνεῦμα, for this word is very little used by Plotinus, and does not stand for anything important in his system. It has the right associations. We think of Spirit as something supremely real, but incorporeal, invisible, and timeless. Our familiarity with the Pauline and patristic psychology makes us ready to accept Spirit, Soul, and Body as the three parts of our nature, and to put Spirit in the highest place.[2] St. Paul also teaches us to regard Spirit as super-individual, not so much a part of ourselves as a Divine life which we may share. In all these ways, *Noûs* and Spirit[3] correspond closely. Then, if we call *Noûs* Spirit, τὸ νοητόν (or τὰ νοητά) must be ' the spiritual world.' It is more difficult to find words for the verb νοεῖν, and the substantive νόησις. They are usually translated ' to think,' and ' thought,' which is misleading. ' To think' is λογίζεσθαι, and ' thought' is διάνοια, both of which belong to the life of Soul. We must be content with ' spiritual perception' or ' intuition' for νόησις,[4] and ' perceive,' ' behold,' or ' know,' for the verb. It will be convenient sometimes to retain the Greek words in the text.

In these three—Spirit, Spiritual Perception, and the Spiritual World—we have the trinity in unity in which

---

[1] This does not mean that logic is superfluous in the ascent to the noëtic view of things. Thought is subsumed in the activity of νοῦς.

[2] Keyserling says that this psychology is still familiar to all students in the Eastern Church.

[3] Lossky emphatically prefers ' Spirit ' for νοῦς, and several Germans render by ' Geist.' I am sorry that Mr. Mackenna has chosen the cumbrous and obscure ' intellectual principle.'

[4] Cf. 5. 1. 5, ἔστιν ἡ νόησις ὅρασις ὁρῶσα. Origen (*Contra Celsum*, I. 48) calls it αἴσθησις οὐκ αἰσθητή. Νοῦς, for the Christian Platonists, is almost equivalent to λόγος and πνεῦμα, which tend to flow together in their theology.

reality consists. It is true that Soul also is real; but it is real because it can rise into the world of Spirit, and be active there, without ceasing to be itself. For Plotinus, reality is the spiritual world as known by Spirit, or Spirit as knowing the spiritual world. Here only we find the fully real and the completely true.[1] Most commentators on Plotinus have not emphasised this nearly enough. They have made either the Absolute, or Soul, their starting-point, and have taken one of these as the pivot of the whole system; or they have opposed the spiritual and sensible worlds to each other as if Plotinus meant them to be two real worlds set over against each other.[1] They have left untested the popular errors that Platonism is a philosophy of dualism, and Neoplatonism a philosophy of ecstasy, and have neglected the numerous passages which should have taught them that both these statements are untrue. We shall not understand Plotinus unless we realise in the first place that $ο\dot{υ}σία$ corresponds nearly to what in Mr. Bradley's philosophy is called reality as opposed to appearance, and, secondly, that this reality is neither thought nor thing, but the indissoluble union of thought and thing, which reciprocally

---

[1] The unity of νοῦς, νόησις, and νοητά is well brought out in a passage of Maimonides, quoted in a French translation by Bouillet. ' Tu connais cette célèbre proposition que les philosophes ont enoncée à l'égard de Dieu, savoir qu'il est l'intellect, l'intelligent, et l'intelligible, et que ces trois choses, dans Dieu, ne font qu'une seule et même chose, dans laquelle il n'y a pas multiplicité. Comme il est démontré que Dieu (qu'il soit glorifié !) est intellect en acte, et comme il n'y a en lui absolument rien qui soit en puissance, de sorte qu'il ne se peut pas que tantôt il perçoive et tantôt il ne perçoive pas, et qu'au contraire il est toujours intellecte en acte, il s'ensuit que lui et la chose perçue sont une seule et même chose, qui est son essence ; et que cette action de percevoir, pour laquelle il est appelé intelligent, est l'intellect même qui est son essence. Par conséquent, il est perpétuellement intellect, intelligent, et intelligible. Il est clair aussi que si l'on dit que l'intellect, l'intelligent, et l'intelligible ne forment qu'un en nombre, cela ne s'applique pas seulement au Créateur, mais a tout intellect. Dans nous aussi l'intellect, l'intelligent, et l'intelligible sont une seule et même chose, toutes les fois que nous possédons l'intellect en acte ; mais ce n'est que par intervalles que nous passons de la puissance à i'acte.'

[2] The following passages, among others, throw light on this point : 5. 4, 2, νοῦς δὴ καὶ ὂν ταυτόν ; id. αὐτὸς ὁ νοῦς τὰ πράγματα ; 3. 8. 8, πᾶσα ζωὴ νόησίς τις.

imply each other.[1] Οὐσία is defined[2] as that which belongs
to itself, or is an essential part of that which belongs to
itself. It possesses Bradley's two criteria of reality—
that is to say, universality and inner harmony. It needs
neither supplementing nor rearrangement : it exists
eternally and in perfection. Spiritual perception (νόησις)
is the apprehension of incorporeals ;[3] it is a seeing of the
invisible.[4] It is the activity of Spirit ;[5] a phrase which
might suggest to a modern idealist that νοῦς creates the
νοητά. But this is certainly not the meaning of Plotinus.
He says,[6] quoting the *Timaeus* of Plato, that ' Spirit sees
the Ideas which dwell in real being.' What Plato calls
the living being (ζῷον) is not νοῦς but νοητόν. Spirit
sees the Ideas which dwell in the spiritual world. Are
these Ideas external to the Spirit which sees them ?
If they were, it could only possess the images of them,
not the Ideas themselves ; there would be no direct
contact between thought and thing. But we cannot
admit this ; for though doubtless Spirit and the spiritual
world are distinguishable (ἕτερον ἑκάτερον), they are not
separate or separable. Plato, when he says that νοῦς sees
the νοητά, means that it possesses them in itself. The
νοητόν is νοῦς, but νοῦς in a state of unity and calm,
while the νοῦς which perceives this νοῦς abiding in itself
is an energy proceeding from it. In contemplating it, it
becomes like it, and ' is its νοῦς because it perceives
(νοεῖ) it.' It is in one aspect νοῦς, in another νοητόν.
The Spiritual World, he says in another place,[7] cannot
be outside Spirit, for then what link could unite them ?
How then could we distinguish νόησις from αἴσθησις,
which only beholds types and images of reality ? Can we
be satisfied to say that justice, beauty, and goodness, the
Ideas which Spirit beholds, are strangers to itself ? On
the other side, the Spiritual World (νοητά) must either

---

[1] 6. 3. 4.
[2] C. C. Webb (*The Relations of God and Man*, pp. 157–159) has some
excellent remarks on true knowledge as inherent in Νοῦς.
[3] ἀμεγεθῶν ἀντίληψις, 4. 7. 8.   [4] 5. 5. 1.
[5] 5. 4. 2.   [6] 3. 9. 1.   [7] 5. 5. 1.

be deprived of life and intelligence, or it must have Spirit. In the latter case, the νοητά make up one thing with Spirit, and this thing is ' the first Spirit ' (ὁ πρῶτος νοῦς), ' Are not then Spirit, the Spiritual World, and Truth[1] all one ? ' If we wish to preserve the reality of νοῦς, νοητά, and truth and to make true knowledge possible, we must concede to νοῦς the intimate possession of reality. ' Therefore Spirit, the whole of reality (=τὰ νοητά), and truth, are one nature.'[2] Yet the relation between them is not bare identity. ' The perceiving Spirit must be one and two, simple and not simple.'[3] That is to say, if νοῦς and νοητά were diverse, they could not come together ; if absolutely one, there could be no thought. ' Each of them (of the νοητά) is Spirit and Being, and the whole is all Spirit and all Being. Spirit by its power of perception posits Being, and Being, by being perceived, gives to Spirit perception and existence. The cause, both of spiritual perception and of Being is another,' i.e. their common principle, the One.[4] The relation between them is one of essential identity actualised under the form of essential reciprocity. That the two sides of reality are of equal rank, and not one derived from the other, is plain from what has been quoted, and from several other passages.[5] ' Spirit, in beholding reality (τὰ ὄντα) beheld itself, and in beholding entered into its proper activity, and this activity is itself.'[6] ' Spirit perceives, not as one

---

[1] 'Αλήθεια is strictly the correspondence between θεωρία and τὸ θεωρητόν. Practically, it is an equivalent of νόησις. Αἴσθησις, he says, conveys not ἀλήθεια, but δόξα, because it is passive (5. 5. 1). 'Truth' requires the activity of the perceiving mind. In 5. 5. 2 ἀλήθεια is defined as self-consistency, and identified with νοῦς.

[2] 5. 5. 3, μία τοίνυν φύσις νοῦς, τὰ ὄντα πάντα καὶ ἀλήθεια.

[3] 5. 6. 1, τὸ νοοῦν δεῖ ἓν καὶ δύο εἶναι. ἁπλοῦν καὶ οὐχ ἁπλοῦν δεῖ εἶναι.

[4] 5. 1. 4, ἕκαστον δὲ αὐτῶν νοῦς καὶ ὄν ἐστι καὶ τὸ σύμπαν πᾶς νοῦς καὶ πᾶν ὄν, ὁ μὲν νοῦς κατὰ τὸ νοεῖν ὑφιστὰς τὸ ὄν, τὸ δὲ ὄν τῷ νοεῖσθαι τῷ νῷ διδὸν τὸ νοεῖν καὶ τό εἶναι. τοῦ δὲ νοεῖν αἴτιον ἄλλο, ὃ καὶ τῷ ὄντι.

[5] e.g. 5. 2. 1, ὁμοῦ νοῦς γίνεται καὶ ὄν (=νοητόν). Zeller (p. 568), who mistranslates νοῦς by ' Denken,' tries to prove that for Plotinus ' Denken ' is prior to its object. On this Richter (Neoplat. Stud. 3. 74, 75) says rightly: 'Wenn in der geistigen Welt der Begriff und das gedachte Ding identisch sind, so ist das nicht so zu verstehen, als ob der Begriff des Dinges das Ding selbst ist, sondern vielmehr das Ding, als Gedanke angefasst, ist Begriff.' [6] 5. 3. 5.

that seeks, but as one that already possesses.'[1] 'The being of Spirit is this beholding ' of itself in the spiritual world.[2] Because this activity is the very essence of Spirit, its activity and actuality are identical. Νοῦς and νόησις are one[3]; and νόησις is the activity of νοῦς. The νοητά, however, are the product not of νοῦς but of the One. The whole spiritual nature (νοητὴ φύσις) proceeds, like the rays from the sun, direct from the One, and not through the medium of νοῦς.[4] ' Reality is that which is seen, not the act of seeing.'[5] If Plotinus were a modern idealist, there would be no need of a super-essential all-transcending principle. Monism would be achieved, or rather aimed at, as in so many modern systems, by whittling away one of the terms. We have seen how far Plotinus is from attempting this solution.

These quotations are perhaps enough to show that the famous dictum, ' the spiritual world is not outside Spirit ' (οὐκ ἔξω νοῦ τὰ νοητά), does not bear the sense which it would have in the mouth of a post-Kantian idealist. But the problem puzzled Plotinus' own disciples. Porphyry wrote an essay in refutation of the doctrine which he attributed to his master, hoping in this way to induce Plotinus to explain himself more clearly. But Plotinus only smiled, and asked Amelius to ' remove the misunderstanding.' A controversy followed between Amelius and Porphyry, which resulted in the submission and recantation of the latter. These essays have of course perished ; but in dealing with so important and difficult a point in the Neoplatonic philosophy, it may be worth while to let Plotinus explain his doctrine more at length.

' We must not regard the objects of spiritual perception as things exterior to Spirit, nor as impressions stamped upon it, thus refusing to Spirit the immediate possession of truth ; to do so would be to condemn the

---

[1] 5. I. 4, νοεῖ οὐ ζητῶν ἀλλὰ ἔχων.
[2] 5. 3. 10.   [3] 5. 3. 5   [4] 5. 3. 12.
[5] 6. 2. 8, τὸ βλεπόμενον τὸ ὂν οὐχ ἡ βλέψις.

Spirit of ignorance in spiritual things, and to destroy the reality of Spirit itself. If we wish to maintain the possibility of knowledge and of truth, and the reality of existence, and knowledge of what each thing is, instead of confining ourselves to the simple notion of its qualities, which only gives us an image of the object, and forbids us to possess it, to unite ourselves with it and become one with it, we must allow to true Spirit the possession of everything. So only can it know, and know truly, and never forget or wander in search, and the truth will be in it, and reality will abide with it, and it will live and know. All these things must appertain to the most blessed life ; for where else shall we find the worthy and the noble ? On this condition only will Spirit have no need of demonstration or of faith ; for so Spirit is itself, and clear to itself ; so Spirit knows that its own principle [the One] is above itself, and that that which comes next after the One is itself ; and none else can bring it any surer knowledge than this about itself—it knows that it exists in very truth, in the spiritual world. Absolute truth, therefore, agrees not with any other, but with itself ; it says nothing outside itself ; it *is*, and what it is, that it says.'[1]

The same argument is developed in the ninth book of the Fifth Ennead,[2] which I will translate in an abbreviated form. ' Spirit is not only in potentiality. It does not become knowing after being ignorant ; it is always active and always Spirit. It exercises its power from itself and out of itself, which implies that it *is* what it knows. We must not separate the knowing Spirit from the objects of its knowledge ; it is only our habit in dealing with the things of sense that makes us prone to make separations in the world of Spirit. What then is the activity of Spirit, in virtue of which we may say that it is the things which it knows ? Plainly, since Spirit has real existence, it knows and posits reality. Spirit therefore *is* all that really exists. . . . The objects of

[1] 5. 2. 2.　　　　[2] 5. 9. 5–8.

spiritual knowledge cannot be in the world of sense, for sensible objects are only derivative. The νοητά existed before the world ; they are the archetypes of sensible things, and they constitute the true being or reality of Spirit. . . . Spirit is the first lawgiver, or rather it is itself the law of being. This is the meaning of the saying ' To know is the same as to be ' ; and *the knowledge of immaterial things is identical with the things known*. . . . Thus Spirit and the real world are one. Spirit contains all things in itself, not locally, but as it possesses itself. Yonder all things are together and yet remain distinct, as the Soul may possess many sciences without confusion. . . .

' The sciences (ἐπιστῆμαι) which exist in the reasoning Soul are some of them of sensible objects (though this kind of knowledge ought rather to be called opinion) : these are posterior to the facts, being images of them ; others are of spiritual things ; and these are true sciences, coming from Spirit into the reasoning Soul, and not concerned with the objects of sense. In so far as they are scientific knowledge, they are identical with their objects, and have within them both the spiritual object and the faculty of spiritual vision. For the Spirit is within ; it is always companying with itself, and always active, though not needing to acquire anything, as the Soul does ; but Spirit stands in itself and is all things together. But the objects in the spiritual world were not brought into being by Spirit ; God, for example, and movement, did not come into existence because Spirit thought them. So when it is said that the Ideas are νοήσεις, if it is meant that the spiritual world only exists because Spirit thought it, the statement is untrue. The object of this knowledge must exist before knowledge of it.[1]

' Since then νόησις is knowledge of what is immanent in Spirit, that which is immanent is the Form (εἶδος)

---

[1] True knowledge (ἐπιστήμη, νόησις) implies both the objective reality of the thing known and its complete possession by the knower.

and νόησις is the Idea (ἰδέα).[1] What is this? Spirit
and spiritual being (νοερὰ οὐσία). Each idea is not
different from Spirit, but each idea is Spirit. ' And the
whole of Spirit is all the forms, and each form is each
Spirit, as the whole of science is the sum of its theories ;
each theory is a part of the whole, not separated locally
but having its power in the whole. This Spirit is in itself,
and possessing itself in constancy is the plenitude of
things. If Spirit had been thought of (προεπενοεῖτο)
as prior to being (i.e. before the νοητὰ existed), we should
have had to say that the activity and the thought of
Spirit produced and perfected all existences ; but since
we are obliged to think of being as prior to Spirit, we
must insist that all existences are in the preceding Spirit,
and that activity and νόησις come to existences, as the
activity of fire joins itself to the essence of fire, so that
the existences, being immanent in Spirit,[2] have Spirit as
their activity. But being is also activity ; the activity
of both then is one, or rather both are one. *Therefore
Being and Spirit are one nature,* and so are all existences
and the activity of being and the corresponding Spirit ;
in this sense, νοήσεις are the form and shape of being
and its activity. In separating by our thought being and
Spirit, we conceive of one of them as prior to the other.
For the Spirit which separates is in fact another ; but
the unseparated and unseparating Spirit is being and all
things.'

This last chapter is as important as it is difficult. Spirit
as it is in itself does not attempt to separate itself from
the spiritual world ; we go wrong as soon as we think of
the two as subject and object, still more if we think of
them as Form and Matter, or as creator and created.
But ' our Spirit,' which is Soul exercising its highest
faculties, cannot help using the categories of subject and

---

[1] I am not sure of the meaning of this difficult sentence. Creuzer,
Taylor, and Bouillet read ἐν ὄντος for ἐνόντος, wrongly I think.

[2] Volkmann and Müller keep ἐν ἵντα. But I have no doubt that
Ficinus is right in reading ἐνόντα.

object. We cannot help thinking of an eye which sees something—and the eye ' cannot behold itself ' ; or of a mind taking knowledge of something which it certainly did not create by thinking. And so we involuntarily ' conceive of one as prior to the other ' ; we either think as subjective idealists, or we affirm that ' the spiritual world is outside Spirit.' The Spirit that ' neither divides nor is divided ' is no part of us ; we pass into it only when we ' awake out of ourselves ' and find ourselves in the presence of the One which is beyond existence. For Spirit, when it is absolutely undivided and undividing, is indistinguishable from the Absolute.

A few more quotations may be added, though my contention has already been fully proved. ' If Spirit-in-itself (αὐτονοῦς) were the creator, the created would have to be inferior to Spirit, but close to Spirit and like Spirit ; but since the creator [the Absolute] is beyond Spirit, the created must be Spirit. But why is the creator not Spirit ? Because νόησις is the activity of Spirit.'[1]

' Thus νοῦς and νοητόν and Being (τὸ ὄν) are one and the same thing, and this is the First Being : it is also the First νοῦς possessing all realities (τὰ ὄντα), or rather identical with them.[2] But if νόησις and νοητόν are one and the same, how will τὸ νοοῦν be able in this way to know itself ? (πῶς νοήσει ἑαυτό). For νόησις will, as it were, embrace τὸ νοητόν, or it will be identical with it, but one does not yet see how νοῦς can know itself. This is the answer. Νόησις and νοητόν are the same, because νοητόν is an activity (ἐνέργεια) and not a mere potentiality (δύναμις) ; life is not a stranger to it nor adventitious ; τὸ νοεῖν is not an accident to it as it would be to a stone or lifeless body ; and νοητόν is the First Reality (οὐσία ἡ πρώτη). Now if νοητόν is an activity, and the first activity, it must be

---

[1] 5. 4. 2.   The argument is that since νόησις, which is the activity of νοῦς, is ' perfected ' and ' defined ' by its object (the νοητόν), νοῦς cannot be the creator.   [2] 5. 3. 5.

the noblest νόησις, and objectively real (οὐσιώδης νόησις). And as this νόησις is completely true, and the first νόησις, it must be the first νοῦς. It is not νοῦς only potentially, nor can it be distinguished from νόησις; otherwise its essence (or reality, τὸ οὐσιῶδες αὐτοῦ) would be only potential. If then it is an activity and its essence (οὐσία) is activity, it must be one and the same with this activity. But Being and νοητόν are also one and the same with their activity. Therefore νοῦς, νοητόν, and νόησις are all the same thing. Since the νόησις of νοῦς is τὸ νοητόν and τὸ νοητόν is νοῦς, νοῦς will know itself. It will know, (νοήσει) by the νόησις which is itself, the νοητὸν which is also itself.[1] It will know itself, both as being νόησις and as being νοητόν; and the νόησις with which it knows is also itself.'

Plotinus, it will be seen, is not content with making Spirit and the Spiritual World correlatives implying each other. He asserts something like what Christian theologians, in discussing the attributes of the Trinity, and the two natures of Christ, called περιχώρησις and communicatio idiomatum. Spirit and the Spiritual World flow over into each other. In another chapter[2] he says: ' νόησις is the activity of νοῦς. But νόησις seeing τὸ νοητόν, and turning towards it and perfecting itself, as it were, from it, is itself indeterminate (ἀόριστος) like vision (ὄψις), but is determined by τὸ νοητόν. For which reason it has been said that forms and numbers come from the indeterminate Dyad and the One;[3] and forms and numbers are νοῦς. Wherefore it is not simple, but many, and exhibits a synthesis, but within the spiritual order, and it sees many things [i.e. it sees things as distinct from each other, not as one]. It is itself νοητόν, and also νοῶν; so that it is two. There is further another νοητόν after it. But how does νοῦς arise from τό νοητόν ? Thus, the νοητόν remaining in itself and needing

---

[1] αὐτός ἐστιν ἃ νοεῖ, 5. 9. 5; νοῦς ἐστὶ τὰ ὄντα, ibid.   [2] 5. 4. 2.
[3] This appears to be a quotation, but I cannot trace it. A doctrine of this kind is attributed to Plato in the *Metaphysics* of Aristotle.

nothing, differing in this from the seeing and knowing faculty, is not without consciousness, but is self-contained and independent, and has complete power of self-discernment ; it has life in itself and all things in itself, and it knows itself by a kind of self-consciousness in an eternal stability and intuition, other than the intuition of νοῦς.[1] If then anything comes into being, while the νοητόν remains in itself, this comes from νοητόν when the νοητόν is most itself. So then, when νοητόν remains in its proper character, that which comes into being comes from it, without any change in the νοητόν. When then it remains as νοητόν, that which comes into being comes as νόησις ; and this being νόησις and deriving its power of thought from its source (νοοῦσα ἀφ᾽ οὗ ἐγένετο)—for it has none other—becomes νοῦς, another νοητόν, as it were, an imitation and image of the first.' In this difficult passage the order of priority is νοητόν, νόησις, νοῦς. But this precedence is only possible because Plotinus begins by making νοητόν include νόησις and νοῦς. In 5. 9. 7 he says that the ideas (εἴδη) are not strictly νοήσεις ; ' or if they are, we must give τὸ νοούμενον a priority before this νόησις.'

These quotations show one thing very clearly—that Plotinus is no slave to his own technical terms. They are not rigid. They seem to throw out ' organic filaments,' as if to prove the doctrine that the whole is implicit in each part. It would be a mistake to stiffen classifications which their author has deliberately left fluid. He was well aware that sharp distinctions and hard boundary-lines belong to the logical faculty (διάνοια), not to νοῦς, and that these methods are inappropriate when we are considering the stage above the discursive intellect. In the relations of νοῦς and νοητά we see a complete reconciliation of the One and the Many, of Sameness and Otherness ; and if this is so, it is manifestly impossible to give distinct characters to Spirit on the one side and

---

[1] ἡ κατανόησις αὐτοῦ αὐτὸ οἰονεὶ συναισθήσει οὖσα ἐν στάσει ἀϊδίῳ καὶ νοήσει ἑτέρως ἢ κατὰ τὴν νοῦ νόησιν. Mr. Ross suggests αὐτοῦ for αὐτό.

the Spiritual World on the other. Reality is not to be identified either with Thought, or with a kind of transcendental physical world which is the object of Thought ; nor can we arrive at it by forming clean-cut ideas of these two, and saying that they are ' somehow ' joined together. Reality is eternal life ; it is a never-failing spiritual activity ; it is the continual self-expression of a God who ' speaks, and it is done, who commands, and it stands fast.' The dialectic may, as Greek philosophy claims, lead us up to the threshold of the eternal world and beyond it ; but within that world a principle prevails, which logic is powerless to analyse ; for the Divine Ideas penetrate each other, and defy every attempt to treat them as intellectual counters.[1]

The Ideas

The usual word for the Ideas is εἴδη, which I have frequently translated ' Forms.' In one place, as we have just seen, Plotinus says that the νοητά immanent in νοῦς are the εἴδη, and νόησις the ἰδέα. It is easier to say what the Ideas or Forms meant to Plotinus, than what they meant to Plato. Plato's Ideas are explained as self-existing substances by Herbart, Pater, and Zeller. Stallbaum, Richter, and others say that they are ' God's thoughts.' Others again, as Kant, Trendelenburg, Lotze, Achelis, and many recent writers, interpret them as a kind of notions of the human mind. Perhaps the soundest discussion of the subject may be found in Burnet and A. E. Taylor, who are in substantial agreement. It can hardly be denied that Plato's own views changed considerably. In the *Republic* the theory of Ideas is no longer a hypothesis, as in the *Phaedo*, but an ascertained

---

[1] Aristotle's *Psychology* illustrates the Plotinian doctrine of νοῦς and νοητά at many points. Aristotle anticipates Plotinus when he says ἐπὶ τῶν ἄνευ ὕλης τὸ αὐτό ἐστι τὸ νοοῦν καὶ τὸ νοούμενον. Wallace, in his fine Introduction to this treatise, shows that Aristotle is nearer to Plato than his rather carping criticisms of his master seem to suggest. We must remember that they are criticisms from *within* ; Aristotle did not break with Platonism.

truth. There are Ideas of justice, beauty, and the good ;
these are always the same, and are an unity of particulars.
Our knowledge of the Ideas is clearer than of sensible
things ; they are independent of the senses ; they are
known by a faculty which is variously called γνώμη,
γνῶσις, ἐπιστήμη, νόησις, νοῦς, τοῦ διαλέγεσθαι δύναμις.
The verbs used are ἰδεῖν, ἅπτεσθαι, θεᾶσθαι, all expressing
immediate and infallible knowledge. The Idea of the
Good is ' beyond existence ' ; it is ' the cause of science
and truth, as known.' Students of the lower sciences
' dream about real existence (τὸ ὄν), but cannot see it in
their waking moments.' The queen of the sciences is
dialectic (which means metaphysics), because it deals
with real existence. The Idea of the Good is the final
cause of the universe ; it enables Plato to bridge over the
chasm between the One and the Many. Plato's objective
idealism is most clearly defined in the *Symposium* and
Phaedo ; in the *Republic* it is less uncompromising. In
the *Theaetetus* the categories take the place of the Ideas,
which means that the Ideas are tending to become forms
of thought.[1] As Plato grew older, the vision faded ; he
attached more importance to the dialectic and less to
intuition. He seems now to allow movement in the Ideas
corresponding to progress in the thinker's mind. In the
Sophist it is suggested that true being is that which has
the power of acting and being acted upon (ποιεῖν καὶ
πάσχειν). But the definition is not explicitly accepted
by the Eleatic stranger, who seems to represent Plato
himself. At the same time, the value of outward impressions is increasingly recognised, and the notion of
being is extended to individual things. Being is sometimes absolute, sometimes relative, while not-being is
always relative, since it arises from a disharmony of
notions. Thus not-being is not one of the categories

---

[1] The change from εἴδη to γένη seems to point in this direction ;
but I do not mean to imply that for Plato the μέγιστα γένη were ever
only subjective.

(γένη). Error is a mistake as to how the Ideas are related to each other. The doctrine at this stage is that the sensible world is built up according to the Ideas which exist in the mind of God, and which pass thence into our minds by the observation of concrete particulars. In the *Timaeus* the Ideas are the models according to which the Demiurge brought order into the world.

But how can an individual Soul ' participate ' in an Idea ? The difficulty for Plato was not that the Idea is a concept, and the Soul a self-contained Person ; for neither of these statements is true. The difficulty arises from the residuum of materialism in the notion of Soul ; and this Plato is trying to shake off. Is the Idea divided among the Souls who participate in it ? This is impossible ; but if not, we must cease to think in terms of extension and quantity ; we must rise to the conception of a spiritual world, which has its own laws. The doctrine of Ideas belongs to the philosophy of mysticism ; and in Plato, as he grew older, the logician and metaphysician gained at the expense of the mystic. If the mystic in him had been slain, he might have turned his Ideas into mere concepts, the creations of the human mind, as some of his modern interpreters have done for him ; but as soon as he sees his argument leading him in that direction, he breaks out in revolt against it. ' In heaven's name, are we to believe that movement and life and soul and intelligence are not present in the ultimately real ? Can we imagine it as neither alive nor intelligent, but that, grand and holy as we hold it to be, it is senseless, immovable, and inert ? '[1] In the *Parmenides* the theory of Mentalism[2] is explicitly raised. Socrates suggests that the puzzle about the unity and plurality of Forms may be solved if the Forms are taken to be only ' thoughts

[1] Plato, *Sophist*, 249.
[2] A useful word coined by Sidgwick, instead of the ambiguous ' Idealism.' The reference to the *Parmenides* is p. 132.

in Souls '—i.e. as merely subjective, as we say. On this
theory, the common nature which unites the particulars
in any class, and the relations between these particulars,
are the work of the human mind, and have no existence
except such as is conferred by our thought. The refutation of this suggestion is so concise and complete that it
may be quoted. ' Can there be individual thoughts which
are thoughts of nothing ? ' ' Impossible.' ' Thought
must be of something ? ' ' Yes.' ' Of something which
is, or which is not ? ' ' Of something which is.' ' Must
it not be of a single something, which thought recognises
as attaching to all, being a single form or nature ? '
' Yes.' ' And will not the something which is apprehended as one and the same in all, be an Idea ? ' ' From
that again there is no escape.' ' Then if you say that
everything participates in the Ideas, must you not say
that everything is made up of thoughts, and that all
things think; or else that there are unthinking
thoughts ? ' ' The latter view is no more rational than
the previous one.'[1] A thought must always be a thought
of something ; it cannot create its own object by willing
to think of something which does not yet exist. An
Idea is not the process of thinking, but the object of
thought. There was never a time when Plato did not
hold this view. The Eleatic disputants in this dialogue
are not combating the existence of Forms as the objects
of knowledge; they are only raising a doubt whether
Socrates has succeeded in establishing a connexion
between the Ideas and the objects of sense. Parmenides
and Zeno wish to discredit sense-perceptions ($\kappa\alpha\tau\alpha\beta\acute{\alpha}\lambda\lambda\epsilon\iota\nu$
$\tau\grave{\alpha}\varsigma\ \alpha\grave{\iota}\sigma\theta\acute{\eta}\sigma\epsilon\iota\varsigma$), and they maintain that Socrates has not
succeeded in rehabilitating them. Plato's object in this
dialogue seems to have been to suggest that Socrates'

---

[1] I agree with Professor Taylor, who has sent me a most illuminating essay by himself on this subject, that ' unthought thoughts ' is
inadmissible as a translation of $\dot{\alpha}\nu\acute{o}\eta\tau\alpha\ \nu o\acute{\eta}\mu\alpha\tau\alpha$. Burnet, however
(*Thales to Plato*, p. 258), takes the other view.

theory of ' participation ' needed more clearing up, a view which he certainly held.[1]

Critics like Natorp, who have fathered their modern psychologism on Plato, seem to me to have introduced great confusion into the study of Platonism. Plato certainly did not hold that νοητά depend for their reality on αἰσθητά, nor that Soul alone is real. The statement that the Ideas are ' simply force,' is in my opinion very far from Plato's manner of conceiving them, at any period of his life.

If the Ideas are not general concepts, and not the activity of our own Souls, what are they ?

Professor Taylor objects to saying that the Ideas are ' thoughts of God,' and does not believe that Plato ever held this opinion. He has successfully demolished the notion that subjective idealism can be found in Plato ; and he argues that we cannot escape from the objections which have proved fatal to this philosophy by supposing the world to consist of Divine, and not human thoughts.[2] He quotes from Bolzano a paragraph which expresses his own view and, as he thinks, Plato's ; ' It follows no doubt from the omniscience of God that every truth, even if it is neither known nor thought of by any other being, is known to him as the omniscient, and perpetually present in his understanding. Hence there is not in fact a single truth which is known to no one. But this does not prevent us from speaking of truths in themselves as truths in the notion whereof it is nowise presupposed that they must be thought by some one. For though to be thought

---

[1] Prof. Taylor says : ' Simplicius says in a scholium on Aristotle's Categories, 8.a.31, that the subjectivist view was held in Plato's time by the Eretrian school of Menedemus. . . . On the scanty evidence we possess, Grote's conjecture that Plato's refutation of [subjective] idealism is meant to refer to the views of Menedemus seems to me the best that can be made.'

[2] I believe that my difference from Professor Taylor is only a slight difference of emphasis. I should say that God cannot ' think ' without *ipso facto* actualising His thought. As Proclus says (*In Parmen.* 844) ὡς νοεῖ ποιεῖ, καὶ ὡς ποιεῖ νοεῖ, καὶ ἀεὶ ἑκάτερον. Proclus defines the Ideas as νοεροὶ λόγοι.

is not included in the notion of such truths, it may still
follow from a different ground, i.e. from the omniscience
of God, that they must at least be known by God, if by
no one else. . . . A thing is not true because God knows
it to be true ; on the contrary, God knows it to be true
because it is so.   Thus, e.g. God does not exist because
God thinks that He exists ; it is because there is a God
that God thinks of Himself as existing.'   Professor Taylor
illustrates this argument by the example of the discovery
of Neptune by Adams and Leverrier.   Neptune of course
existed long before there were any human astronomers,
and if there were no astronomers on other planets within
sight of Neptune, it existed none the less, though observed
by no finite intelligence.   He proceeds, ' And though it
may be reasonable to believe in an omniscient God who
did know about the perturbations [of Uranus] and their
cause before we suspected either, it is pure nonsense to
say that God's knowledge of the existence of Neptune
is what we mean by the existence of Neptune.   For we
should then have to say that what Adams and Leverrier
discovered was not Neptune but the fact that God knew
about Neptune.'   I do not think that Bolzano's words
represent at all accurately the relation between the
Divine mind and its objectified thoughts, as conceived
by Plotinus.   Bolzano, in his polemic against subjective
idealism, seems to me to have fallen into precisely the
error which Plotinus requested Amelius to explain to
Porphyry, the error of placing the νοητά ' outside νοῦς.'
God does not know of Neptune because He has observed
a planet revolving round the sun in an outermost ring ;
He knows of Neptune because He made Neptune, and
without His sustaining will Neptune could not exist for
an instant.   Plotinus would say that the real Neptune is
neither a lump of gases and minerals, nor a notion in the
mind of God, but a realised θεώρημα, in which it is
impossible to separate the creative will from the thing
willed.   The archetypal Neptune is of course (to the

Platonist) immaterial. The Neptune of science is *not* an independently existing congregation of atoms, but an imperfect likeness, constructed and perceived by Soul, of the archetypal Neptune. Soul, as Proclus says, *is* the living world. It is not thought as opposed to thing ; it is its own world, as Spirit is its own world. It is just within the confines of real existence (οὐσία) ; but it is more loosely integrated than the world of Spirit, and therefore the particulars which compose it are not, when taken apart, what they seem to be. The world of Soul—the κόσμος ζωτικός—is real ; but it cannot be pulled to pieces without admixture of error. The planet which Leverrier observed is part of the κόσμος ζωτικός. Science finds that it takes its place in an ordered universe, and infers that God (or νοῦς) knows of Neptune, which means that Neptune really exists.[1]

Platonism is not consonant with the fashionable pluralism, which divides the world into minds, which exist for themselves, and things, which exist only for minds. Against this philosophy it is worth insisting, with Eucken, that a spiritual world is not the same thing as a world of spirits, which these thinkers are content to leave in a non-spiritual environment. The difficulty of deciding whether (e.g.) a lobster has an objective existence—or wherever else the pluralist chooses to draw his arbitrary line—is enough to discredit the whole theory. Nature knows no sharp dividing line between conscious and unconscious life ; the distinctions between animate and inanimate, organic and inorganic, are apparently breaking down under modern investigation.[2] But these difficulties do not affect Platonism or Neoplatonism. No Platonist ever supposed that there is a separate Soul or

---

[1] Plotinus did not think it ' pure nonsense ' to say, ἃ δ' ἐστὶν ἄϋλα, εἰ νενόηται, τοῦτ' ἐστὶν αὐτοῖς τὸ εἶναι. 6. 2. 8.

[2] This is still hotly denied, even by some distinguished scientists. But the study of colloids, giant molecules, seems to indicate a bridge between living and non-living matter (Moore, *Origin and Nature of Life*).

an Idea of a pebble or a pen.[1] ' All things are in various degrees endowed with Soul '—so Plotinus says with Spinoza, but this kind of panpsychism is very different from pluralistic idealism, which is often disguised materialism. We do not get rid of materialism by merely banishing the word. Proclus, instead of ' all things think,' says ' all things pray.'

The doctrine of Plotinus is that so far as every thought in Spirit is also an eternal Form of being, all the thoughts of Spirit are Ideas. Spirit embraces all the Ideas, as the whole its parts. Each Idea is Spirit, and Spirit is the totality of the Ideas. The Kingdom of the Ideas is the true reality, the true beauty. They are unity in diversity, and diversity in unity.[2] Their number cannot be infinite, though it is immeasurably great, for beauty and order are inseparable from limitation, and the number of possible Forms is not, strictly speaking, infinite.[3] There are as many Ideas Yonder as there are Forms Here. The only objects Here which are not represented Yonder are such as are ' contrary to nature.' There is no Idea of deformity, or of any vie manquée.

Chaignet[4] thinks that the Platonic doctrine of Ideas is ' not organic ' in the sytem of Plotinus, and that it is perhaps only retained out of respect for Plato. It is certainly not easy to distinguish the Ideas from Spirits, and from the creative Logoi. Zeller says that in the Enneads, as in Philo, the Ideas ' verdichten sich ' into Spirits, which are not merely thoughts in the great Spirit, but ' spiritual Powers, thinking Spirits.' The relation between the Ideas and Νοῦς cannot, he adds, be more closely defined ' without bringing to light the contradiction which vitiates Philo's doctrine of Powers— namely, that of ranging substances under each other, sometimes in the relation of logical subordination, some-

---

[1] Plotinus holds that there are no Ideas of artefacts.
[2] 6. 5. 6.   [3] 5. 7. 1–3 ; 6. 6. 18.   [4] Vol. 4, p. 298.

times in that of parts to a whole. Kirchner blames Zeller for identifying the Ideas with Spirits, and the two words are certainly not interchangeable. Perhaps the most important thing that can be said about the εἴδη of Plotinus is that he has found in the creative Reason which is at once in our minds and the formative principle in the world, the bridge between thought and thing. Spirit does not create the spiritual world ; but it does create the ordered universe as known by the reason, and the reason which knows it.

Categories (γένη) of the Spiritual World

In Plato's later dialogues the Categories, as has been said, tend to displace the Ideas. The first table of Categories is in the *Theaetetus*, repeated and enlarged in the *Sophist* and *Parmenides*. The first place in all enumerations is given to οὐσία (τὸ εἶναι, ὄν) and its opposite τὸ μὴ εἶναι. The Same and the Other, Similarity and Dissimilarity, are also common to the three. The One and the Many are dropped in the Sophist ; Permanence and Change (Stability and Movement) are omitted in the Theaetetus. ' Not-Being ' is to be dropped, as it turns out to be only another word for ' Otherness.' These γένη are not identical with the Ideas. There is no place among them for Truth, Beauty, or the Good. The older intuitive vision gives way to an analytic investigation of a given universe. Lastly in the *Timaeus* we have almost the Aristotelian list.[1]

Aristotle's Categories have been very severely criticised by modern philosophers ; [2] and Plotinus subjects them to

---

[1] The references are—Theaetetus, p. 185 ; Sophist, p. 254 ; Parmenides, p. 136 ; Timaeus, p. 37.   [2] Cf. Vol. 1, p. 191.

an acute and hostile examination in the first book of the
Sixth Ennead.   It is the more remarkable that the later
Neoplatonists, except Syrianus, passed over Plotinus'
work, and preferred the Aristotelian treatment.   The
fact is, I think, that, as Ravaisson says, ' Les genres de
Plotin sont des attributs inséparables de l'être ; c'est ce
qu'il nomme, par une fausse analogie avec les catégories
d'Aristote, les premiers genres de l'être.'[1]   I am much
more disposed to agree with Zeller, who minimises the
importance of the *Kategorienlehre* in Plotinus, than with
Steinhart and Richter, who find in it the key to the
whole system.   The long discussion of the Categories in
the Sixth Ennead seems to me, at any rate for our purpose
in these lectures, the least interesting part of the whole
book.

There are, according to Plotinus, three pairs of categories, each pair consisting of opposites, which are reconciled in the spiritual world.   These are, Spirit and Being,
or Thought and Thing (νοῦς and ὄν) ;   Difference and
Identity (ἑτερότης and ταὐτότης) ;   Stability and Movement, or Permanence and Change (στάσις and κίνησις).[2]
But he is not quite consistent about this classification.
Sometimes he omits the first pair and makes four categories ;[3] sometimes, as in the important passage which
follows,[4] he enumerates five, leaving out νοῦς.   ' We
must lay down these three categories, since Spirit knows
each of them separately—Being, Movement, and Stability.
In knowing them, it posits them, and in being thus seen,
they exist.   Those things the existence of which is bound
up with Matter, have not their existence in Spirit ; but we
are now speaking of the non-material, and of non-material
things we say that their existence consists in being known
by Spirit.   Behold then pure Spirit and look at it earnestly,

---

[1] Ravaisson, *Essai sur la Métaphysique d'Aristote*, Vol. 2, p. 412.
[2] 5. 1. 4, γίνεται οὖν τὰ πρῶτα νοῦς, ὄν, ἑτερότης, ταὐτότης δεῖ δὲ καὶ
κίνησιν λαβεῖν καὶ στάσιν.
[3] 6. 2. 15, 19.   [4] 6. 2. 8.

not with your bodily eyes. You behold the hearth of Reality (οὐσίας ἑστίαν) and a sleepless light shining in it ; you see how it stands in itself, united and yet divided ; you see in it permanent life and spiritual vision which is directed not on the future but on the present, or rather on the eternal Now and the always present, and on itself, not on anything external. In this spiritual vision or knowledge reside activity and movement ; in the fact that it is directed on itself reside reality and being (ἡ οὐσία καὶ τὸ ὄν) ; for in this self-knowledge both subject and object are known as truly existing, and that on which it rests is known as truly existent.[1] For activity directed on itself is not Reality (οὐσία), but the source and object of the activity is being (τὸ ὄν) ; for being is that which is seen, not the act of seeing ;[2] but the act of seeing also possesses being, because its source and object is being. Now since being is in act and not in potentiality (ἐνεργείᾳ, οὐ δυνάμει), it[3] connects the two terms again and does not separate them, but makes itself being, and makes being itself. Being is the most stable of all things, and the foundation of stability in all other things, and possesses nothing that is not absolutely its own. It is also the goal of spiritual knowledge, as a stability that had no beginning, and the starting-point of it, as a stability which never began to move ; for movement cannot arise from movement nor end in movement. The Idea (ἰδέα) further belongs to the category of stability as being the term of Spirit, but Spirit is its movement ; so that all things are one, movement and stability, and are categories which exist in all beings. Each of the beings posterior to these is a definite being, a definite stability, and a definite movement.' He goes on to say that if we analyse these three categories, Being, Stability, and Movement, we shall find that they are both identical

---

[1] Viz. the νοητόν, which calls νοῦς into activity.
[2] τὸ γὰρ βλεπόμενον τὸ ὄν, οὐχ ἡ βλέψις, an important statement.
[3] νοῦς connects subject and object.

and different ; so that we must add Identity and Difference, making up five categories in all. In this chapter Plotinus follows Plato's Sophist, without introducing clearness into a very obscure argument.

Plotinus elsewhere distinguishes carefully between Being (ὄν) and Reality (οὐσία). ' Being and Reality are different. Being is found by abstraction from the others (i.e. the other two pairs of categories) ; but Reality is Being together with Movement, Stability, Identity, and Difference.' We have seen that Being (ὄν) is identical with νοητόν in abstraction from νοῦς. Therefore it has the same relation to νοῦς as στάσις to κίνησις. But it is surely an error to make νοῦς and νοητόν a pair of categories by the side of the other two pairs. For the antithesis of Stability and Movement, and of Identity and Difference, belongs to the sphere of discursive reason, the Soul-world. They only become categories of Spirit when their contradictions are harmonised by being taken up into a higher sphere. But when they thus cease to be contradictories, they cease to be themselves. That which is always in motion and yet always at rest, is neither in motion nor at rest, in the common sense of the words. It is true that motion and rest are ideas which imply each other ; but the very fact of their real interdependence, combined with their apparent mutual exclusiveness, stamps them as imperfect ideas, which are transcended rather than reconciled in the life of Spirit. Change and Permanence are ideas which belong obviously to that range of thought of which time and place are necessary forms. Identity and Difference are contradictory relations which, if they can both be asserted of the same terms, prove that the terms have been imperfectly understood, or wrongly divided. But the unity in duality of νοῦς and νοητόν belongs to the sphere of real existence. It is only transcended in the Absolute, which is ' beyond existence.' The third pair of categories, we may venture to say, ought to be Thought (διάνοια) and its Object, which present the same kind of difficulties as the other two pairs. And all three pairs are not strictly γένη τοῦ ὄντος, but forms of thought in the Soul-world.[1]

The Same and the Other (ταὐτὸν—ἕτερον)

External nature appears to us as a collection of objects in juxtaposition, with no inner connexion. The main task of Soul, and above that, of Spirit, is to systematise and unify. In a sense Identity and Difference are not so much categories by the side of the other pairs, as (taken together) the relation in which each member in the other pairs stands to its correlative. Or we might say that the antithesis between Identity and Difference is the most fundamental, and that until we understand how it can be transcended, we cannot hope to understand how Change and Permanence, Thought and its Object, can be unified in the world of Spirit.

The great doctrine which Plotinus expresses as the reconciliation of ' the same ' and the ' other,' is that all the barriers which break up experience into fragmentary and opposing elements must be thrown down, not in order to reduce life to a featureless mass of undifferentiated experience, but in order that each element in

---

[1] Aliotta, whose *Idealistic Reaction against Science* (1912) is one of the ablest of recent philosophical books, defends the Platonic categories. ' Certain categories are presupposed in our ideal reconstruction, but they do not include cause, substance, quantity, time, or mathematical space, but rather other categories which are really primitive and fundamental, and are conditions essential to the thinkableness of any form of experience. Such are Identity and Diversity. . . . And we have presupposed the category of Being, that is to say, the affirmation of facts as existing.' Plotinus (6. 2. 18) refuses to place νοῦς among the γένη, because it is ' made up of all the others ' (σύνθετον ἐκ πάντων). ' True νοῦς is Being with all the others and already the whole of existence, but ὄν taken alone and isolated (μόνον καὶ ψιλὸν λαμβανόμενον) is an element (στοιχεῖον) of Spirit.' This is as much as to say that ὄν when used as a category is not the same as νοητόν. If so, it is difficult to say what it is, or what room there is for it in Plotinus' system. For a short summary of controversies about Being in scholastic theology see Rickaby, *General Metaphysics*, Book I.

experience may be realised in its true relations, which
are potentially without limit.   Otherness and sameness
help to define and emphasise each other.   The whole, as
Plotinus tells us repeatedly, is in each part.   Individual
Spirits are not parts of the one Spirit.   They exist ' in '
each other ; each is the whole under a particular form.
The universal is implicit in the particular.   The νοητά are
' many in one and one in many and all together.'[1]   They
are not separated in the slightest degree from each other ;
the whole Spirit lives in each centre of life.[2]   There must
be differentiation ;   otherwise no communion of Spirits,
no interaction on the spiritual plane, would be possible.
It would not be enough that distinctions exist on the
plane of Soul ; for then Spirit would need Soul in order
to come to life.   ' Spirit itself is not simple,'[3] any more
than the Soul.

Aliotta[4] says, ' The perception of differences by the
Soul is not ethical valuation, or æsthetic, or any kind of
preference, but qualitative as opposed to quantitative
difference.   Without qualitative difference all individuality is illusory.'   The question here arises whether there
can be a recognition of qualitative differences without
ethical or æsthetic valuation, or any kind of preference.
I am inclined to think that there cannot.   I believe that
judgments of value enter necessarily into every cognitive
process of the Soul.   It seems, however, to be true that
in contemplating the eternal or spiritual world we are
able to recognise different aspects of perfection, without
assigning *comparative* values to them.   No kind of preference need be felt.   In the spiritual world the different
aspects of perfection illuminate and do not interfere
with each other.   In that world, as Plotinus says, ' all
is each, and each is all, and infinite the glory.'   ' It is
necessary to recognise that there must be diversity as
well as unity in the intelligible world.   In the same
way Christian theology, which is just Platonism applied

[1] 6. 5. 6.   [2] 3. 2. 1 ; and cf. 5. 8. 4.   [3] 6. 7. 13.
[4] Aliotta, *The Idealistic Reaction against Science*, p. 10.

to the interpretation of the beliefs of the first Christians, came to recognise that the relation of God to the world and to man cannot be thought out, unless in the Divine nature itself there is diversity and not merely abstract unity.'[1] Spirit is simple in the sense that it is not discerptible; but for that very reason it has everywhere a rich content, which becomes explicit and differentiated in the Soul which proceeds from it. It is only when the creative power reaches the limit of its activity that we find simplicity, in the sense of poverty of content;[2] in Spirit the principles of all differentiation are contained. It is absolutely necessary to trace back the sources of plurality, on the lower planes of being, to the inner nature of Spirit itself. Spirit not only engenders all things; it is all things.[3] Though it does not become anything that it was not, Spirit is in a state of constant inner activity; it ' wanders among realities (ἐν οὐσίαις πλανᾶται), on the field of truth, remaining always itself.' This ' field of truth ' (πεδίον ἀληθείας) is everywhere complex and diversified; it is also subject to incessant movements. There is no standing still; for where there is standing still, there is no thought (or spiritual perception); and where there is no thought, there is no being. Reality and νόησις are identical; the journeys (πορεῖαι) which Spirit makes in ' the field of truth ' are all ' through life and living things,' and all within its own domain. Plotinus deals with the same subject in the Fifth Ennead.[4] ' The being of Spirit is seeing.'[5] But seeing involves duality; and if the seeing is also an activity, it involves plurality and movement as well. Thus Spirit is one in many, and many in one. We cannot even say ' I am this ' without acknowledging at the same time identity and difference. If the relation is one of absolute identity, we no longer have νόησις, but that immediate and

---

[1] Ritchie, *Philosophical Studies*, p. 202.

[2] 6. 7. 13, τοῦ μὲν γὰρ ἐσχάτου ἡ ἐνέργεια ὡς ἂν λήγουσα ἁπλῆ, τοῦ δὲ πρώτου πᾶσαι.

[3] *Ib.*, οὗτος τὰ πάντα ἐγέννα, μᾶλλον δὲ τὰ πάντα ἦν.

[4] 5. 3. 10.   [5] τὴν οὐσίαν αὐτοῦ ὅρασιν εἶναι.

unthinkable union which belongs to the Absolute. The element of plurality belongs not only to the νοητά, but to νοῦς which perceives them. We may speak of νόες as well as of νοῦς.

Movement and Stability (κίνησις and στάσις)

This antinomy is another form of the last. That which changes and yet remains the same, that which moves and yet abides unshaken, is at once 'the same' and 'another' in its relation to itself. Greek philosophy had recognised long before Plotinus that Movement and Stability are complementary ideas, which imply each other.[1] As Kant says,[2] 'Only the permanent and substantial can change.' It is only in a being which 'participates' in eternity that change has any meaning. Recent writers of the activist school have ignorantly represented Plato as the prophet of pure staticism. This is very far from the truth. In the *Theaetetus* and *Parmenides* first appears the notion of κίνησις as change, as well as movement in space. The distinction of these two kinds of movement is introduced as a discovery of Socrates. The starting-point of this theory was the recognition of κίνησις as a principle of being, justified in the *Phaedrus*, mentioned as known in the *Theaetetus*, and

---

[1] I entirely agree with Aliotta, who expresses his astonishment that Bergson should think it possible to return to the crudest belief in movement pure and simple, as the nature of reality. ' Bergson's fantastic mysticism reduces the world to a perennial stream of forms flowing in no definite direction, a shoreless river whose source and mouth are alike unknown, deriving the strength for its perpetual renewal from some mysterious, blind, and unintelligent impulse of nature, akin to the obscure will of Schopenhauer' (*Op. cit.* p. 128).

[2] 'To arise and pass away are not changes of that which arises and passes away. Change is a way of existing that follows on another way of existing of the very same object. Hence whatever changes is permanent and only its state alters' (*Critique of Pure Reason*, Müller's transl. p. 164). Plotinus expresses this by saying ἔστιν εἰς ὃ λήγει ἡ νόησις οὐκ ἀρξαμένη στάσις, καὶ ἀφ᾽ οὗ ὥρμηται οὐχ ὁρμήσασα στάσις. οὐ γὰρ ἐκ κινήσεως κίνησις, οὐδ᾽ εἰς κίνησιν. In opposition to Müller and Bouillet, I think that ἀρξαμένη and ὁρμήσασα agree with νόησις, not with στάσις. Plotinus wishes us to remember that νοήσεις are not, properly speaking, in time (6. 2. 8).

reconciled with the opposing principle of στάσις in the *Sophist*. The inclusion of these two under one primary kind is (says Lutoslawski)[1] one of Plato's most wonderful anticipations of modern philosophy. In the *Sophist*[2] he repudiates staticism with something like indignation.

It will be remembered that for Plotinus Spirit is perfect activity. Activity is defined by Bradley[3] as self-caused change. He proceeds to argue that nothing can be active without an occasion or cause, which makes it, so far, passive, not active ; that activity implies finitude, and a variety of elements changing in time. His conclusion is that activity is only appearance. Plotinus would admit that the activity which consists in changes in time is only appearance ; but he would differ from Bradley by saying that the idea of non-temporal activity is not meaningless. That this idea is wholly intelligible he would perhaps not venture to assert ; the activity which we can understand is an imperfect likeness of spiritual activity, and it needs to be supplemented by harmonising the idea of Stability with that of Movement. Plotinus does not like Aristotle's statement that ' Movement is imperfect activity ' (ἀτελὴς ἐνέργεια) ; [4] because there is Movement in the world of Spirit.[5] ' If no diversity awakened Spirit into life, Spirit would not be activity.'[6] It does not follow that there is Time in the spiritual world ; for ' Movement does not need Time, which only measures the quantity of Movement.'[7] Movement, in the spiritual as in the phenomenal world, implies the operation of will ; not, however, in order to become activity, but in order to accomplish something from which it is quite distinct. ' It is not itself made perfect, but the object at which it aimed.'[8] Movement in the spiritual world is

---

[1] Lutoslawski, *Plato's Logic*, p. 364, sq.
[2] p. 248, quoted above.
[3] Bradley, *Appearance and Reality*, p. 64.
[4] 6. 1. 16.
[5] 6. 7. 13 and 35.   τὸ νοεῖν κίνησίς τις ἦν.
[6] 6. 7. 13.   [7] 6. 1. 16.
[8] 6. 1. 16 and 6. 3. 22.   κίνησις is defined as ἡ ἐκ δυνάμεως ὁδὸς εἰς ἐκεῖνο ὃ λέγεται δύνασθαι.

not antithetic to stability ; its activity is not a development of itself into something that it was not before. The purposes of Spirit are realised, by its creative power, as processes involving temporal succession. In these processes, subject as they are to time and place, Movement is of course opposed to Stability, though the two are necessary counterparts of each other. But this movement, which might truly be called imperfect activity (ἀτελὴς ἐνέργεια), is also imperfect movement, if we compare it with the movement of Spirit, which does not need Time (οὐ δεῖται χρόνου).[1]

Plotinus recognises[2] that continuous and regular movement is a form of stability. The real change would be for the machine to stop. Are we then denying the truth of the kinetic aspect of reality when we postulate unvarying laws of nature ? This thought is the starting-point of the vitalistic philosophies of the present day, such as that of Bergson. It is said that if reality consists of unvarying general laws, illustrated by transient manifestations which in no way affect the eternal steadfastness of the laws, the time-process is without significance, and the universe has no history. Our answer is that history is always a description of the changes within some one finite unitary whole, and that these changes have a meaning only when regarded as states of some abiding reality which persists through and in them all. They are the expression of the life and purpose which constitute the unity of the whole in which they are embraced. In the life of Soul there is no standing still,[3] but continual movement, and movement with a meaning. Within any unitary whole there may be developments of what we call laws as well as in the processes which exhibit their working ; for the laws are only the methods of operation

---

[1] 4. 4. 1, ἄχρονος πᾶσα ἡ νόησις.

[2] 4. 4. 32 and cf. 5. 1. 4.

[3] There is no στάσις here below, but only ἠρεμία, ' the negation of local movement,' 6. 3. 27.

adopted by the Universal Soul, and are uncontrolled by any necessity. Whether, as a matter of fact, the laws of nature are uniform, is to be decided by observation. But when we consider the subordination of the individual to the larger processes of the world-order, it is most improbable that our private volition should be able so to modify the course of events as to give the world the appearance of a ' wild ' system, which by its unaccountable behaviour administers shocks even to its Creator, as William James would have us believe.

In spiritual things, Plotinus says, persistence (στάσις) is their form (μορφή) and determination (ὁρισμός).[1] When we remember the superiority of Form to Matter in his system, we seem here to find an assertion of the superiority of persistence to change, though Movement is a property of Reality no less than Stability ; and this, as has been said, has been regarded by many as a characteristic of Platonism. So Eucken says, ' The ultimate basis of life is here always taken for granted ; in the full development of this, human activity has an important task assigned to it, but at the same time an impassable goal. When this goal is reached, activity ceases to be a mere striving, and is transformed into a state of rest in itself, into an activity fully satisfied by its own exertion and self-expression. . . . Hence the chief problem of life is life itself, as the complete unfolding and effective co-ordination of its own nature ; as the poet says,[2] the important thing is to become what one is.'[3] He contrasts this conception of life, as something which we should see as perfect, if we knew all that it contains, with what he considers the Christian view of life as in need of redemption and radical change. In Christianity, he says, eternity enters into time, and ' temporal happenings thus gain a value for the deepest ground and the ultimate fate

[1] 5. 1. 7.
[2] The reference is no doubt to Pindar's remarkable maxim, γένοιο οἷος ἐσσι μαθών. *Pyth.* 2. 131.
[3] Eucken, *Life of the Spirit* (Engl. Tr.), p. 113.

of reality.' But the Plotinian view is nearer to Christianity than the pseudo-scientific doctrine of perpetual progress which often passes for Christian. In the Christian scheme a term is set, not only to the activities of each individual, but to the world-order itself. ' Heaven and earth shall pass away,' not into nothingness, but into a state in which no further development and change can be asserted.[1] Both individual souls and any larger scheme which has a unitary value in God's sight, have their places in the eternal order, when their task is done here on earth. Nor is it the Christian doctrine that ' temporal happenings have a value for the ultimate fate of reality.' The ultimate fate of reality never hangs in the balance; God does not evolve, and suffers no loss, though He may feel sorrow, in the failures of His creatures. Temporal events determine the ultimate fate of the souls that animate bodies, but they do so not as external happenings, but as the outward expression of that upward or downward movement of the Soul which conducts it to its own place. A man is not damned for what he does, but for what he is. Modern critics of Platonism seem to assume that if progress has its pre-ordained limit, it must be illusory. This is the result of forcing eternity into the category of time, and envisaging it as an endless series. This is, no doubt, the kind of immortality that many look for—' the wages of going on, and not to die.' But this is not eternal life either in the Platonic or in the Christian sense; nor is it the destiny which science allows us to anticipate for the individual, or the race, or the planet itself. We are not in a position to assert or deny that there may be other tasks for the Soul in other lives. But if there are, that is not eternal life, but at best a kind of image of it, a mode of appearance.

---

[1] I have already spoken of the latest astronomical theories of the ultimate fate of the universe, and have said that they are at least unwelcome to the Neoplatonist. Traditional Christian cosmology is catastrophic and anti-evolutionary; it asserts a beginning and end of the universe in time. I am defending not this view, but the belief in an eternally perfect spiritual world, which is common to Platonism and Christianity.

The problem of change and permanence is so important, and is so vitally connected with the debates of modern philosophy, that a few more reflections may be offered upon it. Plato, like Spinoza, was deeply impressed by the timeless immutability of mathematical truth, which therefore became for him the type of the unchangeable eternal Ideas. The Soul which is in communion with the unchangeable must have itself an unchangeable element. So Kant postulated an extra-temporal ' noumenal ' self as a background for our knowledge of the temporal, and T. H. Green argued that knowledge of succession in time can only arise for a mind which is not itself involved in the time-series.[1] It is because the Soul is in its deeper self outside the time-series that it regards the fleeting shows of phenomenal life as either vain or tragic, and identifies itself willingly with those parts of experience which can defy ' the wreckful siege of battering days.' But I believe that what the Soul values in these objects of experience is not their extreme longevity, but their quality of everlastingness. Hegel bids us ' banish from our minds the prejudice in favour of duration, as if it had any advantage as compared with transience,'[2] a counsel which perhaps goes too far, since ability to go on at the highest level is surely a mark of superiority ; but it brings out the main point, that there may be more of the eternal in fifty years of Europe than in a cycle of Cathay, in a life of thirty years greatly lived than in a selfish or vacuous existence prolonged to extreme old age.

> A lily of a day
> Is fairer far in May,
> Although it fall and die that night—
> It was the plant and flower of light.
> In small proportions we just beauties see ;
> And in short measures life may perfect be.'[3]

[1] In this paragraph I am indebted to G. F. Barbour in *Hibbert Journal*, Oct., 1907.
[2] *Philosophy of History* (Engl. Tr.), p. 231.
[3] Ben Jonson.

Belief in the persistence of effort through unending æons does not console us for the perishing of the finest flowers which that effort produces ; nor does it justify the ambition to produce new values, which will be equally transient. Faith can be satisfied with nothing short of Plotinus' confidence that ' nothing that truly is can ever perish ' ;[1] and this belief compels us to assert the existence of an eternal, unchangeable background, of which an unending temporal series would be at best only a symbol. Even the most definitely historical and ethical religions, such as Judaism, are rooted in faith in an Eternal Being, who is ' God from everlasting, and world without end, before the mountains were brought forth or ever the earth and the world were made.'

Bradley has shown very clearly that progress and evolution can only be movements within a unitary whole. ' There is of course progress in the world, and there is also retrogression ; but we cannot think that the Whole moves either on or backwards. The improvement or decay of the universe seems nonsense, unmeaning or blasphemous.'[2]

The difficulty is to prevent the two aspects of reality, Change and Permanence, from falling apart again after we think that we have reconciled them. Plato himself, in the *Parmenides*, anticipates one of the criticisms which have been most often made against his philosophy. ' If God has this perfect authority, and perfect knowledge, his authority cannot rule us, nor his knowledge know us, nor any human thing.'[3] This is an objection of Parmenides, the Eleatic, to the doctrine of Ideas as expounded by the young Socrates. If the Ideas are objective existences independent of phenomena, the two systems must be cut off from each other. Plotinus, as we have seen,

---

[1] So Paul Sabatier says; 'Ce qui a vraiment vécu, une fois revivra.'
[2] *Appearance and Reality*, p. 499.
[3] *Parmenides*, 134. The best answer to the question, ' If like can only be known by like, how can God know his creatures ? ' is perhaps that given in 6. 7. 10. Νοῦς can perceive the lower things because they are δυνάμει spiritual, though not ἐνεργείᾳ.

holds that the world of the Ideas is by no means one of
stationary immobility, though there are, strictly, no
inner changes in spirits. In the world of Soul the Ideas
are polarised, not only into a multiplicity of forms, but
into a series of successive states within unitary processes.
It is, in fact, only by understanding this soul-world, the
world of the One and Many, that we can rise to understand the world of the One-Many, the world of Spirit. In
making this ascent, we by no means exchange the kinetic
for the static view of reality ; but we are strengthened
in our conviction that the whole meaning of movement
and change is to be sought in the direction taken by the
movement, and in the values which the movement,
taken as a whole, succeeds in realising. These values are
themselves above the antithesis of rest and motion ;
they belong to the eternal world. To us, who are ex-
posed to the stress of conflict, they abide in a haven of
peace and calm beyond our reach, and it is no small part
of the longing which we have to enter into that haven,
that in it each particular task is in turn finished and
then kept safe for ever. For the Soul, it may be, there is
no doffing of its armour, but only a temporary repose.
But a life's battle, if won, is won for ever. Its unitary
purpose, if achieved, has its home secure in the world of
real being. Thus our attitude towards life should be
that of Browning's *Rabbi ben Ezra*.

> ' Therefore I summon age
>   To grant youth's heritage,
> Life's struggle having so far reached its term ;
>   Thence shall I pass, approved
>   A man, for aye removed
> From the developed brute ; a god though in the germ.

> And I shall thereupon
>   Take rest, ere I be gone
> Once more on my adventure brave and new ;
>   Fearless and unperplexed
>   When I wage battle next,
> What weapons to select, what armour to endue.'

The moods of the religious mind vary. Sometimes we say with Faber :—

> ' O Lord, my heart is sick,
>   Sick of this everlasting Change ;
>   And life runs tediously quick
> Through its unresting race and varied range.
> Change finds no likeness of itself in Thee,
> And makes no echo in thy mute eternity.'

Sometimes we agree with George Macdonald :—

> Blame not life ; it is scarce begun ;
> Blame not mankind ; thyself art one ;
> And Change is holy, O blame it never ;
> Thy soul shall live by its changing ever ;
> Not the bubbling change of a stagnant pool,
> But the change of a river, flowing and full ;
> Where all that is noble and good will grow
> Mightier still as the full tides flow,
> Till it join the hidden, the boundless sea
> Rolling through depths of eternity.'

But on the whole surely Keyserling is right when he says that if life had no temporal end it would not be ' *ein ewiges Sein,* but *ein perpetuelles Werden.*' And this would mean that we must live for ever in the consciousness of an unfulfilled purpose, doomed never to attain our heart's desire.

' The whole system of Eckhart ' (says Delacroix) ' is a long and passionate effort to place life and movement in Being itself, and to spread the Supreme Being over the multiplicity of the acts the synthesis of which can alone constitute it. Hardly has he affirmed the absolute reality of Being, when he occupies himself in penetrating its depth and discerning its richness. His God is not an immobile God, but the living God ; not abstract Being, but the Being of Being. The reality of God is his work, and his work is, before the birth of things, his own birth.' . . . ' So in developing created things in the world of becoming, Spirit makes them enter into eternity. In God progress and regress, coming and returning, are closely united ; they are at bottom one and the same act, the act by which God penetrates himself and finds himself wholly in himself. Thus divine movement is at bottom repose. Becoming is eternal ; that is to say, its change alters nothing in eternity. God is immobile in himself and so abides.'[1]

Ruysbroek thus unites and distinguishes Work and Rest in God. ' The Divine Persons who form one God are in the fecundity of their nature ever active ; and in the simplicity of their essence they form the Godhead and eternal blessedness. Thus God according to the Persons is eternal Work ; but according to His essence and perpetual stillness, He is eternal Rest. Now love and fruition lie between this activity and this rest. Love would work without ceasing, for its nature is eternal work with God. Fruition is ever at rest, for it dwells higher than the will and the longing for the well-beloved, in the well-beloved, in the divine nescience and simple love . . . above the fecundity of nature.'[2]

If, before leaving this subject, we turn for a moment to the æsthetic aspects of Change and Permanence, we observe the curious fact that the beauty perceived by sight is mainly stationary, while that perceived by hearing requires change. The most exquisite note of a prima donna, if prolonged for two or three minutes, would compel us to stop our ears ; but there is no satiety in gazing at a fine landscape or a noble picture, until the optic nerves become fatigued. The Greeks, though they did not undervalue music, were on the whole more impressed by the beauties of visible form ; their greatest triumphs were in sculpture, an art in which they remain unapproachable. It may not be an accident that in this race of sculptors we find also our pioneers in the cult of

---

[1] ' Gotlich nature is ruowe.' Esse ipsum dat quietem et facit in seipso et solo ipso quiescere omnia quae citra ipsum sunt. Igitur deus in se quiescit et in se quiescere facit omnia.' ' Ipsum esse est quies et quietans omnia et ipsum solum.' Delacroix, *Le Mysticisme en Allemagne*, pp. 192, 176.
[2] *De Septem Gradibus Amoris*, Chap. xiv. Underhill, *Mysticism*, p.521.

'eternal form, the universal mould.' On the other hand, the Jews, in whom the sense of visible form is singularly blunt, have been great musicians, and also strong upholders of the belief that it is in history that God reveals Himself.

The Spiritual World as a Kingdom of Values

The whole discussion of the Categories of the spiritual world in the Enneads leaves me dissatisfied. It seems to me that when we reach the plane of the eternal verities, the κόσμος νοητός, we should leave these dialectical puzzles behind, and recognise that what we now have to deal with is a kingdom of *absolute* values. The whole philosophy of Plotinus is an ontology of moral, intellectual, and æsthetic values. These values are not merely ideals ; they are the constituents of Reality, the attributes under which God is known to man.[1] Whether they should be called categories is a question which does not matter much ; they are the qualities which all spiritual things possess, and in virtue of which they hold their rank as perfect being.

The highest forms in which Reality can be known by Spirits, who are themselves the roof and crown of things, are *Goodness, Truth*, and *Beauty*, manifesting themselves in the myriad products of creative activity. Things truly *are*, in proportion as they ' participate ' in Goodness, Truth, and Beauty. These attributes of Reality, which, so far as can be known, constitute its entire essence, are spiritual ; that is to say, they belong to a sphere of supra-temporal and supra-spatial existence, which obeys laws of its own, and of which the world of common experience is a pale copy.

I venture to think, audacious as the suggestion undoubtedly is, that Plotinus ought, when dealing with the spiritual world, to have made a clean sweep of the Platonic and Aristotelian categories,[2] and to have said

---

[1] Compare Ravaisson, quoted p. 58.

[2] Bradley, as is well known, takes most of the Aristotelian categories m detail and convicts them of being mere Appearance. That is to say they are not categories of the κόσμος νοητός.

that the three attributes of οὐσία are Goodness, Truth, and Beauty—ἀγαθότης, ἀλήθεια, and κάλλος. Let us examine his reasons for refusing to do this ; for he does not leave the question unconsidered. ' Why do we not include among the first categories the Beautiful, the Good, the Virtues, Science (true knowledge), and Spirit ?[1] If by the Good we mean the First Principle, that of which we can affirm nothing, but which we call the Good because we have nothing else to call it, it cannot be a category ; for we cannot affirm it of anything else. . . . Besides, the Good is not in existence, but beyond existence. But if by the Good we mean the quality of goodness, we have shown that Quality is not one of our categories. The nature of Reality is good, no doubt ; but not as the First Principle is good ; its goodness is not a quality, but an attribute.[2] But, it will be said, you have told us that the One has all the other categories in it, and that each of these is a category because it is common and is seen in many things. If then the Good is seen in every part of Reality or Being, or in most of them, why is it not included in the first categories ? The reason is that it is present in different degrees ; there is a hierarchy of goods all depending on the First Good. . . . But if by the Good which is in Being we mean the natural activity which draws it towards the One, and say that this is its Good, to gain the form of Good from the One, then the Good in this sense will be activity directed towards the Good, and this is its life. But this activity is Movement ; and Movement has been named as one of the categories.'[3]

The answer to these various objections is that in the first place when we call Goodness an attribute of νοῦς and νοητά, we certainly do not mean the Absolute, ' which we only call the Good because we have nothing else to call it," but Goodness in its proper sense ; in the

---

[1] This is a direct contradiction of 5. 1. 4, in which νοῦς appears as one of the categories. He is certainly right in excluding νοῦς, but the same arguments are fatal to its correlative ὄν, which he retains among them.

[2] οὐχ ὡς ποιόν, ἀλλ' ἐν αὐτῷ.   [3] 6. 2. 17.

second place that this Goodness is not a quality, but a
constitutive attribute of Reality as such ; in the third
place that the hierarchy of degrees in Goodness is also
a hierarchy in degrees of Reality, the two being inseparable ; and lastly that though the striving towards
the Good is itself a good for the Soul, the good of the
Spirit is not a κίνησις, but a form of activity ' within
the field of truth,' in which movement and stability are
reconciled. The whole argument is hardly worthy of
Plotinus.

Proceeding to the Beautiful, he uses the same arguments with no better effect. Of ἐπιστήμη, which nearly
corresponds to the attribute which we have called Truth,
he says, ' Knowledge is Movement-in-itself (αὐτοκίνησις),
as being a vision of Reality and activity, but not its
possession ; it may be subsumed under Movement, or
Stability, or both.' It is contrary to Plotinus' own
doctrine to say that in the spiritual world there can be
ὄψις without ἕξις.

We have seen already that the disciples of Plotinus
were dissatisfied with his spiritual categories. It was
satisfactory to me to find that the view which had already
occurred to me has the powerful support of Proclus, the
ablest thinker of the school next to Plotinus himself.
' There are three attributes (he says) which make up the
essence of Divine things, and are constitutive of all the
higher categories—Goodness, Wisdom, Beauty (ἀγαθότης,
σοφία, κάλλος) ; and there are three auxiliary principles,
second in importance to these, but extending through
all the divine orders—Faith, Truth, and Love ' (πίστις,
ἀλήθεια, ἔρως).[1] In another place[2] he explains the
relationship between these two triads. Goodness, Wisdom, and Beauty are not only the constitutive attributes
of the Divine nature as such ; they are also active causes.
When they are exerting their activity, they take respec-
tively the forms of Faith, Truth, and Love. ' Faith gives

---

[1] Proclus, *Theol. Plat.* I. I.
[2] Proclus, *In Alcib.* 2, p. 141.

all things a solid foundation in the Good.[1] Truth reveals knowledge in all real existences. Love leads all things to the nature of the Beautiful.'

The ultimate attributes of Reality are values. And it is an unmixed advantage, in considering them, to get rid of the quantitative categories which are only valid of temporal and spatial relations. The intellectual puzzles about sameness and otherness, movement and stability, do not help us at all to understand the spiritual world. They only convince us of the inadequacy of the discursive reason to comprehend the things of the Spirit. The attributes of Reality are values. But values are nothing unless they are values of Reality. Truth, for example, is, subjectively, a complete understanding of the laws and conditions of actual existence.[2] It is the true interpretation of the world of sense, as knowable by Soul when illuminated by Spirit. Objectively, it is an ordered harmony or system of cosmic life, interpreted in terms of vital law, and nowhere contradicted by experience. If, as is notoriously the case, perfect law and order are not to be found in the world of ordinary experience ; if perfect Beauty and Goodness are not to be discerned by the Soul except when it turns to Spirit, we have to suppose that these imperfections are partly due to our faulty apprehension, and partly to the essential conditions of a process which is doubly split up by Space and Time, and which is so disintegrated precisely in order that spiritual values may be realised through conflict with evil.

The great difficulty in this scheme is one which is by no means created by the scheme itself. It is rather a fundamental problem of all philosophy ; and a system

[1] Cf. Epistle to the Hebrews, 11. 1. But Proclus tends to identify Faith with the mystical vision.

[2] Neoplatonism throughout assumes that Truth is ' the conformity of Thought to Thing.' In spite of the heavy guns that have been brought to bear on this first principle of scholastic epistemology, I see no reason to abandon it. It is what we all *mean* by Truth ; and I agree with Fechner that in philosophy ' there comes a point where a man must trust himself.'

which brings it out clearly is so far superior to a system which ignores or conceals it. The difficulty is that judgments of value give us an essentially *graduated* world ; while judgments of existence are not so easily graduated. In judgments of value every object is what it is only in a relation of better or worse as compared with other objects, or of estimated defect in relation to an absolute standard. But judgments of existence are not naturally arranged in an ascending or descending series. An object either is or is not. The quantitative measurements with which science is occupied establish no generic difference between the smaller and the greater. The scientific intellect would be satisfied with a single realm of objective reality, all on the same plane, as distinguished from a shadow-world of false opinions (ψευδεῖς δόξαι), to be suppressed wherever recognised. Science has no business with the categories ' good ' and ' bad,' ' beautiful ' and ' ugly,' and has no absolute standard whereby to approve or condemn any phenomenon. It is true that, as its enemies are now beginning to point out, it has frequently set up an absolute standard, that of universal continuity or invariable sequence, often erroneously called causation, and has treated as a scandal or an enigma the deviations from complete regularity which the investigation of nature brings to light. This, however, is only one of many instances in which judgments of value intrude unnoticed into an abstract method of inquiry when it attempts to deal with the concrete actual. The unconscious assumption is that the order of nature must be perfect, and that the perfect is the absolutely regular. This assumption obliges the scientist to distinguish between normal and abnormal phenomena, and to recognise degrees of abnormality. But these are value-judgments : the abnormal phenomenon is, so to speak, convicted as a law-breaker, although its existence is in truth not a breach of the law but a confutation of it. However, a severer dependence upon observed facts, and a distrust of generalisation, are now characteristic of scientific research. Speaking generally, the scientist aims at a valuation which shall nowhere be contradicted by experience ;[1] while the metaphysician endeavours so to interpret experience that it shall nowhere contradict his valuation. But this latter can only be achieved if the contents of experience are arranged on a graduated scale, according to their relative approximation to an absolute standard not realised in finite experience. Morality and Art can face the possibility that their ideals are not fully realised anywhere or at any time, though in admitting this possibility they confess their faith in a supra-spatial and supra-temporal kingdom of spiritual existence. The Platonist believes that he has the witness of the Spirit to the eternal reality as well as to the validity of his ideals, and he resolutely rejects the expedient of throwing them into the future, as if there were a natural tendency in the universe to improve itself. His ontology therefore compels him to identify Reality with achieved perfection ; and this involves the difficulty of postulating degrees of existence corresponding with degrees of value. No one will pretend that he has succeeded in clearing this conception of its inherent difficulties. It is tempting to say, with Bradley, that graduation belongs only to Appearance ; but are we not then in danger of breaking the link which connects the world of phenomena with the world of Spirit ? There is, in point of fact, no graduation given to us in the physical world ; graduation is entirely the work of our value-judgments interpreting phenomena. But these value-judgments claim to be also judgments of existence ; for that which has no existence has no value. If then graduation is only Appearance, we are left, it seems to me, with a perfect world of the Ideas over against an undifferentiated world of Matter. The former, it would seem, has no existence, and the latter no value ; nor is it possible to bring them together.

The solution offered by a spiritual philosophy, such as

[1] This clause is from Münsterberg.

that of Plotinus, is that the world is most adequately conceived under the form of spiritual values, rather than under the form of commensurable quantities. It is only when we think of ponderable quantities that the dilemma ' to be or not to be ' leaves no escape. Science is in truth occupied with certain values—those which Plotinus calls order and limit (κόσμος or τάξις and πέρας), and looks for them in the objects which it examines. From this point of view, all real irregularity is a problem, and the only solution of the problem is to show that the irregularity is only apparent. Similarly the apparent ' failures of purpose,' as Aristotle calls them, in soul-life, are problems for the philosopher. But the notion of ' imperfect existence,' taken in itself, does not seem to me to involve any contradiction when applied to immaterial things.

It is also a principle of the philosophy of Spirit that since all the world of becoming is radically teleological, it can only be understood by the method of valuation. As Lotze says in a very fine passage : ' All the increase of knowledge which we may hope to attain, we must look for, not from the contemplation of our intelligent nature in general, but from a concentration of consciousness upon our destiny. Insight into what ought to be will alone open our eyes to discern what is ; for there can be no body of facts, no course of destiny, apart from the end and meaning of the whole, from which each part has received not only existence but also the active nature in which it glories.'[1]

The three attributes of the Divine nature, Goodness, Truth (or Wisdom), and Beauty, are ultimates, in our experience. They cannot be fused, or wholly harmonised. There is a noëtic parallelism between them, with that character of mutual inclusion which belongs to spiritual existences.[2]   Popular theology quite justifiably fuses

[1] Lotze, *Microcosmus*, Bk. 3, Chap. 5.
[2] A very clear and thoughtful treatment of this theme may be found in Mr. Clutton Brock's little book, *The Ultimate Belief* (1916).

them, with the help of a quasi-sensuous imagery, into a kind of unity, in which all three suffer equal violence. The aim of popular religion is practical; it gives us a working hypothesis and a rule of conduct; but its science, ethics, and æsthetics are all demonstrably faulty. The philosophy of Plotinus does not permit us to acquiesce in such accommodations. It shows us why we must expect to find some difficulties insuperable, by insisting that there is a stage, which we have not yet reached, where they will disappear. ' Now we see through a glass darkly, but then face to face.' Meanwhile we have our revelation, imperfect though it is, of these three attributes of God, a threefold cord not quickly broken.

It follows from this conception of the spiritual world as a kingdom of values, that it is the goal of the will and of the intellect together. We need not try to separate these two faculties, which work together. The ' ought to be ' is an element of spiritual perception; but the ethical ideal which is here realised is of no private interpretation. It is not *my* will, but the will of God, which is done Yonder.

In concluding this section, we may mention that Eucken and Münsterberg both regard a self-contained system of pure values as one of the desiderata of modern philosophy. Would it not be true to say that if *Life* is the supreme category of the world as constituted by and known to Spirit, harmony must have the form of teleology, unity of love, joy of creation, and goodness of virtue ?

See especially p. 20. ' The philosophy of the spirit tells us that the spirit desires three things and desires these for their own sake and not for any further aim beyond them. It desires to do what is right for the sake of doing what is right; to know the truth for the sake of knowing the truth; and it has a third desire which is not so easily stated, but which I will now call the desire for beauty without giving any further explanation of it. These three desires and these alone are the desires of the spirit; and they differ from all our other desires in that they are to be pursued for their own sake, and can indeed only be pursued for their own sake.'

The Great Spirit and Individual Spirits

We have followed the explanations of Plotinus with regard to the Universal Soul and its relations to individual Souls.[1] We shall not be surprised to find Universal Spirit holding much the same position in relation to particular Spirits. The chief passage in which he deals with ' the Great Spirit ' is in the second chapter of the Sixth Ennead.[2] Let us suppose, he says, that Spirit is not yet attached to any particular being. We may find an analogy in generalised Science, which is potentially all the sciences, but actually none of them. So Universal Spirit, enthroned above particular Spirits, contains them all potentially, and gives them all that they possess. The Great Spirit exists in itself, and the particular Spirits exist equally in themselves ; they are implied in the Universal Spirit, and it in them. Each particular Spirit exists both in itself and in the Great Spirit, and the Great Spirit exists in each of them as well as in itself. The Great Spirit is the totality of Spirits in actuality (ἐνερ-γείᾳ), and each of them potentially (δυνάμει). They are particular Spirits ἐνεργείᾳ, and the Great Spirit δυνάμει. As to the source of particular Spirits, he says that when the Great Spirit energises within itself, the result of its activity is the other Spirits, but when outside itself, Soul. Thus the Great Spirit is exactly analogous to the Universal Soul on the next rung of the ladder.

The Great Spirit, as the manifestation of the ineffable Godhead in all its attributes, is the God of Neoplatonism.[3] This fact is obscured both by the completeness with which it is divested of all anthropomorphic attributes, and by the mystical craving for union with the Godhead itself, which has been commonly supposed to be the

---

[1] See especially 4. 3. 4.   [2] 6. 2. 20, 21, 22.

[3] Plotinus seems to call the One ὁ θεός in 1. 1. 8 ; Arnou (' Le Désir de Dieu dans la Philosophie de Plotin, pp. 120–127) gives other possible examples ; but those modern critics who habitually speak of the Neoplatonic Absolute as ' God ' only mislead their readers. Νοῦς is formally identified with God in 6. 9. 6; 4. 7. 10 ; 1. 8. 7; 3. 5. 6; 5. 5. 3.; 3. 7. 5.

starting-point and the goal of this philosophy. But it is only as Spirit that the Godhead is known to us as a factor in our lives. We have the power of rising above our psychic selves to share in the life of Spirit ; and this communion, which may be the directing principle of our inner and outer life, is, except in rare moments of ecstasy, the highest degree of worship and spiritual joy to which a human being can attain. The life of religion consists in communion with the Father of Spirits ; and it is here that philosophy also reaches her goal. Those Christian philosophers who, following the deepest doctrine of the Fourth Gospel, have placed salvation in communion with the Logos-Christ, are in a position to understand the Plotinian doctrine of Spirit. Such similes as that of the vine and its branches, and such sayings as ' Abide in me, and I in you,' illustrate the relation of the Great Spirit to other Spirits in Neoplatonism.

In ascending to Spirit, the Soul loses itself in order to find itself again. We present ourselves a living sacrfice, not to death but to life ; and this is possible because our highest life-principle is supra-personal. The ideal unity is truer than the concrete individuality. Love joins the discontinuity of living beings to the continuity of life, and mirrors in the subjective sphere the objective unity of individuals. Love is the psychical expression of the natural unity of living creatures, and of their union with God. This doctrine is common to Neoplatonism and Christianity.

The consciousness of eternal values, and love for them, are primary and instinctive affections of the Soul. And since these values are not coincident with individual advantage, this fact is inexplicable unless the ultimate reality is supra-personal. We do not, in our consciousness, begin with the individual and then pass by abstraction to the general, but the general works in us as such immediately. We see resemblances before we see the objects which resemble each other. The objective interconnexion of life is a fact, and the highest expression of each individual life is not itself but the totality of life. The physiology of birth and infancy indicate how little independent the individual is. We are drawn into supra-personal life whenever we find it impossible to rest in the present moment, which alone belongs to us ; whenever we rise above the mere animal plane, we in truth forget ourselves and enter into a larger life. The fact that our psycho-physical ego is for all of us object not subject (this is indisputably true) is itself a sufficient proof that *we*, in our deepest ground, are far more than it.[1]

And yet the individual is not a link in the chain. He is the chain itself. The whole is not ' the race,' as known to the historian or anthropologist. The race, so studied, is an organism more loosely integrated, and therefore of a lower type, than the personal life. But in the spiritual world the race is one ; ' each is all,' as Plotinus says in the passage quoted below.

The differences which keep spiritual things from fusing completely are qualitative differentiations ; but, as Plotinus says in an interesting passage, they are ἐνέργειαι and λόγοι rather than qualities.[2] These distinctions, which do not involve separation, are a good thing,[3] be-cause they add to the richness of the real world, which includes not only the diverse (διάφορα), but opposites (ἐναντία).[4] It is not easy to answer the question whether there are differences of *value* among the νοητά.[5] Their common life is so much more than their individual life that the question has not much meaning. The inferior values, if such there be, are raised to the level of perfection by their intimate unity with the whole spiritual world. On the lower levels real inferiority exists, because

---

[1] So Eckhart says, ' Men differ according to flesh and according to birth ; but according to Thought (=νοῦς) they are one man, and this one man is Christ.' Delacroix, p. 203.

[2] 6. 1. 10.   [3] 6. 7. 8-10, οὕτω βέλτιον.   [4] 3. 2. 16.

[5] Plotinus says that beings in the eternal world are unequal, but not imperfect (6. 7. 9). Each has realised the ' nature ' which it was intended to attain ; but there is a natural hierarchy there, as here. And see 2. 9. 13, καὶ ἐκεῖ ψυχὴ χεῖρον νοῦ : and 2. 6. 1 for qualitative differences ἐκεῖ.

the avenues of intercourse with things Yonder are obstructed.

It is plain that the individual νοῦς is the same life as the individual ψυχή, only transformed into the Divine image and liberated from all baser elements.[1] Individuality is maintained by the 'something unique' in each Spirit ;[2] but it is no longer any bar to complete communion with all that is good, true, and beautiful in others. And this state, so far from being a mere ideal, is the one true reality, eternal and objectively true existence, the home of the Soul, which has its citizenship in heaven.

Mr. Bosanquet says,[3] 'In every true part—hence in every member—of an infinite whole there is something corresponding to every feature of such a whole, though not repeating it. . . . It would certainly be true of a genuine infinite that if we speak of whole and parts at all, the whole represents itself within every part.' This is exactly the doctrine of Plotinus with regard to νοητά. Their characteristic in relation to each other is ' mutual inclusion,' which is another way of saying that 'the relations between psychical states cannot be expressed quantitatively.'[4] 'Each part of the whole is infinite.'[5] 'Each νοητόν is intrinsically multifold.'[6] 'Each is a whole, and all everywhere, without confusion and without separation.'[7] In a fine passage,[8] one of the noblest in Plotinus, the condition of beatified spirits is thus described. 'A pleasant life is theirs in heaven ; they have the Truth for mother, nurse, real being, and nutriment ; they see all things, not the things that are born

---

[1] In 4. 3. 5 he says that individual souls are the λόγοι of particular νόες within νοῦς, ' made more explicit.'

[2] 4. 3. 5, ἀπολεῖται οὐδὲν τῶν ὄντων, ἐπεὶ κἀκεῖ οἱ νόες οὐκ ἀπολοῦνται, ὅτι μή εἰσι σωματικῶς μεμερισμένοι, ἀλλὰ μένει ἕκαστον ἐν ἑτερότητι ἔχον τὸ αὐτὸ ὃ ἐστιν εἶναι.

[3] The Value and Destiny of the Individual, p. 298.

[4] Lindsay, The Philosophy of Bergson, p. 50.

[5] 6. 7. 13.   [6] 5. 3. 10.

[7] 1. 8. 2, ὅλον ἐστὶν ἕκαστον καὶ πανταχῇ πᾶν. καὶ οὐ συγκέχυται ἀλλὰ οὐ χωρίς. The editors follow the MSS. in reading αὖ χωρίς, but surely οὐ must be right.   [8] 5. 8. 4.

and die, but those which have real being ; and they see
themselves in others. For them all things are transparent,
and there is nothing dark or impenetrable, but everyone
is manifest to everyone internally, and all things are
manifest ; for light is manifest to light. For everyone
has all things in himself and sees all things in another ; so
that all things are everywhere and all is all and each is
all, and the glory is infinite. Each of them is great, since
the small also is great. In heaven the sun is all the stars,
and again each and all are the sun. One thing in each is
prominent above the rest ; but it also shows forth all.
There a pure movement reigns ; for that which produces
the movement, not being a stranger to it, does not trouble
it. Rest is also perfect there, because no principle of
agitation mingles with it.'

William Penn, the Quaker, shows how Love can anticipate the state of beatified Spirits here on earth. ' They
that love beyond the world cannot be separated by it.
Death cannot kill what never dies. Nor can Spirits ever
be divided that love and live in the same Divine Principle,
the root and record of their friendship. Death is but
crossing the world, as friends do the seas ; they live in one
another still. For they must needs be present, that love
and live in that which is omnipresent. In this Divine
glass they see face to face ; and their converse is free as
well as pure. This is the comfort of friends, that though
they may be said to die, yet their friendship and society
are in the best sense ever present, because immortal.'

Life in the Spiritual World

The most attractive description of the state of beatified
Spirits is that quoted above, from the eighth book of the
Fifth Ennead. Another brief passage may be added.[1]
' After having admired the world of sense, its grandeur,
and beauty, the eternal regularity of its movement, the
gods, visible or invisible, the dæmons, the animals and

[1] 5. 1. 4.

plants which it contains, we may rise to the archetype
of this world, a world more real than ours is ; we may
there contemplate all the spiritual objects which are of
their own nature eternal, and which exist in their own
knowledge and life, and the pure Spirit which presides
over them, and infinite wisdom, and the true kingdom
of Kronos, the God who is κόρος and νοῦς. For it
embraces in itself all that is immortal, all Spirit, all that
is God, all Soul, eternally unchanging. For why should
it seek to change, seeing that all is well with it ? And
whither should it move, when it has all things in itself ?
Being perfect, it can seek for no increase.' It is much
the same as Plato's description in the *Phaedo* : ' When the
Soul returns into itself and reflects, it passes into another
region, the region of that which is pure and everlasting,
immortal and unchangeable ; and feeling itself kindred
thereto, it dwells there under its own control, and has
rest from its wanderings, and is constant and one with
itself as are the objects with which it deals.'[1] Aristotle
is really not far from the same conception of spiritual
life. ' We ought not to pay regard to those who exhort
us that as we are men we ought to think human things
and to keep our eyes upon mortality. Rather, as far
as we can, we should endeavour to rise to that in us which
is immortal, and to do everything in conformity with
what is best for us ; for if in bulk it is small, yet in power
and dignity it far exceeds all else that we possess. Nay,
we may even think of it as our true self, for it is the
supreme element and the best that is in us. If so, it would

---

[1] We may quote a parallel from a modern Platonist, who by an
early and glorious death has passed into the better world which was
often in his thoughts.

[We will] there
    Spend in pure converse our eternal day ;
      Think each in each, immediately wise ;
    Learn all we lacked before ; hear, know, and say
      What this tumultuous body now denies ;
    And feel, who have laid our groping hands away ;
      And see, no longer blinded by our eyes.
                    (Rupert Brooke).

be absurd for us to choose any life but that which is properly our own.'[1]

In the spiritual world finite beings exist as pulse-beats of the whole system ; finite relations are superseded by complete communion. All the faculties of the Soul must be transmuted to suit these eternal conditions. There can be no reasoning (λογισμός) Yonder ; a constant activity (ἐνέργεια ἑστῶσα) takes the place of dubitative reasoning.[2] Nor can there be any memory ; for all νόησις is timeless.[3] In the spiritual world all is reason (λόγος) and wisdom ;[4] Spirits pass their existence in ' living contemplation ' (θεωρία ζῶσα).[5] ' The calm of the Spirit is not an ecstatic condition, but a state of activity.'[6] Its rest is unimpeded energy.

This raises a question, which affects the roots of the Neoplatonic philosophy, whether even in heaven there can be satisfaction without tension. For if there be no such thing as unimpeded activity, the only escape from this troublesome world of change and chance would be into the formless Absolute and the dreamless sleep of Nirvana. We should lose the κόσμος νοητός, and with it almost all that makes Plotinus an inspiring guide. The world would be cut into two halves, both of which could be proved by analysis to be unreal. The answer, I think, is that in the spiritual world the opposition between tension and free action, like that between rest and motion, is transcended. Of course the Spirit cannot energise *in vacuo ;* but the condition which calls out the expenditure of its energy is willed and accepted, so that if there is tension, there is no strife. We must not forget that there is a close parallelism between the world Yonder and that which we know Here below. ' All that is there is here,' as Plotinus says. The difference is that what we see here in a state of partial disintegration,

---

[1] Aristotle, *Ethics*, Bk. x.   [2] 4. 3. 18.
[3] See the long discussion in 4. 4.   [4] 3. 3. 5.   [5] 3. 8. 8.
[6] 5. 3. 7. This is one of many passages which show how far Plotinus was from the *Schwärmerei* of the extreme mystics.

amid a war of jarring elements, is there known as vigorous
and harmonious life. The forces which 'here' seem to
thwart the operations of the Universal Soul are not
destroyed 'there,' but minister to the triumphant and
healthful activity of Spirit.

Plotinus raises the curious question, what room, if
any, there is for the arts and sciences in heaven.[1] His
answer is, that in so far as these aim at symmetry and
harmony, they are rooted in spiritual reality, and have
their place in the higher sphere. Greek æsthetics always
overvalued the importance of symmetry and proportion
in art. A modern Platonist would be right in enlarging
this answer, and saying that all art which expresses an
eternal or spiritual meaning has its place in the eternal
world of Beauty, while all science which succeeds in the
discovery of nature's laws belongs to the eternal world
of Truth.

In heaven 'the Soul is the Matter of Spirit,'[2] which
means that the self-transcendence of the Soul is achieved
by making itself the passive instrument of Spirit, turning
its gaze steadily towards God and heaven, and trying,
as a medieval mystic says, 'to be to God what a man's
hand is to a man.' When it thus turns to God, it finds
that 'there is nothing between.'[3] It comes to Spirit, is
moulded by Spirit, and united to Spirit. Nor does it
lose its individuality, or its self-consciousness, though it
is one and the same with the world of Spirit ; and from
this blessed state it will not change.[4]

'In knowing God, the Spirit knows also itself ; for it
will know what it receives from God, what God has given
to it, and can give. In knowing this, it will know itself ;

---

[1] 5. 9. 11. 'In heaven '=ἐκεῖ. Plotinus uses οὐρανὸς=ὁ κόσμος, τὸ
ὅλον ζῷον, τὸ πᾶν, τὸ ὅλον. See Bouillet, Vol. 1, p. 243. But he also
uses οὐρανὸς of an intermediate sphere between ἐκεῖ and ἐνταῦθα, in which
memory first appears, 4. 4. 5. I have sometimes translated ἐκεῖ 'in
heaven,' because I wish to emphasise that it is the home of beatified
Souls.   [2] 3. 9. 3.
[3] 4. 4. 2, στραφεῖσα οὐδὲν μεταξὺ ἔχει. Cf. also 5. 1. 6.
[4] 4. 4. 2, οὕτως οὖν ἔχουσα οὐκ ἂν μεταβάλλοι, ἀλλὰ ἔχοι ἂν ἀτρέπτως πρὸς
νόησιν ὁμοῦ ἔχουσα τὴν συναίσθησιν αὐτῆς, ὡς ἐν ἅμα τῷ νοητῷ ταὐτὸν γενομένη.

for it is itself one of God's gifts, or rather the sum-total of them. If then the Spirit will know him and his powers, it will know itself as having come from him and derived from him all that it can do. If it cannot see him clearly, it is because seer and seen are the same. For this reason Spirit will know and see itself, because to see is to become oneself the thing seen.'[1]

Thus the Soul can pass without any abrupt change into the eternal world, and find itself at home there. ' There is nothing between,' as Plotinus says again and again. It is only a question of words whether we call ' the pure Spirit in the Soul ' ' our Spirit,' or whether we still call it Soul.[2] ' We are kings when we are in the Spirit.'[3] Nay, we are no longer mere men, when we ascend to that height, ' taking with us the best part of the Soul.' The understanding (διάνοια) can discern the handwriting, as it were, of Spirit. It judges things by its own canons, which are given to it by Spirit, and testify that there is a higher region than its own. It knows that it is an image of Spirit, and that the handwriting which it deciphers in itself is the work of a writer who is Yonder. Will it then be content not to go higher ? No. It will proceed to the region where alone complete self-consciousness and self-knowledge exist—the realm of Spirit.[4] So ' the διάνοια of the true Soul is Spirit in Soul.'[5]

It is difficult to picture to ourselves a state of existence in which we shall no longer reason, because we know intuitively ; in which we shall not talk, because we shall know each other's thoughts ; a state in which we shall be ' all eye.'[6] St. Augustine uses the same language and applies it to the angels and beatified Spirits.[7] Origen has much the same doctrine about the relation of Soul to Spirit that we find in Plotinus ; but, like almost all

---

[1] 5. 3. 7.
[2] In I. 6. 6. he says that the Soul is ὄντως μόνον ψυχή when it becomes νοῦς.   [3] 5. 3. 4.   [4] 5. 3. 4.
[5] He also uses νοῦς ἐν ἡμῖν, νοῦς λογιζόμενος, νοῦς ἐν διαστάσει καὶ κινήσει, νοῦς μεθεκτός.   [6] 4. 3. 18.
[7] Augustine, De Civitate Dei, 10. 29 ; 22. 29.

Christian philosophers, he follows St. Paul in calling the higher principle πνεῦμα, not νοῦς. ' When the Soul is lifted up and follows the Spirit, and is separated from the body, and not only follows the Spirit but becomes in the Spirit, must we not say that it puts off its soul-nature, and becomes spiritual ? '[1] But Plotinus will not let us forget that Soul is the child of Spirit ; and that the higher principle never is, or can be, barren. The felicity of Spirit always flows over into Soul, which is the Logos and activity of Spirit.[2] As Shakespeare says :—

> ' Heaven doth with us as we with torches do ;
> Not light them for themselves : for if our virtues
> Did not go forth of us, 'twere all alike
> As if we had them not. Spirits are not finely touched
> But to fine issues : nor Nature never lends
> The smallest scruple of her excellence,
> But, like a thrifty goddess, she determines
> Herself the glory of a creditor,
> Both thanks and use.'[3]

It is necessary for us to be carefully on our guard against interpreting the Neoplatonic ' Yonder ' as merely the *future* life. It is intimately bound up with present experience. Every worthy object of human activity, including the mechanical arts, belongs at least in part to the eternal world.[4] Spirit is the *universal* element in all worthy occupations. Spirituality means a persistent attitude of mind, which will never be immersed in the particular instance. The Soul is able to recognise spiritual law in the natural world, and in recognising it, Soul itself becomes more spiritual. Escape from the thraldom of change and chance is always open ; and the return journey, which is the magnetic attraction of Spirit, is always open too.

---

[1] Origen, *De Oratione*, 10.   [2] 5. 1. 3.
[3] Shakespeare, *Measure for Measure*, Act I, Sc. I.
[4] 5. 9. 11. And cf. 5. 5. 2, where it is stated explicitly that Spirit knows the life of Soul.

Eternity (αἰών)

' Spirit possesses all things at all times simultaneously.
It possesses all things unchanged in identity. It *is* ; it
knows no past or future ;[1] all things in the spiritual world
co-exist in an eternal Now. Each of them is Spirit and
Being ; taken together, they are universal Spirit, universal Being.'[2]

' In virtue of what attributes do we call the spiritual
world immortal and perpetual ? [3] In what does perpetuity (ἀϊδιότης) consist ? Are perpetuity and eternity
identical, or is a thing eternal by being perpetual ?[4] In
any case eternity must depend on one common character,
but it is an idea composed of many elements, or a nature
either derived from the things Yonder or united to them,
or seen in them, so that all spiritual objects taken together make one eternity, which nevertheless is complex
in its powers and in its essence. When we look at its
complex powers, we may call it Being or Reality, as the
substratum of spiritual objects ; we may call it Movement, as their life ; Rest, as their permanence ; as the
plurality of these principles, we may call it Difference ; as
their unity, Identity.[5] A synthesis of these principles
brings them back to life alone, suppressing their differences, and considering their inexhaustible activity, the
identity and immutability of their action, their life, and
their thought, in which there is no change or break. In
contemplating all things thus, we contemplate eternity ;
we see a life which is permanent in its identity, which
possesses all things at all times present to it, which is
not first one thing and then another, but all things at

---

[1] Mr. Bertrand Russell (*Mysticism and Logic*, p. 21) quotes as
typical of the mystical attitude towards time the following from a
Persian Sufi : ' Past and future are what veil God from our sight.
Burn up both of them with fire. How long wilt thou be partitioned
by these segments as a reed ?'
[2] 5. 1. 4.   [3] 3. 7. 3.
[4] In 1. 5. 7 he says we must not confound τὸ χρονικὸν ἀεὶ τῷ αἰωνίῳ.
[5] Plotinus thus finds in eternity all the γένη τῆς οὐσίας.

once ; which is perfect and indivisible.[1] It contains all things together, as in a single point, without anything passing from it ; it remains identical and suffers no change. Being always in the present, because it has never lost anything nor will acquire anything, it is always what it is. Eternity is not the substratum ;[2] it is the light which proceeds from it. Its identity admits of no futurity ; it is always now, always the same. . . . That of which we cannot say, ' It was,' or ' it will be,' but only, ' it is ' ; that, the existence of which is immovable, because the past has taken nothing from it and the future can bring nothing to it, that is eternity. Therefore the life of the real in reality, in its full, unbroken, and absolutely unchanging totality, is the eternity which we are seeking.

' Eternity is not an extraneous accident of spiritual reality ; it is with it and of it. It is closely bound up with reality, because we see that all the other things which we affirm to exist Yonder are from and with reality. For the things which hold the first rank in being must be in and with the highest existences. This is to be said of the Beautiful, and also of Truth. Some of these qualities are as it were in a part of the whole of Being, while others are in the whole ; because this whole, being a true whole, is not composed of parts, but engenders the parts. Further, in this whole, Truth does not consist in the agreement of one thing with another, but with that of which it is the Truth. The true whole must be a whole not only in the sense that it is all things, but in the sense that nothing is wanting to it. If so, it can have no future ; for to say that anything *will be* for it is to imply

---

[1] Augustine expounds the doctrine of Plotinus in his own words. ' Ad quam [Sapientiam] pertinent ea quae nec fuerunt nec futura sunt sed sunt; et propter aeternitatem in qua sunt, et fuisse et esse et futura esse dicuntur sine ulla mutabilitate temporum. Non enim sic fuerunt ut esse desinerent, aut sic futura sunt quasi nunc non sint, sed id ipsum esse semper habuerunt semperque habitura sunt. Manent autem non tamquam in spatiis locorum fixa veluti corpora, sed in natura incorporali sic intelligibilia praesto sunt mentis aspectibus, sicut ita in locis visibilia vel contrectabilia corporis sensibus.' *De Trinitate*, 12, 14.

[2] Plotinus uses this Aristotelian term ($\dot{v}\pi o\kappa\epsilon i\mu\epsilon\nu o\nu$) both of Matter as the receptacle of Forms, 2. 4. 1, and, as here, of $\nu o\eta\tau\dot{a}$. Cf. 6. 3. 4.

that something is wanting, that it is not yet the whole. Again, nothing contrary to its nature can happen to it ; for it is impassible. And if nothing can happen to it, it has no future and no past.

'In the case of created things, if you take away their future you take away their existence, which consists in continual growth ; but in things that are not created you cannot apply the idea of futurity without ousting them from their position in Reality. For they could not belong originally to the world of real being, if their life were in a becoming and in the future. . . . The blessed beings which are in the highest rank have not even any desire for the future ; for they are already all that it is their nature to be ; they possess all that they ought to possess ; they have nothing to seek for, since there is no future for them, nor can they receive anything for which there is a future. . . . The world of Spirit can admit nothing which belongs to not-being. This condition and nature of Reality is what we mean by eternity ; the word αἰών is derived from τὸ ἀεὶ ὄν, that which exists for ever. . . .[1]

'What then if we do not cease to contemplate the eternal world, if we remain united to it, adoring its nature ; if we do not weary in so doing, if we run to it and take our stand in eternity, not swerving to right or left, that we may be eternal like it, contemplating eternity and the eternal by that which is eternal in ourselves ? If that which exists in this manner is eternal and ever-existing, it follows that that which never sinks to a lower nature, and which possesses the fullness of life . . . must be perpetual. . . . Eternity then is a sublime thing ; it is identical with God. *Eternity is God manifesting his own nature ;* it is Being in its calmness, its self-identity, its permanent life. We must not be surprised to find plurality in God ; for everything Yonder is multiple on account of its infinite power. That is

---

[1] This etymology was generally accepted. It appears in the pseudo-Aristotelian *De Mundo*, 1. 9.

infinite which lacks nothing ; and that of which we speak is essentially infinite, because it loses nothing. Eternity then may be defined as life which is infinite because it is universal and loses nothing of itself, having no past and no future. . . .

' Since this nature, so all-beautiful and eternal, exists around the One, from the One, and to the One, never leaving it, but abiding around it and in it and living like it, Plato speaks with profound wisdom when he says that " eternity abides in One."[1] In these words he implies that Eternity not only reduces itself to unity with itself, but that it is the life of Reality around the One. This is what we seek, and that which so abides is eternity. That which abides in this manner, and which remains the same, that is to say, the activity of this life which remains of itself turned towards the One and united to it, and which has no illusory life or existence, must be eternity. For true being consists in never not being and never being different ; that is to say, in being always the same without distinctions. True being knows no gaps, no developments, no progress, no extension, no before or after. If it has no before or after ; if the truest thing that we can say about it is that it *is ;* if it is in such a way as to be Reality and life, we are again brought to the notion of eternity. We must add, however, that when we say that " Being is for ever," that there is not one time when it is and another when it is not, we are speaking with a view to clearness ; " for ever " is not used quite correctly. If we use it to express that Reality is indestructible, we may mislead ourselves by using words applicable only to the many, and to persistence in time.[2] It might be better to call eternity " that which is," simply. But as " that which is " is an adequate equivalent of " Reality," and as some writers have called

---

[1] Plato, *Timaeus*, 37.

[2] πλάνῳ ἂν τὴν ψυχὴν εἰς ἔκβασιν τοῦ πλείονος καὶ ἔτι ὡς μὴ ἐπιλείψοντός ποτε. A very obscure sentence ; I am not sure that I have given the meaning rightly.

Becoming " Reality," the addition of " for ever " seemed necessary.'[1]

It is plain from this passage, and from all that Plotinus says about the eternal world, that his conception of eternity is widely different from the hope of continued existence in time, to which many persons, though by no means so many as is often assumed, cling with passionate desire. Ghost-stories have no attraction for the Platonist. He does not believe them, and would be very sorry to have to believe them. The kind of immortality which ' psychical research ' endeavours to establish would be for him a negation of the only immortality which he desires and believes in. The difference between the two hopes is fundamental. Some men are so much in love with what Plotinus would call the lower soul-life, the surface-consciousness and surface-experience which make up the content of our sojourn here as known to ourselves, that they wish, if possible, to continue it after their bodies are mouldering in the grave. Others recognise that this lower soul-life is a banishment from the true home of the Soul, which is in a supra-temporal world, and they have no wish to prolong the conditions of their probation after the probation itself is ended, and we are quit of our ' body of humiliation.' Nor does Neoplatonism encourage the belief that the blessed life is a state which will only begin for the individual when the earthly course of the whole human race has reached its term. This theory of the ' intermediate state ' as a dreamless sleep finds a beautiful expression in Christina Rossetti :—

' O Earth, lie heavily upon her eyes ;
 Seal her sweet eyes weary of watching, Earth ;
 Lie close around her ; leave no room for mirth
With its harsh laughter, nor for sound of sighs.
She hath no questions, she hath no replies,
 Hushed in and curtained with a blessed dearth
 Of all that irked her from the hour of birth ;
With stillness that is almost Paradise.
Darkness more clear than noonday holdeth her.

[1] 3. 7. 3–6.

> Silence more musical than any song ;
> Even her very heart has ceased to stir :
> Until the morning of Eternity
> Her rest shall not begin nor end, but be ;
> And when she wakes she will not think it long.'

' The morning of Eternity,' it appears, is the beginning of a new series, snipped off at one end but not at the other. And the waiting time before that hour arrives must be a period of unconsciousness, in which the Soul is neither dead nor alive. This unphilosophical conception is very unlike the doctrine of Plotinus. For him, to win admittance into the eternal world, which lives in an everlasting Now, is to awake out of sleep. But the sleep is the surface life of common consciousness. And, as he says, we can take nothing with us which belongs to the dream-world of mortality. The Soul which lives Yonder in blessed intercourse with God is not the ' compound ' ($\sigma\acute{\upsilon}\nu\theta\epsilon\tau\omicron\nu$) which began its existence when we were born. Nothing which can never die was ever born. Our true self is a denizen of the eternal world. Its home is in the sphere of eternal and unchanging activity Yonder, even while it energises in the execution of finite but Divine purposes here below.

Eternity is an experience and a conception partly latent and partly patent in all human life. It is in part defined to our consciousness negatively. Of things in place and time we say : This thing is outside that. They cannot coincide or amalgamate ; hence they are different. And again we say, This thing comes after that. The former must disappear before the latter can arrive ; hence they are different. But our minds tell us that there is a large class of things of which these statements are untrue. These things do not interfere with each other or displace each other. They are alive and active, but they are neither born nor die. They are constant without inertia ; they are active but they do not move.[1] Our

---

[1] See Dr. Schiller's excellent essay on the $\acute{\epsilon}\nu\acute{\epsilon}\rho\gamma\epsilon\iota\alpha$ $\acute{\alpha}\kappa\iota\nu\eta\sigma\acute{\iota}\alpha\varsigma$ in Aristotle, in the volume called *Humanism*.

knowledge of the eternal order is as direct as our knowledge of the temporal order ; but our customary habits of thought and modes of speech confuse us. To be honest, we can think most clearly of eternal life when we divest the conception of its ethical associations ; but this is to cut the nerve which links the temporal and the eternal. It will lead us to acosmism, for this world will then have no meaning ; or, since ' outraged nature has her occasional revenges,' we may swing round into materialism. And the interpenetration of time and eternity in our consciousness, though it may spoil or confound the symmetry of our metaphysics, is, after all, a fact of the soul-nature, in which we live and move. Reason seeks to divide them, assigning to Cæsar and to God what belongs to each ; but in the true spiritual experience they are not divided. Time is a child of eternity, and 're-sembles its parent as much as it can.'[1] The most illum-inating of all prophetic writings are those in which the temporal is set in a framework of eternity, such as the Johannine presentation of the life of Christ, or Words-worth's interpretations of wild nature. And the sense of contrast between the temporal and the eternal exist-ence, which are both ours, has produced some of the noblest utterances of religious meditation. Such is the thought which inspired the 90th Psalm, or the following words of Augustine, ' Thou, O God, precedest all past times by the height of thine ever-present eternity ; and thou exceedest all future times, since they are future, and when they have come and gone will be past time. . . . Thy years neither come nor go ; but these years of ours both come and go, that so they may all come. All thy years abide together, because they abide . . . but these our years will all be only when they will all have ceased to be. Thy years are but one day ; and this thy day is not every day but to-day. This thy to-day is eternity.'[2]

[1] Schopenhauer has the remarkable thought that ' Time is the form in which the variety of things appears as their perishableness.'

[2] Augustine, *Confessions*, 11. 13. See also *Confessions*, 11. 24; *De Trin.* 12. 14 ; *In Psalmos*, 101.

The very transiency of time becomes a stately procession of images across a background of eternal truth. 'This day of ours does not pass within thee, and yet it does pass within thee, since all these things have no means of passing, unless somehow thou dost contain them all.'[1]

The natures of Time and Eternity are so diverse that it is very difficult to bring them into vital relation with each other. We might have expected that Plotinus would have resorted to his favourite expedient of introducing an intermediate category which should ' partake of the nature of both.' I do not find that he has done so.[2] But the Christian schoolmen of the Middle Ages, who on this subject are in direct descent from the Neoplatonists through the highly respected Boëthius, did make this attempt. The analysis of the concept *aevum*, which stands between Eternity and Time, is of great interest to the student of Neoplatonism. The following summary is taken mainly from the work of the very able and learned Jesuit, Bernard Boedder.[3]

In the strict sense, he says, Eternity implies an existence which is essentially without beginning and without end. But no creature can be *essentially* without beginning and end and internal succession. If such a creature exists, it owes its eternity to the will of God. But God is essentially eternal. As the First Cause, He can have had no beginning. Absolute necessity of existence must be identical with His essence ; He can therefore never cease to be. And His existence is unchangeable ; therefore it cannot contain any different successive phases or modes of being. Boëthius defines Eternity as

---

[1] *Id.* 10. 27. We miss in Plotinus what Augustine (*Confessions*, 7. 20, 21) also missed in him, the lesson of Divine love and human humility which the descent of the Eternal into time suggests to the Christian.

[2] Proclus does draw distinctions in his treatment of eternity. The One is προαιώνιος (as it is προ—everything else) ; and τὸ ἀίδιον (perpetuity) is a lower form of τὸ αἰώνιον (eternity). There is an ἀϊδιότης which is κατὰ χρόνον. There are ὄντα which are not in the full sense αἰώνια. This doctrine may have been one of the foundations of the scholastic doctrine of *aevum*.

[3] *Natural Theology*, p. 243 sq.

' a simultaneously full and perfect possession of interminable life.' Eternity, thus defined, is identical with the highest life conceivable, the self-activity of infinite intellectual will. This life is ' interminable,' because it endures of absolute necessity. It is ' simultaneously possessed ' because it is neither capable of development nor liable to defect. In God is neither past nor present nor future. As Boëthius expresses it, ' the passing Now makes time, the standing Now makes eternity.' The duration of God is one everlasting state, the duration of temporal being is liable to a succession of states really distinct from each other.

The duration of created Spirits is called *aevum.* In *aevum* there is no succession, as regards the substantial perfection of a created Spirit. Nevertheless, Spirits are not quite above time or succession ; for though the specific perfection of their substantial being is unalterable, they can pass from one thought and volition to another, and the Creator may cause in them now one and now another accidental perfection. Their essential being is above time, but they are liable to accidental modification of temporal duration. The duration called time belongs properly to Matter. St. Thomas Aquinas says : ' Time has an earlier and a later ; *aevum* has no earlier and later in itself, but both can be connected with it ; eternity has neither an earlier nor a later, nor can they be connected with it.' ' Spiritual creatures,' says Aquinas again, ' as regards their affections and intellections, are measured by time ; as regards their natural being, they are measured by *aevum ;* as regards their vision of glory, they participate in eternity.'

Baron von Hügel[1] has yielded to the temptation to find in the notion of *aevum* an anticipation of Bergson's *durée.* But as Bergson is far from holding the doctrines about Time and Eternity which are common to Neoplatonism and to the Catholic Schoolmen, it is not likely that he should need or acknowledge a conception which

[1] *Eternal Life,* p. 106.

was expressly designed to mediate between them. The scholastic *aevum* is something which 'participates' (in the Platonic sense) in Time and Eternity, as these words are understood by St. Thomas. It is, in fact, the form which belongs to Soul-life, as Time belongs to the changes of Matter, and Eternity to the life of Spirit. A modern Neoplatonist may find the conception useful in explaining the relations of the Soul to Time and Eternity, though it is of little or no value in bridging the chasm between temporal succession and the *totum simul*. 'We prefer to confess,' says another modern interpreter of the Schoolmen,[1] 'that we do not know how to effect the translation of Eternity into Time.' Eternity is above and beyond us, though in it we live and move and have our being. If we understood it, we should understand Time also, and the relation between them. But this cannot be, without transcending the conditions of our finite existence.

Eternity is, on one side, an ethical postulate. Without it, the whole life of will and purpose would be stultified.[2] All purpose looks towards some end to be realised. But if time in its course hurls all its own products into nothingness—if there is no eternal background against which all happenings in time are defined, and by which they are judged, the notion of purpose is destroyed. The existence of human will and reason becomes incomprehensible. Our minds travel quite freely over time and space ; they are not confined to the present ; whether we realise it or not, in every thought we imply that Reality is supratemporal. Both Time and Eternity are involved in every act of our moral and rational life. And it is through our experience of Time that we come to know Eternity. As Baron von Hügel says,[3] ' Time is the very stuff and

---

[1] John Rickaby, *General Metaphysics*, p. 214.
[2] Cf. Rothe, *Stille Stunden*, p. 219. ' He who believes in a God, must also believe in the continuance of life after death. Without this there would be no world which would be thinkable as an object (*Zweck*) for God.'
[3] *Eternal Life*, p. 386 sq.

means in and by which we vitally experience and apprehend eternal life. . . . A real succession, real efforts,
and the continuous sense of limitation and inadequacy
are the very means in and through which man apprehends
increasingly (if only he thus loves and wills) the contrast-
ing yet sustaining simultaneity, spontaneity, infinity,
and pure action of the eternal life of God.' Duration is
not eternal life, though in its entirety and meaning it is
very near to it. It may be called the eternity of the
phenomenal world. This thought has been very nobly
expressed in a fine sonnet by Sidney Lanier :—

> ' Now at thy soft recalling voice I rise
> Where thought is lord o'er Time's complete estate,
> Like as a dove from out the grey sedge flies
> To tree-tops green where coos his heavenly mate.
> From these clear coverts high and cool I see
> How every time with every time is knit,
> And each to all is mortised cunningly,
> And none is sole or whole, yet all are fit.
> Thus, if this age but as a comma show
> Twixt weightier clauses of large-worded years,
> My calmer soul scorns not the mark : I know
> This crooked point Time's complex sentence clears.
> Yet more I learn while, friend, I sit by thee :
> Who sees all time, sees all eternity.'

Eternity is that of which duration is the symbol and sacrament. It is more than the totality of that which strives
to express and ' imitate ' it. But Time ' resembles it as
far as it can.' All that we find in Time exists, ' in an
eminent sense,' in eternity. We must therefore beware,
when we tread the mystic's negative road, lest we cut
ourselves off from knowledge of God. When we say that
God, or eternity, is ' not like this,' we mean that Reality
is glimmering through its appearances as something
higher than they, but not as something wholly alien to
them. Therefore we need not discard those modes of
envisaging eternity which clearly depend on temporal
and spatial imagery. Such imagery cannot be dispensed
with ; for the symbols of substance and shadow equally

belong to this world, and do not take us much further than those of co-existence and succession.

Nevertheless it cannot be denied that popular religion, by insisting on its local and temporal imagery, has not only impeded the progress of natural science, but has sadly impoverished the idea of eternal life, and in the minds of very many has substituted a material fairyland for the true home of the Spirit. The Jewish tendency to throw the golden age into the future has its dangers, no less than the early Greek tendency to throw it into the past.

LECTURES XVII, XVIII, XIX

THE ABSOLUTE

(τὸ ἕν, τὸ πρῶτον, τὸ ἀγαθόν)

THE goal of the Intellect is the One. The goal of the Will is the Good. The goal of the Affections—of Love and Admiration—is the Beautiful.

These three words will all require close analysis. We shall find that the One is something other than a numeral; that the Good is not merely that which satisfies the moral sense; and that the Beautiful is not merely that which causes æsthetic pleasure.

We have seen that Goodness, Truth, and Beauty are the attributes of Spirit and the Spiritual world. They are the three objects of the Soul's quest. They may be represented as the three converging pathways which lead up the hill of the Lord; and they furnish three lines of proof.[1] The spiritual world *must be*—this is the conclusion of the dialectic, which convinces us that the idea of plurality implies that of unity, that of imperfection a perfect. It *ought to be*—this is the claim of the ethical

---

[1] Bradley is here again a valuable guide to understanding Plotinus. ' The relational form implies a substantial totality beyond relations and above them, a whole endeavouring without success to realise itself in their detail.' [This is the apex of the dialectical pyramid. But the disciple of Plotinus must not take ' realise itself ' in the Hegelian sense.] ' Further, the ideas of goodness, and of the beautiful, suggest in different ways the same result. . . . We gain from them the knowledge of a unity which transcends and yet contains every manifold appearance. . . . And the mode of union, in the abstract, is actually given ' (*Appearance and Reality*, p. 160). We must, however, remember that for Plotinus ' the relational form,' though it points beyond itself, is an essential character of οὐσία. ' We cannot get above νοῦς without falling outside it,' as Plotinus tells us.

sense. *It is*—this is the discovery of direct experience or intuition, made by the Soul yearning in love for its heavenly home.

The Path of Dialectic

The word 'dialectic,' like many other technical terms of Platonism, has helped to confuse modern critics. It means literally the art of discussion, but it has travelled far from its original meaning. Diogenes Laertius[1] quotes Aristotle as saying that the method was invented by Zeno, the Eleatic, from whom it was no doubt borrowed by Socrates. In the Dialogues of Plato it means the art of giving a rational account (λόγον) of things, and more especially the discovery of the general truths and principles which underlie the discoveries of particular sciences. For instance, the results of mathematical and astronomical science need to be examined by the dialectician.[2] In the *Republic*[3] Socrates claims that dialectic alone ' can comprehend by regular process all true existence, and what each thing is in its true nature ; for the arts in general are concerned with the desires or opinions of men, or are cultivated with a view to production and construction, or for the preservation of such productions and constructions ; and as to the mathematical sciences, which have some apprehension of true being, they only dream about being, but never behold the waking reality so long as they leave their hypotheses unexamined and are unable to give an account of them. . . . Dialectic does away with hypothesis, in order to make her own ground secure ; the eye of the soul, which is literally buried in an outlandish slough, is by her gentle aid lifted upwards ; and she uses as helpers and handmaids in the work of conversion the sciences which we have been discussing.' We reach true science only when we ' do

[1] Diogenes Laertius, 9. 25.
[2] Plato, *Euthydemus*, 290.
[3] Plato, *Republic*, 533.

away with the hypotheses ' which belong to some sciences and not to others. Such particular hypotheses are only postulates, and we desire to find the non-hypothetical first principle. Dialectic, thus understood, is the art of discovering the affinities of forms or ideas (εἴδη), and kinds or categories (γένη), with each other. This is why dialectic is specially concerned with the relations of Being, Change, and Permanence. Plotinus follows Plato closely in his treatment of dialectic. ' It is a science which enables us to reason about each thing, to say what it is and how it differs from others, what it has in common with them, where it is, whether it really exists, to determine how many real beings there are, and where not-being is to be found instead of true being. It treats also of good and evil, of all that is subordinated to the Good and to its contrary, of the nature of that which is eternal and of that which is not. It speaks of all things scientifically and not according to simple opinion. . . . It traverses the whole domain of the spiritual, and then by analysis returns to its starting-point.' Then it rests, in contemplation of the One, and hands over logical disquisitions to another art, subordinate to itself. Dialectic receives its clear principles from Spirit, which furnishes Soul with what it can receive. In possession of these principles, it combines and distinguishes its material, till it comes to pure spiritual knowledge. Dialectic is the most precious part of philosophy ; all existing things are ' Matter ' for it ; ' it approaches them methodically, possessing things and thoughts in combination.'[1] Falsehood and sophisms it recognises only to reject them as alien to itself. The lower kinds of knowledge it leaves to the special sciences, seizing the general truth about them by a kind of intuition. Philosophy includes these studies, such as the detailed application of ethical principles : dialectic, which is the same as wisdom (σοφία), is concerned with the principles themselves, on which con-

---

[1] ἅμα τοῖς θεωρήμασι τὰ πράγματα ἔχουσα. In true ἐπιστήμη the correspondence between thought and thing is perfect.

duct depends. But one cannot reach wisdom without traversing first the lower stages.[1]

Dialectic, then, is the study of first principles which leads up to intuitive wisdom. It passes through logic, and at last rises above it. Plotinus is at no pains to separate the intellectual ascent from the moral and the mystical; in fact he refuses to do so. They begin to join long before our journey's end. This view, so disconcerting both to 'intellectualists' (if there are any such people) and to those who try to find intellectualism in the school of Plato, is the outcome of the conception of logic which is common to Plato and Hegel. 'Logic is the supreme law or nature of experience, the impulse towards unity or coherence by which every fragment yearns towards the whole to which it belongs.'[2] The birth of logic is an experience which clamours for completion.

Dialectic, says Plotinus, rests, and worries itself no more (οὐδὲν ἔτι πολυπραγμονεῖ) when it has traversed the whole domain of Spirit. But it does not permit us to stop at the attributes of the spiritual world. Just as Eckhart, the most Plotinian of all Christian philosophers, distinguishes between God and the Godhead, so Plotinus must follow his quest of unity to the utmost limit. The God whom we commonly worship is the revelation, not the revealer. The source and ground of revelation cannot be revealed; the ground of knowledge cannot be known. So the common source and ground of Goodness, Truth, and Beauty must be beyond existence and beyond knowledge.

The Absolute as the One

If the Greeks had had a symbol for zero, and especially if that symbol had been the mystic circle, it may well be that the Pythagoreans and Plotinus would have anticipated John Scotus Erigena, who called the Absolute

---

[1] I. 3. 4–6.
[2] Bosanquet, *The Principle of Individuality and Value*, p. 340.

nihil. Plotinus does call ' the One ' the negation of all number.[1] The earlier Pythagoreans had not learnt to distinguish between numbers and the things counted. For this reason they affirmed that numbers are realities. Plato agreed that numbers are realities, but this is part of his affirmation that there are other kinds of reality besides that of sensible objects.[2] The Monad in Pythagorean arithmetic was not itself a number, but the source in which the whole nature of all numbers is implicit. They thought of the Monad as the undifferentiated whole, out of which particulars branched off. The true whole, as Plotinus said, is that which gives birth to the parts, not a mere collection of the parts.[3] Thus we must be careful not to give ' the One ' a merely numerical sense. In this, the numerical sense, unity and plurality are correlatives, so that we cannot have the former without the latter. In this sense, the Absolute One would be an impossible abstraction. But for Plotinus the One is the source from which the differentiation of unity and plurality proceeds ; it is the transcendence of separability rather than the negation of plurality. In the Fifth Ennead he says that ' the One is not one of the units which make up the number Two.' When we call the Absolute the One, we intend thereby only to exclude the notion of discerptibility.[4]

The unity in duality of Spirit and the Spiritual World points decisively to a deeper unity lying behind them. This is the coping-stone of the dialectic. ' Spirit,' he says,[5] ' cannot hold the first place. There must be a principle above it, such as we have been endeavouring to find. Spirit is at once νοῦς and νοητόν, that is to say, two things at once. If they are two, we must find that which is before this duality. What is this ? Is it Spirit alone ? No ; for there can be no νοῦς without a νοητόν ; separate τὸ νοητόν, and you will no longer have νοῦς. If the principle we are seeking is not νοῦς, it must, if

---

[1] 5. 5. 6.   [2] Burnet, *Early Greek Philosophers*, p. 308.
[3] 3. 7. 4.   [4] 5. 5. 4.   [5] 3. 8. 9.

it is to escape the dualism, be something above νοῦς. Why then should it not be τὸ νοητόν ? Because τὸ νοητόν is as closely joined to νοῦς as νοῦς to it. If then it is neither νοῦς nor νοητόν, what can it be ? We shall answer, the source from which both νοῦς and νοητόν proceed.' The Absolute is therefore inferred from the impossibility of reducing either νοῦς or νοητόν to dependence ; the two are inseparable, and the Absolute can be neither of them. Another reason, for Plotinus, why neither νοῦς nor νοητόν can be the Absolute is that they are themselves multiple. ' The νοήματα are not one but many,' and νοῦς also is many in one. The name ' The One ' is not adequate to express the nature of the Absolute, which cannot be apprehended by any of our senses. If any sense could perceive it, it would be sight ; but how can we see that which has no form ? We say that the Absolute is One as being indivisible ; but this is to introduce a quantitative measurement, which is quite out of place.[1] Without attempting to picture to ourselves the nature of the One, we can understand that as all things participate in unity, in different degrees, and as the path to reality is a progress from lower unities to higher unities, there must be, at the top of the ascent, an absolute unity, a perfect simplicity, above all differentiation. It is not the weakest and poorest of all numbers, but the plenitude of all, and the source of all.

The One as Beyond Existence

In considering the train of reasoning which led the Neoplatonists to place the Absolute ' beyond existence,' we must remember three things. (1) The nature of the Godhead is certainly unknown to us ; we are unable to form any idea of the absolute and unconditioned. (2) It is a principle of this philosophy that we are not cut off from the highest form of life—the eternal and universal life of Spirit. (3) We have, in the mystical

[1] 6. 9. 5, 6

state, an experience of intuition which is formless and indescribable, and which is therefore above the spiritual world of Forms or Ideas.

The doctrine goes back to Plato, and a little further still, for Eucleides of Megara was the first to identify the Good and the One, who is also called God and Wisdom.[1] He seems to have argued that all the Forms may be reduced to One, which alone exists. This line of thought leads straight to the nihilism of some Indian philosophy, for an all-embracing, undifferentiated, solely existing unity has no distinguishable content whatever. Plato, in the *Republic*,[2] seeks to escape this conclusion by relegating the Good, or the One, ' beyond Reality ' ($\epsilon\pi\epsilon\kappa\epsilon\iota\nu\alpha$ $\tau\hat{\eta}\varsigma$ $o\dot{\upsilon}\sigma\iota\dot{\alpha}\varsigma$). The passage, which is isolated in Plato, and is never referred to by Aristotle, had yet an enormous importance for subsequent philosophy, ' The God is not only the author of knowledge to all things known, but of their Being and Reality, though the Good is not Reality, but beyond it, and superior to it in dignity and power.' This remarkable sentence is followed by the famous allegory of the cave, in which the prisoners, when their heads are turned towards the light, see the realities which cast their shadows upon the walls of their den. ' In this world of true knowledge the Idea of the Good appears last of all, and is seen only with an effort ; and when seen is inferred to be the universal author of all things beautiful and right, parent of light and of the lord of light in this visible world, and the immediate source of reason and truth in the spiritual world ; and this is the power upon which he who would act rationally in public or private life must fix his gaze.' This position is half-way between that attributed to Eucleides and the doctrine of Plotinus. The ' Idea of the Good ' still belongs to the world of Real Being, and still, it would seem, subsumes the other Forms under itself ; but the Good itself is ' beyond Reality.'

[1] See Burnet, *Greek Philosophy*, Vol. 1, 230 sq.
[2] p. 509 sq.

It is not clear that Plato sanctions any goal of aspiration beyond this noblest of the Forms.

Alexandrian philosophy before Plotinus had pondered much upon the unknowable Godhead. To Philo, as a Jew, it was a dogma that no man may see God face to face, and live. The created cannot behold the uncreated. 'One must first become God—which is impossible—in order to be able to comprehend God.' Even Moses, though he 'entered into the thick darkness' where God dwells, could perceive nothing, and his prayer was answered only by a vision of the 'hinder parts' of the Eternal. God exists; it is folly to say more about Him than this. He has properties (ἰδιότητες), but no qualities (ποιότητες).[1] We may call Him eternal, self-existent, omnipotent, for these predicates belong to Him alone. But God is 'better than the Good itself and the Beautiful itself: He can be apprehended by Himself alone.' Philo's God is above space and time; but not 'beyond Reality.'

Clement of Alexandria, as a Christian, feels the same objection to saying that God is 'beyond Reality.' Accordingly, he declares that God is or has οὐσία, but outdoes the Neoplatonists by saying that He is 'beyond the One and above the Monad,'[2] a phrase which seems to have no meaning. 'He is formless and nameless, though we sometimes give Him names.' Origen attaches less value than Clement to the 'negative road' as the way to understand God's nature; but he insists that a certain divine inspiration (ἐνθουσιασμός τις) is necessary for the knowledge of Him.

The doctrine has had a long history in later Christian theology. Augustine, whose earlier works are steeped in Plotinus, says that God is *essentia,* not *substantia;* perhaps God alone should be called *essentia.*[3] 'We can know what God is not, but not what He is.'[4] Dionysius

---

[1] ἀποιος properly means *sui generis*, not belonging to any class.
[2] Clement, *Pæd.*, 1.8.71. But Iamblichus and Proclus also speak of a πάντη ἄρρητος ἀρχή above the One.
[3] Augustine, *De Trinitate*, 7. 5.
[4] *De Trinitate*, 8. 2.

the Areopagite describes God the Father as ' super-essential indetermination,' ' the unity which unifies every unity,' ' the absolute no-thing which is above all reality.' ' No monad or triad,' he exclaims in a queer ebullition of jargon, ' can express the all-transcending hiddenness of the all-transcending superessentially superexisting super-Deity.' Erigena is not afraid to follow Plotinus in denying Being to the Absolute. Being, he says, is a defect, since it separates from the superessential Good. ' The things that are not are far better than those that are.' God, therefore, ' *per excellentiam non immerito Nihilum vocatur.*' God is above the category of relation ; and therefore in the Godhead the Three Persons of the Trinity are fused. Eckhart, as we have seen, distinguishes between the Godhead and God. The Godhead is not Being, but the eternal potentiality of Being, containing within Himself all distinctions, as yet undeveloped. ' All things in God are one thing.' But Eckhart is determined not to deprive God of Being and Life. ' If I have said that God is not a Being and is above Being, I do not mean to deprive Him of Being, but to honour Being in Him.'[1] But elsewhere he uses the familiar language of mysticism, calling the Godhead the silence, the darkness, or the desert. His theory of creation resembles that of Plotinus. ' We were in God eternally, like a work of art in the mind of a master.' His distinction between God and the Godhead enables him to insist, like a modern Hegelian, on the immanence of God in the world. Without the creatures, God ' would not be God.'

Plotinus makes the same distinction between the Absolute and the knowable God, though he is more careful than Eckhart to maintain that the creation of the lower orders of Being is ' necessary ' because the higher order is what it is, not at all in order that it may become what it ought to be. He is quite clear that the One must be independent of the world of Forms.

The One is ' beyond οὐσία, beyond activity, beyond

---

[1] Cf. Delacroix, *Le Mysticisme en Allemagne*, p. 174.

νοῦς and νόησις.[1] It is 'an activity beyond νοῦς and
sense and life.'[2] We may call it First Activity,[3] or First
Potency;[4] since in the One there is no difference between δύναμις and ἐνέργεια;[5] but strictly δύναμις and
ἐνέργεια belong to οὐσία, and cannot properly be predicated of the Absolute. It has no limit or boundary,[6]
but is fundamentally infinite.[7] It is, in short, ineffable.[8]
We can say what it is not, but not what it is. After
ascribing to it the highest attributes that we can conceive,
we must add, ' yet not these, but something better.'

We must not ascribe Will to the Absolute, if Will
implies the desire for something not yet present.[9] But
we may say, ' It is what it willed to be,' for it is its own
author.[10] In a more detailed discussion, he says that
the One is ' all Will,' and that ' there is nothing in him
that is prior to his Will.' There is no real resemblance
between this doctrine and the blind unconscious Will of
Schopenhauer and von Hartmann. The One in Plotinus
is not unconscious, but superconscious. It possesses a
higher form of consciousness than the discursive reason,
or even than the intuitive perception of Spirit. Plotinus
calls it immediate apprehension (ἀθρόα ἐπιβολή).[11] He is
careful to explain that when we speak of Will in the
Absolute, we are using words incorrectly. What we mean
to assert is that the One posits himself (ὑφίστησιν ἑαυτόν),
that there is no chance or contingency in him, and that he
could never wish to be other than he is. In one curious
passage he says that ' he is what he wishes (θέλει, not
βούλεται) to be, or rather he projects (ἀπορρίπτει) what
he wishes into the world of Reality.' The Absolute is
essentially Will only as being his own cause : he is all
Will, because there can be nothing outside him. He is

---

[1] 5. 4. 2 ; 1. 7. 1. [2] 6. 8. 16.
[3] 5. 6. 6. It is ἐνέργεια ὑπὲρ νοῦν, 6. 8. 16; ἐνέργεια ἡ πρώτη ἄνευ
οὐσίας, 6. 8. 20 ; ἐνέργημα ἑαυτοῦ αὐτός, 6, 8. 16.
[4] 5. 4. 1. [5] 2. 9. 1. [6] 4. 3. 8 ; 6. 7. 17.
[7] 6. 5. 12, βυσσόθεν ἄπειρον. [8] 5. 3. 13, ἄρρητον τῇ ἀληθείᾳ.
[9] 5. 3. 12. [10] 6. 8. 13.
[11] Aliotta (p. 32) says truly enough that Hartmann endows his
' Unconscious ' with the same faculty. But in him this is a patent
inconsistency.

also *all* necessity, because there can be no contingency in his life. Plotinus would have agreed with Mr. Bosanquet,[1] that ' for the Absolute to be a Will, or purpose, would be a meaningless pursuit of nothing in particular.' The Absolute is all necessity, as being subject to no necessity. Being absolutely free, He is the cause of freedom in the world of Spirit. We may rightly call the One ' the giver of freedom ' (ἐλευθεροποιόν). All teleology belongs to the finite world of becoming, in which the thoughts of God are transmuted into vital law. Nevertheless, the purposes which constitute the reality of psychical life, and which live as achievement in the spiritual world, flow directly from the One, who ' is what he willed to be.' Plotinus does not bind us to the frozen passivity of the God of Angelus Silesius :—

> ' Wir beten : es gescheh, mein Herr und Gott, dein Wille ;
> Und sieh, er hat nicht Will', er ist ein ewge Stille.' •

Eckhart is nearer Plotinus when he says, ' He is God naturally, but not from nature ; willingly, but not from will.'

Plotinus also answers in the negative the question whether the One thinks (νοεῖ).[2] But he certainly does not mean that his Absolute is wrapped in eternal slumber. It has a ' true νόησις,' different from that of νοῦς.[3] He has ' self-discernment ' (διακριτικὸν ἑαυτοῦ), which implies a sort of self-consciousness.[4] It differs from νόησις as being more instantaneous, the subject-object relation being quite transcended. The only reason why νόησις, and ordinary self-consciousness (συναίσθησις), are denied to the Absolute is that these actions imply a sort

---

[1] *Principle of Individuality and Value*, p. 391 ; and cf. Bradley, *Appearance and Reality*, p. 483 sq.

[2] 6. 9. 6 ; 6. 7. 37. To these I add 3. 9. 3, where the manuscript reading is ἀλλ' οὐ θεοὶ τὸ πρῶτον ἐπέκεινα ὄντες. It is strange that none of the editors have seen how to restore this corrupt passage. We must read ἀλλ' οὐ νοεῖ τὸ πρῶτον ἐπέκεινα ὄντος. This is the thesis of the paragraph which follows. No sense whatever can be made out of θεοί.

[3] 3. 8. 10 ; 5. 4. 2.

[4] 6. 7. 16 and 5. 1. 7. He has οἷον συναίσθησιν τῆς δυνάμεως, ὅτι δύναται οὐσίαν. He even says that τῇ ἐπιστροφῇ πρὸς αὐτὸ ἑώρα, ἡ δὲ ὅρασις αὕτη νοῦς.

of duality. ' That which is absolutely self-sufficing does not even need itself.'[1] The One abides in a state of ' wakefulness (ἐγρήγορσις) beyond Being.'

We miss in Plotinus any clear statement that, in the words of Thomas Aquinas, ' God, in understanding himself, understands everything else. God sees himself by his essence ; all other things he sees not in themselves but in himself, in so far as he contains in his essence the likeness of all other things that come from him.' Aristotle's God has no knowledge of the imperfect, and Plotinus does not speak decisively on the other side.

The criticism will certainly be made, that Plotinus, after protesting that nothing can be said of the Absolute, tells us a good deal about it or him, investing him in fact with the attributes of a personal God. The attributes of Spirit are, after all, ascribed to the First Principle, only *per eminentiam*, and with apologies for the weakness of human thought. We must not say that the Absolute wills, and yet he is all Will. We must not say that he thinks, and yet he comprehends everything. We must not say that he is conscious, and yet he is more awake than we can ever be. Such a Being, it may be objected, is not the Absolute to whom the dialectic conducts ; he is not ' beyond Reality,' but the reigning monarch of the real world.

I do not see how this criticism is to be met, any more than I can justify the various characteristics which Herbert Spencer gives to the Unknowable, and Hartmann to the Unconscious. The real question for the student of Neoplatonism is not whether the dialectic really leads to an Absolute ' beyond existence.' It does. The question is whether this Absolute can be the object of worship, or of contemplation, without at once descending into the sphere of νοῦς. The mystical vision of the One will be dealt with presently. Here we are concerned with a number of statements about the One, which are intended to make us understand *what* he is, though we know that strictly he is not. Plotinus was well aware that *omnis*

[1] 5. 3. 13.

determinatio est negatio ;[1] but one cannot worship the *a* privative. He would probably not have been seriously troubled by the above criticism, for he has no desire at all to separate his three Divine Principles sharply from each other. He might perhaps have accepted our suggestion that the God of practical religion is the universal Soul, the God of devout and thankful contemplation the Great Spirit, the God of our most inspired moments the Absolute. ' And these three are one.' This is not so for the dialectic, if we treat the dialectic as a logical structure leading to a climax ; but we have seen that for the Platonist, dialectic is the method of acquiring knowledge of the eternal verities ; and scholastic logic, which does not recognise the fluidity and interpenetration of concepts in the spiritual world, gains lucidity and cogency at the price of truth. However, I will not conceal my opinion that Plotinus tells us too much about ' the One.' The inevitable result is that his successors postulate some still more mysterious principle behind the Monad.

The One as Infinite

The One is ' fundamentally infinite.' When we re-member that Matter was also defined as ' the infinite,' we may think that there is a danger of a ' meeting of extremes,' such as, I think, really exists in the philosophy of Herbert Spencer.[2] The abstract idea of absolute fullness has no determinations to distinguish it from the abstract idea of absolute emptiness. If they are different, it may be argued, that is only because in the philosophy of Plotinus ' the One ' has already begun to differentiate himself, and ' Matter ' to receive forms. We are con-fessedly in a region where discursive thought is no longer adequate, and we cannot leap off our shadows. To mount above νοῦς, Plotinus himself warns us, is to fall outside it. There is a profound truth in the observation of Proclus, already quoted, that the extremes (at the top

[1] ἡ προσθήκη ἀφαίρεσιν καὶ ἔλλειψιν ποιεῖ, 3. 9. 3.
[2] Cf. Proclus, Comm. 473. 3. 4. ὡς γὰρ ἡ ὕλη ἀνείδεος, καὶ ὁ θεός· καὶ δὴ καὶ ἄπειρον ἑκάτερον καὶ ἄγνωστον.

and bottom of the scale) are simple, but the intermediate
are complex. But the extremes are no more identical
than the ' religion ' to which, in Bacon's aphorism, depth
in philosophy recalls us, is identical with the religion
from which a little philosophy estranges us. With regard to the conception of the Infinite, it is perhaps true
to say that immeasurableness is revealed in the act of
measuring. The *fact* of limit ($\pi\acute{\epsilon}\rho\alpha s$) only implies the
indefinite ; the *act* of limiting implies the infinite. To
know the infinite is a contradiction ; for to know is to
limit ; but we know the fact of the infinite, for it is
implied in the act of knowing.

It is a common criticism, brought against mysticism
of the Indian type, that it ends in metaphysical nihilism.
The mystic who tries to apprehend the infinite grasps
only zero.[1] As applied to the actual teaching of Indian
thinkers, this criticism is based largely on Western misunderstanding of Eastern thought. Nirvana is not what
Europeans have agreed to paint it.[2] But the danger
certainly exists—and the best writers on mysticism have
fully admitted it—that we may grasp at a premature
synthesis and simplification of experience, and so lose
the rich content of spiritual life. The vacuity, passing
almost into idiocy, of many contemplatives is an object-
lesson in the consequences of this error. But no disciple
of Plotinus is likely to fall into it. He teaches us that
we must gain our soul first, and surrender it afterwards ;
there are no short cuts to the beatific vision. And the
highest experience, if it comes to us, will be light, not
darkness.

The question whether we ought to speak of God as
infinite has often been raised. To the Platonist, infinity
suggests the absence of Form, which in all objects of
thought is an evil ; to others it asserts freedom from all
limitations, and is therefore a proper term to apply to
God. Rothe[3] says, 'Absoluteness and infinitude are in

---

[1] On the different senses in which the One and Matter may be called
$\delta\acute{\upsilon}\nu\alpha\mu\iota s$ $\pi\acute{\alpha}\nu\tau\omega\nu$ see 5. 3. 15.

[2] See A. David, *Le Modernisme Bouddhiste* and Poussin, *The Way
to Nirvana*. [3] *Still Hours*, p. 98.

no way identical conceptions. Infinitude is merely eternity with the idea of self-negation added. It cannot, therefore, in any sense be predicated of God. There is no worse, no poorer definition of the Absolute than the word infinite. God in his immanent being is to be considered as entirely outside space and time, and therefore is just as little infinite as finite.' The root of this objection is that infinitude is an idea which belongs to space ; to ascribe it to God is the same blunder as to explain eternity as endless existence in time. But there is no harm in adopting the frankly metaphorical expression of the Schoolmen (following Augustine) that God has his centre everywhere, and his circumference nowhere.

The One as First Cause and Final Cause

The Absolute as the One is the first cause ; as the Good it is the final cause of all that is. Plotinus is quite explicit in asserting the causality of the Absolute.[1] But it must be remembered that the spiritual and phenomenal worlds are coeternal with the One, so that causality means little more than the assertion of a hierarchy in Reality, leading up to an all-embracing Absolute in which everything is contained, and which in the world of becoming is the primary source and final consummation of every process. The following quotation [2] will show in what relation the One stands to the world of νοητά. ' Whatever is engendered by another resides either in the principle which made it, or in another being, if there is one between it and its source ; for that which springs from another, and needs another to come into existence, needs another everywhere, and therefore resides in another. The lowest things are in the next lowest, the higher in the next highest, and so on up to the first principle. This first principle, having nothing above it, cannot be in another ; but it contains all the others, embracing them without dividing itself among them, and possessing them without

---

[1] The One is ἀρχή, 6. 9. 6 ; αἴτιον τῶν πάντων, 5. 5. 13 ; πηγὴ καὶ δύναμις γεννῶσα τὰ ὄντα ; an ἐνέργεια which is τελειότερον τῆς οὐσίας, δύναμις ὄντως ποιητική, 6. 8. 18. And cf. 3. 8. 9. 10.   [2] 5. 5. 9.

being possessed by them.' The One, he goes on, is everywhere and nowhere ; all things depend on it, and differ in
value according as the dependence is closer or more
remote.

Plotinus was well aware that it is not easy to show
how plurality can emanate from unity, Being from the
super-essential. Physical science is equally unable to
account for differentiation, and professes ignorance as to
whether ether, homogeneous electrons, atoms only
quantitatively different, and elements with very different
properties, are all modifications of some πρώτη ὕλη. The
difficulty is the same whether we begin at the top or the
bottom of the scale. To regard this problem as an inconsistency specially characteristic of Neoplatonism seems
to me unintelligent criticism. The solution offered by
Plotinus is that of *creation*. The Absolute does not cease
to be the Absolute by creating a world wholly dependent
on itself, nor does Spirit lose anything by creating the
Soul-world. To say that the Absolute must be God *plus*
the world seems to me like saying that the real Shakespeare is the poet *plus* the folio edition of his works. As
to the *motive* and *manner* of creation, it is obvious that
we cannot be expected to know much. ' How God
creates the world we can never understand,' says Prof.
Ward ; and many other philosophers have urged that
we cannot expect to know. But if, with Heracleitus, we
assume that the ' road up ' and the ' road down ' must
be the same, and if we can show, as Plotinus has shown,
that there is nowhere any *salto mortale* in the ascent of the
Soul to God, it seems reasonable to infer that there are
no unbridged chasms in the creation of the various orders
of Being by the Absolute, though we cannot understand
the first stages, because we are not God. We have not
even any secure footing in the Spiritual World, the
' second nature ' ; we do not even know our own highest
selves. As Malebranche says very well : ' My inner self
reveals only that I am, that I think, that I desire, that
I feel, that I suffer, etc. ; but it does not reveal to me
what I am, the nature of my feelings, of my passions, of

my pain, nor the relations of all these to one another, because, having no idea of my soul, not beholding its archetype in God, I am not able to discover either what it is, or the modes of which it is capable.'[1] If this is true, any theory which seemed to explain to us the origin of the spiritual world would be justly suspect. Nevertheless, Plotinus throws out some suggestions for countering objections. The existence of the world is due to the necessity of there being 'a second nature' (δευτέρα φύσις).[2] If there were no necessity for each principle 'to give of its own to another,' the Good would not be the Good, Spirit would not be Spirit, and Soul would not be Soul.[3] Without Spirit, the One would have no object for its activities; it would be alone and deserted, at a standstill. For activity is not possible in a being which has no inner multiplicity, unless it acts on another.[4] 'The One could not be alone; if it were, all things would remain hidden, having no form in the One.'[5] There is a 'mysterious power' (ἄφατος δύναμις) which impels each nature to create, and go on creating down to the lowest limit of existence. Thus only can its latent qualities be unfurled (ἐξελίττεσθαι). Why should we suppose that the One would remain standing still in itself? From envy? Or from want of power, though it is the power of all things?[6] The creation is a kind of overflow (οἷον ὑπερερρύη) of the One.[7] It is like the efflux of light and heat from the sun, which loses nothing in imparting itself.[8] Another favourite word is 'dependence' (ἐξαρτᾶσθαι),[9] which comes from Aristotle. There is an unbroken chain from the One to Matter and back. The One is present to all grades, since it penetrates all things with power. The chain is so continuous that 'wherever the third rank is present, there is also the second, and the first.'[10]

[1] Malebranche, *Entretien*, 3.   [2] 3. 2. 2.   [3] 2. 9. 3.
[4] 5. 3. 10. See, however, p. 63. Plotinus seems at times to welcome the idea of an inner reciprocity of Spirits ἐκεῖ.
[5] 4. 8. 6.   [6] 5. 4. 1.   [7] 5. 2. 1.
[8] 5. 1. 6. This unfortunate illustration is now employed by critics to discredit the theistic doctrine of creation.
[9] E.g. 1. 7. 1; 5. 5. 9; 1. 6. 7.   [10] 6. 5. 4.

The passages just quoted have a Hegelian sound. They suggest that the world is as necessary to the Absolute as the Absolute is to the world. Whether this view is right or wrong, it is not the philosophy of Plotinus. He insists upon the complete independence of the One in many places ; the following sentence may serve as a sample.[1] ' The Good is the principle on which all depends, to which all aspires, from which all proceeds, and which all need. In itself it is in need of nothing (ἀνενδεές), sufficient for itself, wanting nothing, the measure and term of all things, giving out of itself Spirit and Reality.' [2] The ' necessity ' which causes the real world to proceed from the First Principle is akin to the necessity for self-expression on the part of an artist ; it is not a vital necessity of growth or self-preservation. The Hegelian view, it need hardly be said, takes the world into the Absolute ; for otherwise the Absolute would need something outside itself, which is a contradiction. Further, it seems to make the time-process an essential factor in the life of the Absolute ; for according to this philosophy, as stated by its founder, God only comes to Himself in human history. It is no doubt difficult to say whether Hegel really means that God becomes, through history, something that He was not before, for he oscillates continually between two different kinds of development, the dialectical and the historical. Some Hegelians repudiate the notion of real progress in the Divine life, and speak instead of self-communication. This brings them much nearer to Plotinus, who himself is found saying that the One ' would have been hidden ' without a world. But the Hegelians, if I understand them, would say that without a world the Godhead would have been hidden *from itself*. This I do not think that Plotinus would admit. In Biblical language God made the world ' to make His glory to be known.' But such an expression has no meaning as applied to the inner life of the One. The activity of

---

[1] 1. 8. 2.

[2] The One is absolute Freedom. Its ὑπόστασις is ἐνέργεια, 6. 8. 7 ; and 6. 8. 20, ἐνέργεια οὐ δουλεύσασα οὐσίᾳ (not bound to any substance) καθαρῶς ἐστὶν ἐνέργεια.

the Absolute is purely one-sided; there is no reaction upon it.

I can imagine a critic saying: 'The One of Plotinus seems to me to be only an objectification of the categories of Cause and Substance, which analysis has driven out of the real world. The infinite regress has led him to take refuge in a citadel beyond the limits of thought, where he is unassailable because he has cut his communications with Reality.'

But for Plotinus there is no infinite regress, because things in time are not causes. Nor is it true that Substance, if by this is meant οὐσία, has been driven out of the real world. It is not the infinite regress of causation, but the infinite progress of aspiration, which leads us to the furthest confines of Reality, and beyond them to the fountain-head of all that is. We cannot ever say: 'Now I have reached the top, and may stop climbing.' '*Un Dieu défini est un Dieu fini.*' But Plotinus is as well aware as any of his critics that his titles for the One are attempts to name the Nameless.

The Path of Beauty

Plotinus calls the Absolute indifferently the One and the Good; he does not call it the Beautiful. In one passage[1] he seems to put the Beautiful in a slightly lower place than the One or the Good; but he half withdraws this judgment. 'A man will first ascend to Spirit and will there behold all beautiful forms, and will say that this (namely, the world of Forms) is beauty; for all things in them are beautiful, being the offspring and essence of Spirit. Beyond this, as we affirm, is the nature of the Good, which radiates the Beautiful in front of itself (προβεβλημένον τὸ καλὸν πρὸ αὐτῆς ἔχουσαν). So that, speaking shortly, the Good is the First-Beautiful. If we wish to make distinctions within the spiritual world, we shall say that the Beautiful in the spiritual world is the place of the ideas, but that the Good is beyond this, as

---

[1] I. 6. 9.

the source and beginning of the Beautiful. Or we may put the Good and the First-Beautiful on the same level.' Other passages seem to show that he does not wish to put the Beautiful on a lower plane, especially that in which he says, ' he who has not yet seen him desires him as the Good, but he who has, admires him as the Beautiful.' [1] It is true that the One ' does not wish to be beautiful ' ; but the One does not ' wish ' to be anything, having in itself the potency of all things.[2] The One is ' the flower of all that is beautiful,' ' beauty above beauty.' [3] It may, as we have seen, be identified with the ' First-Beautiful.' Perhaps the clearest passage about the relations of the One and the Beautiful is 5. 5. 12. We do not begin to perceive and know the Beautiful until we ' know and are awake ' ; but ' the Good is inborn, and present to us even when we are asleep ' ; [4] and ' it does not amaze its beholders, because it is always with them.' The ' unconscious desire ' (ἀναίσθητος ἔφεσις) for the Good proves it to be ' more original ' (ἀρχαιότερον) than the Beautiful. Further, all are satisfied with the Good ; but not all with the Beautiful, which some think is ' advantageous for itself, not for them.' Beauty, too, is more superficial and subjective ; people are satisfied to be *thought* beautiful, but not to be *thought* good. Again, the enjoyment of Beauty is exciting and mixed with pain ; that of the Good is a calm delight. Even Yonder, the Beautiful needs the Good, not the Good the Beautiful.

These reflections are rather surprising, at any rate till we remember that ' the Good ' is not to be identified with ' the morally good.' On this more must be said presently. The curious opinion that the enjoyment of Beauty is ' mixed with pain ' seems to come from Plato,[5] for whom sex-love, ἔρως γλυκύπικρος, is the type of spiritual love. The position of inferiority here ascribed to the Beautiful is revoked in 1. 6. 6. ' When the Soul is raised to Spirit,

---

[1] 1. 6. 7. [2] 6. 8. 10. [3] 6. 7. 8.
[4] We may compare Psalm 127. 3, ' Even in sleep God gives his gifts to his beloved.'
[5] *Phaedrus*, 251 ; and cf. *Philebus*, 48, where he says that great works of art bring tears to the eyes.

it becomes more beautiful. Spirit, and the gifts that flow from Spirit, are its proper Beauty, for only when it becomes Spirit is Soul truly Soul. Wherefore it is rightly said that, for the Soul, to become good and beautiful is to be made like God, because from Him comes the beautiful and the other part of reality.[1] Or rather we should say that Reality is Beauty, and " the other nature " is the Ugly. The Ugly and the First-Evil are the same, and, on the other hand, Good and Beautiful are the same, or the Good and Beauty. We may therefore study Beautiful and Good together, and Ugly and Bad together. *We must give the primacy to Beauty, which is also the Good. Then follows Spirit, which is identical with the Beautiful.* Soul is beautiful through Spirit ; other things that are beautiful are so through the Soul which forms them, including beautiful actions and practices. Even bodies, which are reckoned beautiful, are the creation of Soul ; for being a Divine thing, and as it were a part of the Beautiful, it makes all that it touches and controls beautiful, so far as they are able to receive it.' Thus he distinguishes Beauty (καλλονή), which he *identifies* with the One, from the Beautiful (τὸ καλόν), which is Spirit. The One, being formless (ἄμορφον καὶ ἀνείδεον) could hardly be τὸ καλόν. ' Beauty is not embodied in forms ' (τὸ κάλλος οὐ μεμόρφωται),[2] but τὸ καλόν is. ' The First-Beautiful, and Beauty, are formless, and Beauty Yonder is the nature of spiritual Good.' [3] The one is ' the beginning and end of Beauty.'

When we take these passages together, we find that Plotinus has three names for his Absolute—the One, the Good, and Beauty. These are the three attributes of Spirit, carried up to their primary source, above the place where the streams divide and assume those determinations which, as Spinoza says, are always negations. There is a certain awkwardness in correlating ' the One ' and ' the Good,' not with ' the Beautiful,' but with ' Beauty ' ; but the reasons for it will now be apparent.

---

[1] i.e the higher part ; but see the next sentence.
[2] 6. 7. 32.   [3] 6. 7. 33.

A more serious criticism is that the One, thus character-ised, is a Triad of Platonic Ideas, and not the hidden source from which all the Ideas flow. Plotinus is, I think, well aware of this. Strictly, though, the three attributes of Spirit, however exalted to their ideal per-fection, are the first determinations of the Absolute, and not the Absolute itself. The ' Spirit in love ' worships the One as the fountain of these Divine ideals, which are the highest things that we can know. Plotinus might, no doubt, have given more consideration to the relations of Goodness, Truth, and Beauty to each other, especially as the rival claims of these three ideals give rise to some serious practical and moral problems. He has not thought it necessary, because it has never occurred to him to isolate the intellect, or the artistic sense, or the moral consciousness, in the way that some modern thinkers have done.

The Path of Perfection

' It is essential to the understanding not only of Plato but of Greek philosophy generally, to realise the place held by " the Good." ' [1] Three ideas are here inseparable: (1) the Good is the supreme object of all desire and aspiration. (2) The Good is the condition of knowledge ; it is that which makes the world intelligible. (3) The Good is the creative and sustaining cause of the world. ' The Good ' did not in the first instance involve any moral qualities. It meant the object of desire—that which we most want. Our Good is that for which we would give up everything else. Man is always a creature of means and ends ; he is a rational being, who lives for something. This explains the connexion between reason and the Good. Greek thought is intensely teleological, not in the sense that the world was made for men, for ' the universe contains many beings more divine than man,' but ' the nature of a thing is its end,' the object or

[1] R. L. Nettleship, *Lectures on Plato's Republic*, p. 218.

ideal which it strives to realise.   The good life is directed towards the most worthy end, and the pursuit of this end is the immanent principle which gives life its meaning and character.   'Virtue' (ἀρετή) is not necessarily a moral quality ;   it is that which makes anything good of its kind.   Thirdly, the Good *makes* things what they are. The reality of things is what they *mean*, what they are 'good for' ;   and it is the Good which gives them their place, and assigns them their proper task (ἔργον).

It has been said that Plotinus alters Plato's doctrine of the Good, inasmuch as for Plato the Good is within the circle of the Ideas, while for Plotinus it is above them. But this overstates the difference.   For Plato the Good is the supreme source of light, of which everything good, true, and beautiful in the world is the reflexion.[1]   In the *Republic* [2] he says that we must look at all other Forms in the light of the Form of the Good, which is the starting-point of knowledge.   The Good is beyond knowledge and being, or at least beyond our knowledge of being.   Beauty and Truth are the Good under certain forms.   The question has often been raised whether in Plato the Form (or Idea) of the Good is the same as God.   The discussion is not a very profitable one, for θεός is by no means an equivalent of the God of the modern theist.   But the identification is impossible, because for Plato God is a Soul, not a Form.   The Form of the Good is rather the pattern which the Creator copies in making the world.

It is undoubtedly true that Plotinus exalts 'the Good' to a more inaccessible altitude than Plato has done.   It is not for us only, but for the highest intelligence, that the Good is 'beyond being.'   But if the Good is the Absolute, the question at once arises whether we can rightly use such a name for it as 'the Good.'   Plotinus insists that the Absolute cannot be 'the Beautiful,' but Beauty, or the source of the Beautiful.   Why does he not say that it cannot be the Good, but Goodness, or the

[1] Nettleship, p. 81.
[2] Plato, *Republic*, pp. 505–509.   Cf. Burnet, *Greek Philosophy*, p. 169.

source of the Good?[1] In fact, this is his view; but in loyalty to Plato he retains the name, and explains that in reference to *us* the One is the Good, and so may be called by this name, though it is not strictly accurate.

Plotinus dissociates 'the Good' from the idea of mere moral excellence. 'Virtue is not the Good, but a Good.'[2] It is undoubtedly true that morality, as such, must be transcended in the Absolute. Morality lives in a radical antithesis ; it is what it is only in contrast with its opposite. So Rothe[3] says that the good in God is not moral good. Moral good is becoming and is destined to become real good, but it has not yet attained perfection. In attaining this perfection it ceases to be moral good. But that which only exists as one side of an antithesis cannot be the Absolute, or even fully real. We must therefore be careful not to give a strictly ethical sense to the Good as a name of the One. The Good, for Plotinus, is *unity as the goal of desire.*[4] This desire, he says, is universal.[5] The Good is the fulfilment of the natural desire (ὄρεξις) for self-completion and self-transcendence, which every finite centre of consciousness feels. Our life indeed *is* that desire ; all life is a *nisus* towards its proper goal. This unity which is the Good of all finite life is also the source of all individual being. All being begins and ends in the Good. Spirit flows over into Soul, unconsciously. Soul returns to Spirit, consciously ; and Spirit is rooted in the One. 'From the great deep to the great deep he goes.'

Perhaps we should understand Plotinus' supreme category better if we called it 'the Perfect' instead of the Good. It is *valor valorum,* as Nicholas of Cusa says of

---

[1] Origen prefers ἀγαθότης to τὸ ἀγαθόν. Denis, p. 87.
[2] 1. 8. 6.   [3] *Still Hours,* p. 97.
[4] 6. 8. 7, ἡ τοῦ ἀγαθοῦ φύσις αὐτὸ τὸ ἐφετόν. Proclus (Dubner, lvi.) says clearly : ἐστιν ἡ ἀγαθότης ἕνωσις καὶ ἡ ἕνωσις ἀγαθότης. What Plotinus means by the Good is clear from 5. 5. 9, διὸ καὶ ταύτῃ ἀγαθὸν τῶν πάντων. ὅτι καὶ ἔστι καὶ ἀνήρτηται πάντα εἰς αὐτὸ ἄλλο ἄλλως. διὸ καὶ ἀγαθώτερα ἕτερα ἑτέρων, ὅτι καὶ μᾶλλον ὄντα ἕτερα ἑτέρων (' one thing is better than another, in proportion as it *is*—possesses οὐσία—in higher degree than another ').
[5] 6. 2. 11.

God. Its characteristic is that 'it needs nothing.'[1] It is
quite in accordance with his usual method when Plotinus
reminds us that 'the Good' which we recognise as such
is not the Absolute Good, but is relative to the stage
which we have reached ourselves.[2] 'The Good of Matter
is Form ; for Matter, if it were conscious, would receive
it with pleasure. The Good of the Body is Soul ; for
without it, it could neither exist nor persist. The Good
of the Soul is virtue ; then, rising higher, it is Spirit. The
Good of Spirit is that which we call the First Principle.
Each of these Goods produces something in the object
of which it is the Good ; it gives it either order and
beauty, or life, or wisdom and happiness. Finally, the
Good gives to Spirit an activity, which emanates from
the Good, and spreads over it what we call its light.'[3] In
the same chapter he tries to explain how Plato in the
Philebus came to 'mix pleasure with the end [of life],
thereby making the Good not simple, nor in Spirit only.'
'Plato was not trying to determine what is the Good
absolutely, but the Good for man' ; the two are not the
same. He is anxious to prove that Plato's view was
really the same as his own. 'Plato,' he says,[4] 'establishes
three degrees in the hierarchy of beings. Everything is
ranged round the king of all. He speaks here of things
of the first rank. He adds : That which is of the second
rank is ranged round the Second Principle, and that
which is of the third rank round the Third Principle. He
also says that the First Principle is the father of cause—
meaning Spirit by "cause" ; for he makes Spirit the
Demiurge ;[5] and also that Spirit creates Soul in the
"bowl" of which he speaks. The cause being Νοῦς, its
"father" must be the Absolute Good, the Principle above
Spirit and above existence.' He is on safer ground when
he says that the 'pure and unmingled Spirit' of Anaxa-
goras is by definition detached from all sensible things,

[1] 3. 8. 11, οὐδενὸς δεῖται.   [2] 6. 7. 25.   [3] 6. 7. 25.
[4] 5. 1. 8. The reference is to the *Second Epistle*.
[5] Plotinus also calls Spirit the Demiurge, 2. 3. 18.

and that the ' perpetual flux' of Heracleitus is meaningless unless there is also an eternal and unchanging One.
Aristotle, he says truly, by making his highest Principle
' think itself,' places it below the absolute One. The
Pythagoreans, as he sees, are nearest to his own theory.

' Good,' in relation to finite experience, is the perfection
to which each grade in the hierarchy aspires, and having
attained which it passes into the next stage above. ' All
things strive after life, after immortality, and after
activity.'[1] True life and true Spirit are identical, and
both come from the Good. The Ideas—the spiritual
world and its contents—are good, but not the Good.
We cannot stop at the world of Spirit, as if the First
Principle was to be found there. ' The Soul does not
aspire to Spirit alone. Spirit is not our supreme end,
and all does not aspire to Spirit, while all aspires to the
Good ; beings which do not possess νοῦς do not all seek
to possess it, while those which do possess it are not content to stop there. Νοῦς is sought as the result of reasoning ; but the Good is desired before argument. If the
object of desire is to live, to live always, and to act, this
is desired not as Spirit, but as good, as coming from good
and leading to good ; for it is only thus that we desire
life.' It is then natural for the Soul, and still more for
Spirit, to aspire to the absolutely perfect. Nothing else
contents us. ' When a man sees this light, he moves
towards it, and rejoices in the light which plays over the
spiritual world. Even here, we love bodies not for themselves, but for the beauty which shines in them. For each
νοητόν is what it is in itself ; but it only becomes an
object of desire when the Good gives it colour, bestowing
grace upon the object and love upon the subject. As
soon as the Soul receives into itself the effluence from
above, it is moved, it is filled with holy ecstasy, and
becomes love. Before that, it is not moved by the sight
of Spirit, for all its beauty ; its beauty is inactive, till it
receives the light of the Good ; and the Soul lies supine

[1] 6. 7. 20.

before it and wholly inactive, cold and stupid even in the presence of Spirit. But when warmth from the Good enters into it, it becomes strong and wide awake, and though troubled by what lies near at hand, it ascends more lightly to that which a kind of memory tells it to be greater. And as long as there is anything higher than what is present to it, it rises, lifted up naturally by that which implanted the love. Beyond the spiritual world it rises, but it cannot pass beyond the Good, because there is nothing beyond. If it abides in the region of Spirit, it beholds indeed beautiful and noble things, but is not completely in possession of all that it seeks. For the world of Spirit is like a face which does not attract us in spite of its beauty, because no grace plays upon its beauty. Even here we are charmed not by symmetry as such, but by the beauty which shines upon it. A living face is more beautiful than a dead one ; a statue which is full of life, as we say, is more beautiful than one which appears lifeless, though the latter be more symmetrical ; a living animal is more beautiful than a picture of one. This is because the living appears to us more desirable ; it has a soul ; it is more like the Good ; it is so because it is coloured by the light of the Good, and enlightened by it is more wide awake and lighter ; and in its turn it lightens its own environment [the body], and as far as possible makes it good and awakens it.'[1]

This very remarkable passage shows that Plotinus was not insensible to the feeling of chill which repels many moderns from Platonism. The world of ideas, of perfect forms, of stable beauty and perfection—is it not after all ' faultily faultless, icily regular, splendidly null ' ? Is it not too much like the beautiful but cold and motionless marble statues in which the Greek spirit expressed itself so perfectly ?[2] We have seen that Plotinus by no means intended his spiritual world to have this character. It

[1] 6. 7. 22.
[2] Whether this was the effect of Greek statuary when it was new is another question.

is to be a world of life, activity, and ceaseless creativeness. But as the apex of a dialectical pyramid it may even seem almost forbidding. If the Soul, on getting there, were to say, I see all to admire, but nothing to love, what answer should be made ? Some later philosophers have shrunk from the cold white light of the eternal and unchanging, and have willingly embraced the warm colours and rapid changes of the world of appearance—a lower sphere, doubtless, but better fitted for such beings as we are to live in. So Schiller invokes Colour rather than Light to be his companion.

' Wohne, du ewiglich Eines, dort bei dem ewiglich Einen !
  Farbe, du wechselnde, komm' freundlich zum Menschen herab.'

Plotinus could not have made this invocation without being false to the first principle of his philosophy. The Soul is forbidden to acquiesce in any downward move- ment. The only escape from difficulties is to press ever upward, in the confidence that all disharmonies will be resolved, all obstacles left behind, as we resolutely turn our backs upon change and strife, and follow the gleam of the pure and undivided Unity. Even in heaven the Soul is not content with itself. It must still aspire,[1] and its aspiration is purest and keenest when it is in full view of the very highest.[2] It is then that the Soul takes fire, and is carried away by love. The fullest life is the fullest love ; and the love comes from the celestial light which streams forth from the Absolute One, the Absolute Good, that supreme Principle ' which made life, and made Spirit, the source and beginning, which gave Spirit to all spiritual things and life to all living things.' [3] But, we may ask, what is there in the idea of absolute perfec- tion, raised above all forms and all existence, to kindle

---

[1] 3. 8. 11. ἐν τῷ νῷ ἡ ἔφεσις καὶ ἐφιέμενος ἀεὶ καὶ ἀεὶ τυγχάνων. And 5. 3. 10. πόθος τις καὶ ἡ γνῶσις—very fine words.
[2] Cf. Leo, *Ninth Sermon on the Nativity*. ' None draws nearer to the knowledge of the truth than he who understands that however far he advances in divine things there is always a beyond for him to seek. He who thinks that he has reached his goal has not found what he sought.' [3] 6. 7. 23.

this passionate love and adoration in the Soul ? If we have not loved our brother whom we have seen, and this warm world of adventure and change, which claims us as its own, how can we love the Godhead whom no man hath seen or can see, who dwelleth in the light that no man can approach unto ? The best answer to these questions is to consider what Plotinus has to tell us about the vision of the One. For it is unquestionably a genuine experience of his own—this ecstatic love of the Absolute. Moreover, the great army of mystics, Christian, Pagan, Mohammedan, corroborate all that the great Neoplatonist describes to us. The ' Spirit in love ' (νοῦς ἐρῶν) [1] is the culmination of personal religion ; and the object of this adoration is not the limited half-human God of popular religion, but the ineffable mysterious Power to whom we shrink from ascribing any human attributes whatever.

The Vision of the One

We can know the unknowable, because in our deepest ground we are the unknowable.[2] This is the ultimate doctrine of the Neoplatonic metaphysics. There is a mystery in ourselves, and in the objects of our knowledge, which the intellect cannot penetrate. Even the Spirit, while it occupies itself with itself as Spirit, with its intuitive power of seeing as Spirit, and with the world of the One-Many in which the Spirit beholds itself, cannot pierce to the depths of this mystery. Only when the Spirit is carried out of itself by aspiring love, are the unplumbed depths of its being stirred, and it *becomes* for a moment that which it can never *know*, the absolute Ground of all being. In this experience the identification of Thinker and Thought is so complete that we cannot speak of knowledge or consciousness. We may speak of " vision," or ' immediate apprehension,' but these and any other words fail to express what they aim at. Eckhart says,

[1] 6. 7. 35.   [2] 3. 8. 9.

'The eye with which I see God is the same with which God sees me. My eye and God's eye are one eye, and one sight, and one knowledge, and one love.' This can only be true of those rare moments of ecstasy when the saint or seer is 'caught up into the third heaven,' and no longer knows whether he is 'in the body or out of the body.' In this state, the very conditions of conscious-ness are suspended, the Soul being more closely identified with the One than νοῦς is with νοητά ; in other words, the subject-object relation is left behind.

The favourite Christian doctrine, best known in the form immortalised by Pascal, 'Tu ne me chercherais pas, si tu ne m'avais déjà trouvé,' is the Plotinian form of the ontological argument. It occurs in Bernard (*De Diligendo Deo*, 7. 22), 'nemo te quaerere valet, nisi qui prius invenerit.'

But we will let Plotinus expound his doctrine and give us (so far as that is possible) his experience, in his own words.

'What then is there better than this wisest life, exempt from fault and error ? What is better than Spirit which embraces all ? What is better than universal life and universal Spirit ? If we answer, That which made these things, we must go on to ask how it made them ; and if no higher principle manifests itself, the argument will proceed no further, but will stop at this point. But we must go higher, for many other reasons and especially because the principle which we seek is the Absolute which is independent of all things ; for things are incapable of sufficing for themselves, and each of them has a share in the One, from which it follows that none of them is the One. . . . That which makes being and independence is not itself being and independence, but above both. Is it enough to say this and pass on ? Or is the Soul in labour with something more ? Perhaps it must bring forth, filled as it is with travail-pangs, after hastening eagerly towards the Absolute. Nay, we must try rather to charm her, if we can find any magic spell against her pains. Perhaps something of what we have already said, if it were often repeated, might act as a charm. Or where shall we find another, a new charm ? For although it permeates all Truth, and therefore the Truth of which we participate, nevertheless it escapes us when we try to speak of it or even to think of it. For the discursive reason, if it wishes to say anything, must seize first one element of the Truth and then another; such are the conditions of discursive thought. But how can discursive thought apprehend the absolutely simple ? It is enough to apprehend it by a kind of spiritual intuition (νοερῶς ἐφάψασθαι). But in this act of apprehension we have neither the power nor the time to say anything about it ; afterwards we can reason about it. We may believe that we have really seen, when a sudden light illumines the Soul ; for this light comes from the One and is the One. And we may think that the One is present, when, like another god,[1] he illumines the house of him who calls upon him ; for there would be no light without his presence. Even so the Soul is dark that does not behold him ; but when illumined by him, it has what it desired, and this is the true end and aim of the Soul, to apprehend that light, and to behold it by that light itself, which is no other than the light by which it sees. For that which we seek to behold is the light which gives us light, even as we can only see the sun by the light of the sun. How then can this come to us ? Strip thyself of everything.'[2]

'We must not be surprised that that which excites the keenest of longings is without any form, even spiritual form, since the Soul itself, when inflamed with love for it, puts off all the form which it had, even that which belongs to the spiritual.world. For it is not possible to

---

[1] Like one of the gods of the popular mythology. **Commentators** suggest that Plotinus has in mind either Homer, Od. 19. 33, πάροιθε δὲ Παλλὰς Ἀθήνη, χρύσεον λύχνον ἔχουσα, φάος περικαλλὲς ἐποίει, or the *Hymn to Demeter*, 279, τῆλε δὲ φέγγος ἀπὸ χροὸς ἀθανάτοιο λάμπε θεᾶς . . . αὐγῇς δ' ἐπλήσθη πυκινὸς δόμος, ἀστεροπῆς ὥς.

[2] 5. 3. 17.

see it, or to be in harmony with it, while one is occupied
with anything else. The Soul must remove from itself
good and evil and everything else, that it may receive the
One alone, as the One is alone. When the Soul is so
blessed, and is come to it, or rather when it manifests its
presence, when the Soul turns away from visible things
and makes itself as beautiful as possible and becomes like
the One ; (the manner of preparation and adornment is
known to those who practise it ;) and seeing the One
suddenly appearing in itself, for there is nothing between,
nor are they any longer two, but one ; for you cannot
distinguish between them, while the vision lasts ; it is
that union of which the union of earthly lovers, who wish
to blend their being with each other, is a copy. The Soul
is no longer conscious of the body, and cannot tell whether
it is a man or a living being or anything real at all ; for
the contemplation of such things would seem unworthy,
and it has no leisure for them ; but when, after having
sought the One, it finds itself in its presence, it goes to
meet it and contemplates it instead of itself. What itself
is when it gazes, it has no leisure to see. When in this
state the Soul would exchange its present condition for
nothing, no, not for the very heaven of heavens ; for
there is nothing better, nothing more blessed than this.
For it can mount no higher ; all other things are below it,
however exalted they be. It is then that it judges rightly
and knows that it has what it desired, and that there is
nothing higher. For there is no deception there ; where
could one find anything truer than the True ? What it
says, that it is, and it speaks afterwards, and speaks in
silence, and is happy, and is not deceived in its happiness. Its happiness is no titillation of the bodily senses ;
it is that the Soul has become again what it was formerly,
when it was blessed. All the things which once pleased
it, power, wealth, beauty, science, it declares that it
despises ; it could not say this if it had not met with
something better than these. It fears no evil, while it
is with the One, or even while it sees him ; though all

else perish around it, it is content, if it can only be with him; so happy is it.'[1]

'The soul is so exalted that it thinks lightly even of that spiritual intuition which it formerly treasured. For spiritual perception involves movement, and the Soul now does not wish to move. It does not call the object of its vision Spirit, although it has itself been transformed into Spirit before the vision and lifted up into the abode of Spirits. When the Soul arrives at the intuition of the One, it leaves the mode of spiritual perception. Even so a traveller, entering into a palace, admires at first the various beauties which adorn it; but when the Master appears, he alone is the object of attention. By continually contemplating the object before him, the spectator sees it no more. The vision is confounded with the object seen, and that which was before object becomes to him the state of seeing, and he forgets all else. The Spirit has two powers. By one of them it has a spiritual perception of what is within itself, the other is the receptive intuition by which it perceives what is above itself. The former is the vision of the thinking Spirit, the latter is the Spirit in love. For when the Spirit is inebriated with the nectar, it falls in love, in simple contentment and satisfaction; and it is better for it to be so intoxicated than to be too proud for such intoxication.'

'If you are perplexed[2] because the One is none of those things which you know, apply yourself to them first, and look forth out of them; but so look, as not to direct your intellect to externals. For it does not lie in one place and not in another, but it is present everywhere to him who can touch it, and not to him who cannot. As in other matters one cannot think of two things at once, and must add nothing extraneous to the object of thought, if one wishes to identify oneself with it, so here we may be sure that it is impossible for one who has in his soul any extraneous image to conceive of the One while that

[1] 6. 7. 34. The next paragraph is abridged from 6. 7. 35.
[2] 6. 9. 7, to end.

image distracts his attention. Just as we said that
Matter must be without qualities of its own, if it is to
receive the forms of all things, so *a fortiori* must the Soul
be formless if it is to receive the fullness and illumination
of the First Principle. If so, the Soul must forsake all
that is external, and turn itself wholly to that which is
within ; it will not allow itself to be distracted by anything external, but will ignore them all, as at first by not
attending to them, so now last by not seeing them ; [1] it
will not even know itself ; and so it will come to the
vision of the One and will be united with it ; and then,
after a sufficient converse with it, it will return and
bring word, if it be possible, to others of its heavenly
intercourse. Such probably was the converse which
Minos was fabled to have had with Zeus,[2] remembering
which he made the laws which were the image of that
converse, being inspired to be a lawgiver by the divine
touch. Perhaps, however, a Soul which has seen much
of the heavenly world may think politics unworthy of
itself and may prefer to remain above. God, as Plato
says, is not far from every one of us ; he is present with
all, though they know him not. Men flee away from him,
or rather from themselves. They cannot grasp him from
whom they have fled, nor when they have lost themselves can they find another, any more than a child who
is mad and out of his mind can know his father. But
he who has learnt to know himself will know also whence
he is.

‘ If a Soul has known itself throughout its course, it is
aware that its natural motion has not been in a straight
line (except during some deflection from the normal) but
rather in a circle round a centre ; and that this centre
is itself in motion round that from which it proceeds. On
this centre the Soul depends, and attaches itself thereto,
as all Souls ought to do, but only the Souls of gods do
so always. It is this that makes them gods. For a god

---

[1] This I take to be approximately the meaning of the obscure phrase :
πρὸ τοῦ μὲν τῇ διαθέσει, τότε δὲ καὶ τοῖς εἴδεσι.   [2] Odyssey 19, 178–9.

is closely attached to this centre ; those further from it are average men, and animals. Is then this centre of the Soul the object of our search ? Or must we think of something else, some point at which all centres as it were coincide. We must remember that our "circles" and "centres" are only metaphors. The Soul is no "circle" like the geometrical figure; we call it a circle because the archetypal nature is in it and around it, and because it is derived from this first principle, and all the more because the Souls as wholes are separated from the body.[1] But now, since part of us is held down by the body (as if a man were to have his feet under water), we touch the centre of all things with our own centre—that part which is not submerged—as the centres of the greatest circles coincide with the centre of the enveloping sphere, and then rest. If these circles were corporeal and not psychic, the coincidence of their centres would be spatial, and they would lie around a centre somewhere in space ; but since the Souls belong to the spiritual world, and the One is above even Spirit, we must consider that their contact is through other powers—those which connect subject and object in the world of Spirit, and further, that the perceiving Spirit is present in virtue of its likeness and identity, and unites with its like without hindrance. (For bodies cannot have this close association with each other, but incorporeal things are not kept apart by bodies ; they are separated from each other not by distance, but by unlikeness and difference.) Where there is no unlikeness, they are united with each other. The One, which has no unlikeness, is always present ; we are so only when we have no unlikeness. The One does not strive to encircle us, but we strive to encircle it. We always move round the One, but we do not always fix our gaze upon it : we are like a choir of singers who stand round the conductor, but do not always sing in time because their attention is diverted to some external object ; when they

---

[1] καὶ ὅτι ἀπὸ τοιούτου καὶ ἔτι μᾶλλον ὅτι χωρισθεῖσαι ὅλαι. I am not sure whether this is the meaning of this obscure and elliptical sentence.

look at the conductor they sing well and are really with
him.   So we always move round the One; if we did not,
we should be dissolved and no longer exist; but we do
not always look towards the One.   When we do, we
attain the end of our existence, and our repose, and we
no longer sing out of tune, but form in very truth a divine
chorus round the One.

' In this choral dance the Soul sees the fountain of life
and the fountain of Spirit, the source of Being, the cause
of Good, the root of Soul.   These do not flow out of the
One in such a way as to diminish it; for we are not
dealing with material quantities, else the products of the
One would be perishable, whereas they are eternal,
because their source remains not divided among them, but
constant.   Therefore the products too are permanent, as
the light remains while the sun remains.   For we are not
cut off from our source nor separated from it, even though
the bodily nature intervenes and draws us towards itself,
but we breathe and maintain our being in our source,
which does not first give itself and then withdraw, but
is always supplying us, as long as it is what it is.   But
we are more truly alive when we turn towards it, and
in this lies our well-being.   To be far from it is isolation
and diminution.   In it our Soul rests, out of reach of
evil; it has ascended to a region which is pure from all
evil; there it has spiritual vision, and is exempt from
passion and suffering; there it truly lives.   For our
present life, without God, is a mere shadow and mimicry
of the true life.   But life yonder is an activity of the
Spirit, and by its peaceful activity it engenders gods also,
through its contact with the One, and Beauty, and
Righteousness, and Virtue.   For these are the offspring
of a Soul which is filled with God, and this is its beginning
and end—its beginning because from this it had its origin,
its end because the Good is there, and when it comes there
it becomes what it was.   For our life in this world is but
a falling away, an exile, and a loss of the Soul's wings.
The natural love which the Soul feels proves that the

Good is there ; this is why paintings and myths make
Psyche the bride of Cupid. Because the Soul is different
from God, and yet springs from him, she loves him of
necessity ; when she is yonder she has the heavenly
love, when she is here below, the vulgar. For yonder
dwells the heavenly Aphrodite, but here she is vulgarised
and corrupted, and every Soul is Aphrodite. This is
figured in the allegory of the birthday of Aphrodite, and
Love who was born with her.[1] Hence it is natural for
the Soul to love God and to desire union with Him, as
the daughter of a noble father feels a noble love. But
when, descending to generation,[2] the Soul, deceived by
the false promises of a lover, exchanges its divine love for
a mortal love, it is separated from its father and submits
to indignities ; but afterwards it is ashamed of these
disorders and purifies itself and returns to its father and
is happy. Let him who has not had this experience consider how blessed a thing it is in earthly love to obtain that
which one most desires, although the objects of earthly
loves are mortal and injurious and loves of shadows,
which change and pass ; since these are not the things
which we truly love, nor are they our good, nor what
we seek. But yonder is the true object of our love, which
it is possible to grasp and to live with and truly to possess,
since no envelope of flesh separates us from it. He who
has seen it knows what I say, that the Soul then has
another life, when it comes to God and having come
possesses him, and knows, when in that state, that it is in
the presence of the dispenser of the true life, and that
it needs nothing further. On the contrary, it must put
off all else, and stand in God alone, which can only be
when we have pruned away all else that surrounds us.
We must then hasten to depart hence, to detach ourselves
as much as we can from the body to which we are un-

[1] Greek mythology had no authoritative doctrine about the parent-
age of Eros. According to the version here referred to, he was ' begotten on the birthday of Aphrodite,' but Plato (*Symposium*, 178)
makes him ' the eldest of the gods, of whose birth nothing is said.'
[2] I.e. to the fleeting world of births and deaths.

happily bound, to endeavour to embrace God with all our
being, and to leave no part of ourselves which is not
in contact with him. Then we can see Him and ourselves,
as far as is permitted : we see ourselves glorified, full of
spiritual light, or rather we see ourselves as pure, subtle,
ethereal, light ; we become divine, or rather we know
ourselves to be divine. Then indeed is the flame of life
kindled, that flame which, when we sink back to earth,
sinks with us.

‘ Why then does not the Soul abide yonder ? Because
it has not yet wholly left its earthly abode. But the
time will come when it will enjoy the vision without
interruption, no longer troubled with the hindrances of
the body. The part of the Soul which is troubled is not
the part which sees, but the other part, when the part
which sees is idle, though it ceases not from that knowledge which comes of demonstrations, conjectures, and
the dialectic. But in the vision that which sees is not
reason (λόγος), but something greater than and prior to
reason, something presupposed by reason,[1] as is the object
of vision. He who then sees himself, when he sees will
see himself as a simple being, will be united to himself as
such, will feel himself become such. We ought not even
to say that he will *see*, but he will *be* that which he sees,
if indeed it is possible any longer to distinguish seer and
seen, and not boldly to affirm that the two are one. In
this state the seer does not see or distinguish or imagine
two things ; he becomes another, he ceases to be himself
and to belong to himself. He belongs to Him and is one
with Him, like two concentric circles ; they are one when
they coincide, and two only when they are separated. It
is only in this sense that the Soul is other. Therefore this
vision is hard to describe. For how can one describe, as
other than oneself, that which, when one saw it, seemed
to be one with oneself ? [2]

‘ This is no doubt why in the mysteries we are forbidden

---

[1] ἐπὶ τῷ λόγῳ. I am not quite sure of the meaning of this phrase.

[2] Arnou (p. 246) points out that Plotinus is after all very cautious
about asserting complete union. He is fond of inserting οἷον, ὥσπερ, εἰ δεῖ
καὶ τοῦτο λέγειν, καθ᾽ ὅσον δύναται, and similar phrases.

to reveal them to the uninitiated. That which is divine is ineffable, and cannot be shown to those who have not had the happiness to see it. Since in the vision there were not two things, but seer and seen were one (for the seeing was no seeing but a merging), if a man could preserve the memory of what he was when he was mingled with the Divine, he would have in himself an image of Him. For he was then one with Him, and retained no difference, either in relation to himself or to others. Nothing stirred within him, neither anger nor concupiscence nor even reason or spiritual perception or his own personality, if we may say so. Caught up in an ecstasy, tranquil and God-possessed, he enjoyed an imperturable calm ; shut up in his proper essence he declined not to either side, he turned not even to himself ; he was in a state of perfect stability ; he had become stability itself. The Soul then occupies itself no more even with beautiful things ; it is exalted above the Beautiful, it passes the choir of the virtues. Even as when a man who enters the sanctuary of a temple leaves behind him the statues in the temple, they are the objects which he will see first when he leaves the sanctuary after he has seen what is within, and entered there into communion, not with statues and images, but with the Deity itself. Perhaps we ought not to speak of *vision* (θέαμα) ; it is rather another mode of seeing, an ecstasy and simplification, an abandonment of oneself, a desire for immediate contact, a stability, a deep intention (περινόησις) to unite oneself with what is to be seen in the sanctuary. He who seeks to see in any other manner, will find nothing. These are but figures, by which the wise prophets indicate how we may see this God. But the wise priest, understanding the symbol, may enter the sanctuary and make the vision real. If he has not yet got so far, he at least conceives that what is within the sanctuary is something invisible to mortal eyes, that it is the Source and Principle of all ; he knows that it is by the first Principle that we see the first Principle, and unites himself with it and perceives like by like, leaving behind nothing that is Divine, so far as the Soul can reach.

And before the vision, the Soul desires that which remains for it to see.   But for him who has ascended above all things, that which remains to see is that which is before all things.   For the nature of the Soul will never pass to absolute not-being : when it falls, it will come to evil, and so to not-being, but not to absolute not-being.   But if it moves in the opposite direction, it will arrive not at something else, but at itself, and so, being in nothing else, it is only in itself alone ; but that which is in itself alone and not in the world of Being is in the Absolute.   It ceases to be Being; it is above Being, while in communion with the One.   (If then a man sees himself become one with the One, he has in himself a likeness of the One, and if he passes out of himself, as an image to its archetype, he has reached the end of his journey.)   And when he comes down from his vision, he can again awaken the virtue that is in him, and seeing himself fitly adorned in every part he can again mount upward through virtue to Spirit, and through wisdom to the One itself.   Such is the life of gods and of godlike and blessed men ; a liberation from all earthly bonds, a life that takes no pleasure in earthly things, a flight of the alone to the Alone.'

These extracts will be enough to illustrate the character of the Plotinian mysticism.   As a description of a direct psychical experience, it closely resembles the records of the Christian mystics, and indeed of all mystics, whatever their creed, date, or nationality.   The mystical trance or ecstasy is a not very uncommon phenomenon, wherever men and women lead the contemplative life.   Even when the possibility of literary dependence is excluded, the witness of the mystics is wonderfully unanimous.

The psychology of religious ecstasy has lately been studied with a thoroughness which has nearly exhausted the subject.   I do not propose to discuss it here.   The influence of the psychological school on the philosophy of religion seems to me to be on the whole mischievous.   Psychology treats mental states as the data of a science.

But intuition changes its character completely when treated in this way. This is why a chilling and depressing atmosphere seems to surround the psychology of religion. Many persons are pleased to find that on purely scientific grounds the intuitions of faith and devotion are allowed a place among incontrovertible facts, and treated with sympathetic respect. They do not reflect that the whole method is external ; that psychology is a science not of validity but of origins ; and that in limiting itself to the investigation of mystical vision as a state of consciousness, it excludes all consideration of the relation which the vision may bear to objective truth. There are some, no doubt, who regard this last question as either meaningless or unanswerable ; but such are not likely to trouble themselves about the philosophy of Plotinus. Nor would an examination of pathological symptoms, such as fill the now popular books on ' religious experience,' be of any help towards understanding the passages which I have just quoted. The vision of Plotinus is unusual, but in no sense abnormal. To see God is the goal of the religious life, and the vision of the One is only the highest and deepest kind of prayer, which is the mystical act *par excellence*. There is nothing strange in the mentality of Plotinus except his intense concentration on the Soul's supreme quest. Those who will live as he lived will see what he saw.

Mr. Cutten[1] rightly says that ' there are two forms of ecstasy. The one is characterised by wild excitement, loss of self-control, and temporary madness. It is a sort of religious intoxication, indulged in largely for its delightful effects. This usually originates in dancing and other physical manifestations. The other type is intense, but quiet and calm ; it is usually spontaneous in origin, or else comes through mental rather than physical causes.' The author adds, again very justly, that not only auto-suggestion but crowd-contagion plays a large part in the production of religious excitement, while the calm

[1] Cutten, *The Psychological Phenomena of Christianity*, p. 45.

type of ecstasy is experienced in solitude. The latter type, to which, it is needless to say, Plotinus belongs, is also represented by many other scholarly contemplatives, such as the Frenchman, Maine de Biron,[1] who describes its manifestations from his own experience. It is also characteristic of the poets who have drawn spiritual sustenance from the manifestations of cosmic life in nature. The following reflections may help us to understand some of the chief features of Plotinian mysticism, and the points in which it differs from other branches of the great mystical tradition.

Plotinus is not content to give us his own experience of the beatific vision, nor does he wish us to accept it on his authority. He prefers to appeal to the experience of his readers. He has followed, he says, the guidance of a faculty 'which all have, but few use';[2] a faculty which, as we shall see, is not anything distinct from the normal operations of the mind, but arises from the concentration of these on the return of the Soul to its 'Father.' He assumes that his readers are made like himself, and that many of them have followed the same path. 'He who has seen it knows what I mean,' is his excuse for not attempting to describe the indescribable. But he does claim to have given us a real metaphysic of mysticism. He has put the vision of the One in its right place at the apex of a pyramid which ascends, as the dialectic guides us, from the many and discordant to the One in whom is no variableness. He explains clearly why thought cannot reach the Absolute. Thought must have a Thing ; and Thought and Thing can never be wholly one. This argument we have considered ; here I wish to emphasise that the truth which he claims

---

[1] *Anthropologie*, p. 550. ' C'est au moment où le moi triomphe, où la passion est vaincue, où le devoir est accompli contre toutes les résistances affectives, enfin où le sacrifice est consommé, que, tout effort cessant, l'âme est remplie d'un sentiment ineffable, où le moi se trouve absorbé. Un calme pur succède aux tempêtes.'

[2] So John Wesley said : ' I pretend to no extraordinary revelations or gifts of the Holy Ghost, none but what every Christian may receive, and ought to expect and pray for.'

for the vision of the One is absolute, universal, and necessary truth.

The end of the Soul's pilgrimage is the source from which it flowed. As Proclus was afterwards to teach in more precise language, all life consists in a home-stopping, a journey forth, and a return (μονή, πρόοδος, ἐπιστροφή). If the outward journey were considered in isolation, we should have to say that it was not willed, but necessary. If, however, we take the whole course together, as we should do, we may say that Creation was the first act in the drama of Redemption. For the Soul only realises itself in the desire (ἔφεσις), the travail-pangs (ὠδίς), which draw it back towards the source of its being.

The process of simplification (ἅπλωσις) by which we approach the One seems at first sight to be a kind of self-denudation—a figure which indeed Plotinus uses. Just as we are forbidden to affirm anything positive about the One, because we cannot affirm anything without excluding its opposite, and nothing must be excluded from the Absolute, so the Soul must strip itself of all that does not belong to the spiritual world, and finally must, for the time at least, shut its eyes to the manifold riches of the spiritual world itself, in order to enter naked and alone into the Holy of Holies. This 'negative road' (via negativa) is the well-trodden mystic way, and it is the chief stumbling-block of those who dislike mysticism.

Plotinus describes the method in language familiar to all mystics. It consists in removing everything extraneous to the reality which we seek to win and to be. First the body is to be detached as not belonging to the true nature of the Soul; then the Soul which forms body; then sense-perception. What remains is the image of Spirit. When the Soul becomes Spirit by contemplating Spirit as its own principle, the source of all being still remains unexplored. To reach this, 'take away all' (ἄφελε πάντα).[1] The language used makes it clear that

[1] 5. 3. 17.

this ' abstraction ' consists of intense concentration of the mind and will on what are believed to be the essentials of the quest. But the method is based on the conviction that ' all truth is shadow except the last.' All soul-experience half reveals and half conceals reality. So the ascent of the Soul involves a continual rejection of outward shows, and continual self-denial. ' Ideas are always given through something ' ; but what is behind the Ideas is given through nothing ; if it is given at all, it is given in a manner which is too immediate to be described.

The critics have treated the ' negative road ' as if it were a mere ' peeling the onion,' a progressive impoverishment of experience until nothing is left. Royce, who is not unsympathetic towards mysticism, condemns it for ' ignoring the sum of the series, and craving only for the final term.' This is not true of Plotinian mysticism, and theoretically it is not true of Catholic mysticism either ; though there is a practical danger that the cloistered contemplative may live in dreams and lose touch with the external world. We must remember that for Plotinus reality consists in the rich and glorious life of Spirit, in which whatever we renounce in the world of sense is given back to us transmuted and ennobled. It is quite a mistake to suppose that the Neoplatonist desires to get rid of his Soul. He agrees with the author of the *Cloud of Unknowing*.[1] ' In all this sorrow he desireth not to unbe ;[2] for that were devil's madness and despite unto God But him listeth right well to be ; and he intendeth full heartily thanking to God, for the worthiness and gift of his being, for all that he desire unceasingly to lack the witting and the feeling of his being.' This last clause does not mean that the ideal state is a sort of somnambulism ; we have seen, on the contrary, that Plotinus describes the highest experience as a sort of

---

[1] Chapter 44.
[2] Some of the medieval German mystics *have* used phrases like ' Ich bin entworden.'

awaking. A living realisation has taken the place of abstract conceptions. But he does mean that the reference of every experience to a self-conscious psychic self is necessarily an impoverishment of that experience.[1] The less of subjectivity that there is in our experience, the wider and truer it will be. Thus it is not so much the object as the perceiving subject that is constantly reproved and silenced in the ' negative way ' as practised by Plotinus. It is our image of the object which is not good enough to be true. He is no Gnostic, despising this beautiful world ; he wants to see it as it really is, and not through the distorting medium of his lower faculties. He knows that the Soul is perpetually constructing a synthesis out of what it has seen and apprehended ; it is these premature syntheses which frequently have to be destroyed, or they will detain us in a world of shadows. So the words of Goethe are true :—

' Denn alles muss in nichts zerfallen,
    Wenn es in Sein beharren will.'

Some critics [2] have been content to find a patent contradiction in the philosophy of Plotinus, which they attribute to a conflict between his personal piety and his speculative thought. ' In Plotinus' philosophy God is exiled from his world and his world from him, whilst Plotinus' experiences and intuitions find God to be the very atmosphere and home of all souls.' To the ' abstractiveness of his method ' are traced ' his profoundly unsocial conception of man's relation to God, and of the moments when this relation is at its deepest—alone with the Alone—and the exclusion from the Soul's deepest ultimate life of all multiplicity and discursiveness of thought, and of all distinct acts and productiveness of the will.' These strictures on Neoplatonic ethics will be considered in the next chapter. As for the alleged contra-

---

[1] Cf. 6. 7. 33. ἐπεὶ δὲ ὁ νοῦς ἴδιόν τι νοεῖ, ἠλάττωται.
[2] e.g. Eucken, in his *Lebensanschauungen Grosser Denker*, and Baron von Hügel, who seems to be influenced by him. The quotations are from the latter writer's *Eternal Life*. See below, p. 205.

diction between his personal religion and his speculative thought, Plotinus is the last writer in whom we should expect to find such an inconsistency; his metaphysics were no intellectual pastime, as Hume's seem in part to have been, but an earnest attempt to think out his deepest convictions. Nor does the criticism seem to me to be in any way justified. The 'exile of God from the world' is part of the 'extreme dualism' which Caird supposes in Plotinus, but which, I venture to think, no careful student of the Enneads will find there. There are certainly two movements—a systole and diastole, in which the life of the Soul consists. Spiritual progress is on one side an expansion, on the other an intensification or concentration. But it is not true that one is the core of Plotinus' philosophy, the other of his religion.

One aspect of the Plotinian mysticism, which must be strongly emphasised, is that there is no *occultism* in it. There is no 'mystical faculty,' but only the spiritual sense 'which all possess but few use.' There is continuity of development from sense-perception up to the vision of the One. The whole lore of miraculous Divine favours, which fills the records of cloistered mystics, is entirely absent from Plotinus.[1] The psychology of these delusions is still rather obscure; happily they do not concern us here. Suggestion has no doubt much to do with them; sometimes auto-suggestion, sometimes the contagion of a crowd. During some revivals, the patients swoon; in other cases they dance or jerk convulsively. There is, as Mr. Granger well says, a physical hypocrisy as well as a moral one. The best guides in the mystical life warn their disciples against these 'monkey-tricks of the soul,' as the *Cloud of Unknowing* calls them. Some persons, says this wise and quaint writer, 'turn their bodily wits inwards to their bodies against the course of

---

[1] Iamblichus, however, was asked by his disciples whether it was true that he sometimes floated in the air when he said his prayers ! It is melancholy to find that so sane a writer as Granger (*The Soul of a Christian*, p. 110) can still believe these absurdities.

nature ; and strain them, as they would see inwards with
their bodily eyes, and hear inwards with their ears, and
so forth of all their wits, smelling, tasting, and feeling
inwards . . . and then as fast the devil hath power for
to feign some false light or sounds, sweet smells in their
noses, wonderful tastes in their mouths, and many
quaint heats and burnings in their members.' Eckhart
says distinctly that ecstatic auditions are not the voice
of God, who ' speaks but one word, in which are contained
all truths.' It is the subject of the vision who acts and
speaks, and is under an illusion about his own words and
acts. In ecstasy the soul feels a new vigour ; and as it
has before itself no object which it can know, it makes
an object of itself and answers itself, and creates what it
desires, like the sparks which are seen after a blow on
the eye.[1] St. John of the Cross bids us ' fly from such
experiences without even examining whether they be
good or evil. For inasmuch as they are exterior and in
the body, there is the less certainty of their being from
God. It is more natural that God should communicate
himself through the Spirit than through the sense,
wherein there is usually much danger and delusion ;
because the bodily sense decides upon and judges spiritual
things, thinking them to be what itself feels them to be,
when in reality they are as different as body and soul,
sensuality and reason.'[2] Plotinus would have distrusted
' bodily showings ' for the same reason. When the mind
is engaged in contemplating the things of God, strange
quasi-sensual delights or pains could be only a distrac-
tion, and to provoke or welcome them, and describe them
afterwards with luscious recollection, would be folly. To
suppose that divine knowledge could be so communicated
would contradict his epistemology completely.[3]

This repudiation of occultism does not forbid the per-

---

[1] Delacroix, *Le Mysticisme en Allemagne*, p. 212.

[2] Quoted by Herman, *Meaning and Value of Mysticism*, p. 53.

[3] Origen condemns irrational ecstasy even more strongly, imputing
it to evil spirits. See Denis, *La Philosophie d'Origène*, p. 246.

ception of analogies in nature—that vision of spiritual law in nature which inspires such poets as Wordsworth, and gives some encouragement to magic. So Sir Thomas Browne says : ' The severe schools shall never laugh me out of the philosophy of Hermes, that this visible world is but a picture of the invisible, wherein, as in a portrait, things are not truly but in equivocal shapes, and as they counterfeit some real substance in that invisible framework.' On the subject of magic, some further reflections will be found in the next chapter.

It will also be noticed that there is not a trace in Plotinus of the ' dark night of the Soul,' the experience of dereliction. This tragic experience has received much attention from modern psychology. Many writers have regarded it as merely pathological, as a violent reaction from nervous overstrain. There is no doubt that the unnatural life led by the contemplative ascetic, cut off from almost every healthy relaxation, must often produce morbid conditions. Intense introspection is sure to cause fits of melancholy ; and some mystics, like Madame Guyon, cannot be entirely acquitted of a sort of spiritual self-importance which makes them enjoy retailing their inner joys and miseries. Those who believe, with Miss Underhill, that these sufferings are the privilege of the higher order of mystics, the ' great and strong spirits,' will probably experience, or think they have experienced, something like what they have read of. I think this writer somewhat exaggerates the emotional side of mysticism. But I agree with her that the ' dark night of the Soul ' is not to be disposed of as a phenomenon of morbid psychology. As a rule, one may rather distrust the ecstatic who has had no experience of it. As Delacroix says, ' the dark night condenses the whole vision of things into a negative intuition, as ecstasy into a positive.' The Christian struggle for spiritual victory is more intense than the Platonic, because the contrasted blackness of evil is felt far more vividly. Plotinus knows of no devil, and no active malignancy in the nature of things. There is no sense of horror in his philosophy from first to last.   The temper of the Neoplatonic saint is to be serene and cheerful, confident that the ultimate truth of the world is on his side, and that only ' earth-born clouds ' can come between him and the sun.   It is a manly spirit, which craves for no divine caresses and fears no enmity from ' the world-rulers of this darkness.'   The Christian may be reminded that the words of the Johannine Christ, ' Let not your heart be troubled,' reflect the whole tone of Christ's teaching better than the more sombre outlook of many Christian saints.   But the dark night of the Soul means repentance and remorse ; and are these feelings to be sanctioned or discouraged ?   For the Jew, the call to repent means ' Turn,' not ' Grieve ' ; and Spinoza explicitly forbids remorse, as partaking in the cardinal sin of *tristitia.*   ' One might perhaps expect gnawings of conscience and repentance to help to bring men on the right path, and might thereupon conclude (as everyone does conclude) that these affections are good things.   Yet when we look at the matter closely, we shall find that not only are they not good, but on the contrary deleterious and evil passions. For it is manifest that we can always get along better by reason and love of truth than by worry of conscience and remorse.   These are harmful and evil, inasmuch as they form a particular kind of sadness ; and the disadvantages of sadness I have already proved, and shown that we should strive to keep it from our life.   Just so we should endeavour, since uneasiness of conscience and remorse are of this kind of complexion, to flee and shun these states of mind.' [1]   Some of the Christian mystics are here in accord with Spinoza and Plotinus.   It was one of the accusations against Molinos that he discouraged contrition.   ' When thou fallest into a fault,' he says, ' do not trouble oɪ afflict thyself for it.   Faults are effects of our frail nature, stained by original sin.   Would not he be a fool who during a tournament, if he had a fall, should lie weeping on the ground and afflict himself with discourses upon his

[1] Spinoza, *On God, Man, and Happiness,* ii. 10.

misadventure?' Those who believe in what William James calls the religion of healthy-mindedness will fight against every attack of spiritual misery as if it were a disease. But I cannot disregard the testimony of some of the sanest and best mystics that it is often 'speedful' for a man to fall into this state of depression.[1] I find, after all, something academic and unreal in those whose visions and thoughts always affirm an optimism. John Pulsford says wisely : ' Satan can convert illumination into a snare ; but contrition is beyond his art.' We are meant to feel the strength of the forces that would pull us downward as well as of those which draw us upward ; indeed we can hardly know one without the other. ' I strove towards thee,' says St. Augustine, 'and was repulsed by thee that I might taste death. The disturbed and darkened vision of my mind was being healed from day to day by the keen salve of wholesome pains. I became more wretched, and thou nearer.'

The ecstatic state, under whatever names it may be distinguished in its various manifestations, is for the great Neoplatonist an exceedingly rare experience ; and it is noteworthy that we find no tendency to cheapen it in the later writers of his school. For the mystics of the cloister, on the contrary, it was by no means uncommon ; and so far was it from being reserved for the holiest saints in their most exalted moods, that beginners in the ascetic life were warned not to be uplifted by such visitations, which were often granted as an encouragement to young aspirants. Some of the most famous female mystics, especially, were frequently entranced, their ecstasies sometimes lasting for many hours, though half an hour is so often mentioned that it may be regarded as a normal duration of such states. This difference does not seem to be connected with Christianity, which in its pure form gives no encouragement to violent religious emotion. Some of the philosophical Christian mystics, like Eckhart, though they lived in the golden

---

[1] The allusion is to the *Revelations of Julian of Norwich.*

age of monastic Christian mysticism, do not seem to have experienced these abnormal visitations. Others, like Böhme and Blake, certainly were visionaries. Böhme once hypnotised himself by gazing intently on a bright object, a method which, with variations, has been adopted by many Oriental mystics. There is no trace of this self-hypnotisation in Plotinus, though intense abstraction and concentration of thought may doubtless have the same result as protracted gazing upon some chosen object. But Plotinus is careful to insist that the vision must be *waited for*. ' When the Spirit perceives this Divine light, it knows not whence it comes, from without or from within ; when it has ceased to shine, we believe at one moment that it comes from within and at another that it does not. But it is useless to ask whence it comes ; there is no question of place here. It neither approaches us nor withdraws itself ; it either manifests itself or remains hidden. We must not then seek it, but wait quietly for its appearance, and prepare ourselves to contemplate it, as the eye watches for the sun rising above the horizon, or out of the sea. . . . The One is everywhere, and nowhere.'[1] The note of personal experience cannot be missed in these words. The fine simile of the watcher in the early morning, his gaze fixed on the eastern sky, recalls the verse of Malachi : ' Unto you that fear my name shall the sun of righteousness arise with healing in his wings.' But the question has not yet been fully answered, why states of trance are so much more common among the Christian mystics. I believe that a good deal may be attributed to tradition and expectation. Just as young people in some Protestant sects experience ' sudden conversion ' at the age of adolescence, while in other Christian churches this is almost unknown or regarded as a rare phenomenon, so visions and trances come often when they are looked for, and seldom when they are not expected. The whole practice and discipline of the cloister involved a greater

[1] 5. 5. 8.

strain and tension than the traditions of Hellenic moral training would have approved. Attempts to induce the mystical state were frequent and mischievous, and warnings against this practice are found in the best spiritual guides of the Middle Ages. For instance, in the little fourteenth-century manual from which I have already quoted, we have a graphic account of the delusions which often assailed the aspirant after mystical experiences, delusions which in those times were naturally set down to the ghostly enemies of mankind.[1]

The mystical state never occurs except as a sequel to intense mental *concentration*, which the majority of human beings are unable to practise except for a few minutes at a time. Our minds are continually assailed by a crowd of distracting images, which must be resolutely refused an entrance if we are to bring any difficult mental operation to a successful issue. The necessity of this concentration is insisted on by all the mystics, so that it is superfluous to give quotations. Most of them speak of producing an absolute calm in the soul, in order that God may speak to us without interruption. They often tell us that the will must be completely passive, though the stern repression of the imagination which they practise is only possible by a very exhausting effort of the will. Ecstasy is a fusion of the will and imagination, in which the character of both is changed. In preparing for it all external impressions must be ignored ; the contemplative must be impervious to sights and sounds while he is at work. In extreme cases a kind of catalepsy may be produced, from which it is not easy to recover ; but this is not a danger to be apprehended by many. The mystical experience is not necessarily associated with meditation on the being and attributes of God. Any concentrated mental activity may, it seems, produce it. Philo,[2] for instance, thus describes what he has felt himself while engaged in philosophical study. ' Sometimes, when I have come

[1] *The Cloud of Unknowing*, Chap. 52.
[2] *Migrat. Abrah.* 7. Drummond, *Philo Judaeus*, Vol. 1, p. 15.

to my work empty, I have suddenly become full, ideas being in an invisible manner showered upon me, and implanted in me from on high; so that through the influence of divine inspiration I have become filled with enthusiasm, and have known neither the place in which I was nor those who were present, nor myself, nor what I was saying, nor what I was writing, for then I have been conscious of a richness of interpretation, an enjoyment of light, a most keen-sighted vision, a most distinct view of the objects treated, such as would be given through the eyes from the clearest exhibition.' The philosophical problem which he was debating was almost visualised before his mind's eye, as it is with all philosophical mystics. The Platonist does not contemplate 'a ballet of bloodless categories,' but a rich and beautiful world, in which the imagination clothes spiritual thoughts with half-sensuous forms—a world of inspired poetry and glorious vision.

Wordsworth[1] in a well-known passage describes how the vision comes to a poet's mind.

> Sensation, soul and form
> All melted into him; they swallowed up
> His animal being; in them did he live
> And by them did he live; they were his life.
> In such access of mind, in such high hours
> Of visitation from the living God,
> Thought was not; in enjoyment it expired.
> No thanks he breathed; he proffered no request;
> Rapt into still communion that transcends
> The imperfect offices of prayer and praise,
> His mind was a thanksgiving to the power
> That made him; it was blessedness and love.

Dante, in the Thirty-third Canto of the *Paradiso*, tells the same story.

> La mia vista, venendo sincera,
> e più e più entrava par lo raggio
> dell' alta luce, che de sè è vera.
> Da quincì innanzi il mio veder fu maggio
> che il parlar nostro ch' a tal vista cede,
> e cede la memoria a tanto oltraggio.

[1] *Excursion*, Book I.

Qual è colui che somniando vede,
   chè dopo il sogno la passione impressa
   rimane, e l'altro alla mente non riede ;
Cotal son io, chè quasi tutta cessa
   mia visione, ed ancor mi distilla
   nel cor lo dolce che nacque de essa . . .
Così la mente mia, tutta sospensa,
   mirava fissa, immobile ed attenta,
   e sempre del mirar faccasi accessa.
A quella luce cotal si diventa,
   che volgersi da lei per altro aspetto
   è impossibil che mai si consenta—
Pero che il Ben, ch' è del volere obbietto,
   tutto s'accoglie in lei, e fuor di quella
   è diffetevo ciò che li' è perfetto.[1]

Some musicians tell us of a similar experience. Mozart [2]
has left it on record that his symphonies came into his
mind not phrase by phrase, but as a *totum simul*, accom-
panied by a wonderful feeling of exaltation and happiness. 'When and how my ideas come I know not, nor
can I force them. Those that please me I retain in my
memory and am · accustomed, as I have been told, to
hum them to myself. . . . All this fires my soul, and
provided I am not disturbed my subject enlarges itself,
becomes methodised and defined, and the whole, though
it be long, stands almost complete and finished in my
mind, so that I can survey it like a fine picture or a

---

[1] 'My sight, becoming pure, entered deeper and deeper into the
ray of that high light which in itself is true. Thenceforth my vision
was greater than our language, which fails such a sight ; and memory
fails before such transcendence. As he who sees in a dream, and after
the dream the impress of the emotion remains, and the rest returns
not to the mind, such am I ; for almost all the vision fades, and there
yet flows from my heart the sweetness born of it. . . . Thus did my
mind, all in suspense, gaze fixedly, immovable and intent, and was
ever kindled by its gazing. Before that light one becomes such, that one
could never consent to turn from it to any other sight. For the Good,
which is the object of the will, is in it wholly gathered, and outside it
that is defective which in it is perfect.'

[2] Holmes' *Life and Correspondence of Mozart*, p. 317. Quoted by
Rufus Jones, *Studies in Mystical Religion*, p. xxii. It should be said
that some other great musicians seem to have composed in a manner
different from that of Mozart. This letter of Mozart, however, seems
not to be genuine. See Sorley, *Moral Values and the Idea of God*,
p. 255. Lossky (*The World as an Organic Whole*, p. 83) quotes
another passage from Mozart, to exactly the same effect. (No reference
given.)

beautiful statue, at a glance. Nor do I hear in my imagination the parts successively, but I hear them as it were
all at once. What a delight this is I cannot express. All
this inventing, this producing, takes place in a pleasing
lively dream. But the actual hearing of the whole together
is after all the best. And this is perhaps the best gift I
have my divine Master to thank for.' This passage is of
great psychological interest, because beauty of sound
is essentially dependent on temporal succession. If all
the bars of a symphony were played simultaneously, the
result would be anything but beautiful. The *totum simul*
of his compositions which floated before Mozart's consciousness and gave him such exquisite delight was the
idea of the whole piece, which after being worked out
in a succession of sounds, independent of each other as
vibrations of the air, but unified by the Soul as expressing a continuous meaning, were visualised as a rich but
indissoluble idea by Spirit. This last intuition is not
simultaneous but timeless. There are few better illus-
trations of the psychological truth of the Platonic scheme.

In the medieval mystics the ' darkness ' of the vision
is more emphasised. They describe a state in which the
imagination no longer illuminates even the most spiritual
intuitions of the Soul. Angela of Foligno[1] says that at
one time she had had clear and distinct visions of God.
' But afterwards I saw Him darkly, and this darkness was
the greatest blessing that could be imagined. The soul
delighteth unspeakably therein, yet it beholdeth nought
which can be related by the tongue or imagined in the
heart. It sees nothing, and yet sees all things, because
it beholds the Good darkly, and the more darkly and
secretly the Good is seen, the more certain is it, and
excellent above all things. Even when the Soul sees the
divine power, wisdom, and will of God, which I have
seen most marvellously at other times, it is all less than
this most certain Good ; because this is the whole, and
those other things only part of the whole.' She goes on
to say that though she has had the ' dark ' vision of

[1] See E. Underhill. *Mysticism*, p. 418.

God ' countless times,' yet on three occasions only she has been uplifted to the heights of the vision. ' It seems to me,` she adds, ' that I am fixed in the midst of it and that it draweth me to itself more than anything else which I ever beheld, or any blessing which I ever received, so that there is nothing which can be compared to it.' The rarity of the vision, as well as its character, makes Angela's experience very like that of Plotinus.

It is not necessary, for the purpose of this book, to collect recorded experiences of ecstatics and visionaries. The literature of the subject is already large, and much material which till lately was almost inaccessible is now available for those who wish to study the psychology of mysticism. The common impression about Plotinus, that ecstasy is an important part of his system, is erroneous ; it has been thrust into the foreground in the same way in which Western critics of Buddhism have exaggerated the importance of *Nirvana* in that religion. In both cases the doctrines have also been widely misunderstood. Nirvana does not mean annihilation after death, nor does the philosophy of Plotinus culminate (as Pfleiderer supposes) in a ' convulsed state ' which is the negation of reason and sanity.

The vision of the One is the crowning satisfaction of that love and longing (ἔφεσις, *Sehnsucht*) which, as we have seen, ' makes the world go round ' for Plotinus.[1] It is the νοῦς ἐρῶν which sees the vision. But how can anyone love the Absolute ? It seems to me that the emotion which the mystics so describe is not a simple one. There is such a thing as a longing for deliverance from individual life itself, a craving for rest and peace in the bosom of the eternal and unchanging, even at the price of a cessation of consciousness. It is not annihilation that the mystic desires—annihilation of anything that truly exists is inconceivable ; but the breaking down of the barriers which constitute *separate* existence. Unchanging life in

---

[1] 5. 6. 5. ἡ γὰρ ἔφεσις τὴν νόησιν ἐγέννησε καὶ συνυπέστησεν αὐτῇ· ἔφεσις γὰρ ὄψεως, ὅρασις. An important passage. Even the Life of Spirit depends on will and aspiration. Such passages should be considered by those who accuse Plotinus of ' staticism.'

the timeless All—this is what he desires, and this the vision promises him. But when this is the ground of his yearning for the Absolute, he is not content with a momentary glimpse of the super-existent ; he wishes to have done with temporal existence altogether. 'Leave nothing of myself in me,' is his prayer, as it was that of Crawshaw in his invocation of St. Teresa. In this mood he is willing to accept what to many is the self-stultification of mysticism, that the self, in losing its environment, loses also its content, and grasps zero instead of the infinite. All distinct consciousness is the consciousness of a not-self, of externality ; and this is just what he hopes to lose for ever. This love for the Absolute seems to be anti-selfish emotion raised to a passion. It can hardly express itself except by negations, or by such symbols as darkness, emptiness, utter stillness. The Godhead is the divine Dark, the infinite Void, *ein ewige Stille*. But the 'loving Spirit' which has found its bliss and its home in the rich and beautiful world of the Platonic Ideas has no such longing for 'self-noughting.' It desires only to see the eternal fount from which the river of life flows ever fresh and full. The joy of the vision, to such a one, is the joy of overleaping the last metaphysical barrier, that which prevents subject and object from being wholly one. He knows that beyond the subject-object relation there can be no concrete life or consciousness, and he does not dream of finding a permanent home above the spiritual world. But there is for him no joy comparable to the assurance that he *is*, in very deed and truth, all the glory that has been revealed to him—that there is 'nothing between.' There is an unfathomable something in his own heart which claims this final consummation of communion as his own ; and he returns to the harmonious beauty and order of the spiritual world indescribably enriched by that brief initiation.

There is and must be an element of illusion in the vision of the Godhead. It never remains so formless as the contemplative thinks it to be. The imagination at once constructs a form of formlessness—a shoreless ocean, a vast desert, a black night, and the mind which thinks that it contemplates the Absolute really visualises these symbols of the unlimited. But the *idea* of the One, the Godhead, the ultimate source of all that is good and true and beautiful, is capable of inspiring love, and has inspired love in many noble spirits.

A Christian will press the question asked above (p. 132): Is this ' intellectual love of God ' the crown of love to man, or is it sometimes a substitute for it ? What would Plotinus have said to the plain question, ' He that loveth not his brother whom he hath seen, how can he love God whom he hath not seen ? ' I believe that Platonism can answer this challenge better than Indian mysticism, though in practice nothing can be much more beautiful than the gentle and selfless benevolence of the Oriental saint. Love, for Plotinus, passes through a process of purification and enlightenment, like our other affections and faculties. In a sense it becomes depersonalised, more so than many of us would think desirable ; but when a Christian teacher bids us to ' love the Christ in our brethren,' when he repeats the famous saying, ' When thou seest thy brother thou seest thy Lord,' he is saying very much what Platonism says in other words. We begin, St. Paul says, by knowing other men 'after the flesh,' and loving them after the flesh ; but we end, or should end, by knowing and loving them as immortal spirits, our fellow-citizens in that heavenly country where, as Plotinus says, the most perfect sympathy and transparent intimacy exist among blessed spirits. And the doctrine of the One as the supreme object of love really secures this—that human spirits in their most exalted moods may share not only a common life and a common happiness, but a common hope and a common prayer.

Nevertheless, we must admit that the whole character of the mysticism of Plotinus is affected by the fact that the ideal object of the quest is a state and not a person. At no point in the ascent is God conceived as a Person

over against our own personality. (The God whom
Plotinus mainly worships—the Spirit—is transcendent as
well as immanent in the world of Soul, but purely immanent in his own world, Yonder. In that world He is
no longer an object but an atmosphere. The ineffable
Godhead above God is of course supra-personal.) There
is therefore, in the Platonian mysticism, none of that deep
personal loyalty, none of that intimate dialogue between
soul and soul, none of that passion of love—resembling
often too closely in its expression the earthly love of the
sexes—which are so prominent in later mystical literature. Compare, as a favourable example of this type, the
exquisite *Revelations of Julian of Norwich*, full of tender
reverent affection for the heavenly Christ. We do not
feel quite clear what is the *object* which excites the ardour
of the Soul or Spirit in Plotinus. There is an intense
desire to see and realise perfection ; to be quit of all the
contrarieties and contradictions of earthly life ; to return
to the haven where the pangs of home-sickness are no
more. These are the chief objects of his desire ; and for
him and for many they are enough. They were enough
for Spinoza, and for Goethe. ' What specially attracted
me in Spinoza ' (Goethe writes) ' was the boundless
disinterestedness which shone forth from every sentence.
That marvellous saying, " Whoso loves God must not
desire God to love him in return," with all the premisses
on which it rests and the consequences that flow from it,
permeated my whole thinking. To be disinterested in
everything, and most of all in love and friendship, was
my highest desire, my maxim, my constant practice ; so
that that bold saying of mine at a later date, " If I love
thee, what is that to thee ? " came directly from my
heart.'[1] Disinterestedness is exactly what this type of
philosophy, if it is erected into a rule of life, can give
us ; and a very noble gift it is ; but there is another road
of ascent, by personal affection for man, and even (in
many Christian saints) for God or Christ ; and those
whose temperament leads them by this path are likely

---

[1] Goethe, quoted in Hume Brown's *The Youth of Goethe*, p. 210.

to find the mountain-track trodden by Plotinus cold, bleak, and bare. It may even be true that this type of religious philosophy is likely to be specially attractive to those whom circumstances have cut off from domestic happiness and the privilege of friendship, or who are naturally slow to love their kind. In all ages there are some who fancy themselves attracted by God, or by Nature, when they are really only repelled by man. But in dealing with the great mystics such cavils are not only unjust but impertinent. Their loneliness is the loneliness of the great mountain solitudes ; the air which we breathe at those heights is thin but pure and bracing ; and there is in each one of us a hidden man of the heart who can love and be loved super-individually. This is true of the love of the Christian saint for Christ. St. Paul says that even if we begin by ' knowing Christ after the flesh,' that is a stage which must be left behind. As Bengel says, ' *Conversio fit ad Dominum ut Spiritum.*' In fact, the difference between Neoplatonic and Christian devotion may easily be exaggerated. The Christian cannot feel for the exalted Christ the same emotion which he would have felt for the Galilean Prophet ; his love is worship for a divine Being, the source of all that is lovable, and desire for spiritual communion with the living Power who has ' brought life and immortality to light.' The spiritual love of Plotinus is not very different. It is at any rate true to say that the Christian Platonists of Alexandria, the Cappadocian Fathers, and Greek theology generally, regarded the heavenly Christ as a Being with most of the attributes of the Neoplatonic Νοῦς.

LECTURES XX, XXI

ETHICS, RELIGION, AND ÆSTHETICS

EUCKEN says that it is the special glory of Christianity that its ethics are metaphysical and its metaphysics ethical. But this is equally true of Neoplatonism. The connexion of ethics with metaphysics became closer and closer throughout the history of Greek thought. The first Greek philosophy was generalised natural science ; ethical precept at this time was largely handed down in proverbs and aphorisms, as it still is in China. But for Socrates the aim of philosophy was to discover 'how a man may spend his life to the best advantage.' ;[1] and after him this remained to the end of antiquity the avowed object of metaphysical studies. Aristotle, like Spinoza, was entirely convinced that the search for truth is morally the noblest career that a man can choose. It is, he says, the exercise of that which is highest in our nature, and concerned with the highest things (the being and laws of the universe) ; it gives the purest enjoyment to those who practise it ; and it is, of all modes of life, the least dependent on external conditions.[2]

Stoicism and Epicureanism were both, first and foremost, attitudes towards life ; they claimed to regulate conduct in every particular. These two philosophies had the merit of teaching men how to live in this world ; later thought inclined to the contemplative and almost monastic ideal of the philosophic life, and made ethics a study rather of how to live out of society than in it. In

---

[1] Plato, *Republic*, p. 344.
[2] Cf. Carveth Read, *Natural and Social Morals*, p. 42.

Plotinus we are conscious of the same want, on the ethical side, which makes itself felt in medieval books of devotion and spiritual guidance. The concrete problems of social morality receive too little attention, and the tone is that of Plato's dictum, in the *Laws*, ' Human affairs are not worth taking very seriously; the misfortune·is that we have to take them seriously.' It was one of the chief objects of philosophy to teach men not to take them very seriously. It had become the province of the philosopher to administer the consolations of religion to those who were in affliction, or troubled about the health of their souls. In the second and third centuries the philosopher not only claimed to be ' a priest and servant of the gods ' ;[1] his recognised position was that of spiritual guide, father confessor, private chaplain, and preacher. For the educated layman, poetry and philosophy were still the great ethical instructors.

Plotinus has not written a book about ethics, like Aristotle. Even on friendship, which takes such a prominent place in classical morals, he has not much to say. He tells us that the political virtues, which precede the stage of purification in which the ascent is begun in earnest, must by all means be practised first,[2] but he touches upon them very lightly. They teach the value of order and measure, and take away false opinions.[3] His biographer tells us that he induced Rogatianus the senator, one of his disciples, to give up the active life of a high official, and betake himself to philosophic contemplation. It is the ideal of the cloister, already victorious over the Stoic ideal of civic virtue. But in Plotinus the world-renouncing tendency is not carried to its extreme lengths. He himself lived, as we have seen, a strenuous and active life, as a valued counsellor of emperors, a beloved teacher and spiritual guide, and a conscientious guardian and trustee. Even the later Neoplatonists who were contemporary with the craze

---

[1] ἱερεύς τις καὶ ὑπουργὸς θεῶν, Marcus Aurelius, 3, 4.
[2] I. 3. 6.   [3] I. 2. 2.

for eremitism among the Christians, insisted that the philosopher must qualify as a good citizen before aspiring to higher flights.[1] In the life of Proclus by Marinus, the biographer includes under the 'political virtues' of his hero, contempt for filthy lucre, generosity, public spirit, wise political counsel, friendship, industry, and all the cardinal virtues. Nevertheless, Plotinus never asks the very important question which Plato (in the *Republic*) did ask, in a form which shows a very just apprehension of its gravity. 'How can the State handle philosophy so as not to be ruined?' It is the question which for us takes the form, 'How can a State take the Sermon on the Mount for its guide without losing its independence and therewith the opportunity of having an organic life at all?'

Purification (κάθαρσις) is the first stage of the ascent, when the 'political virtues' have been mastered. In most of what he says about this stage, Plotinus has been closely followed by Augustine.[2] To purify the Soul signifies ' to detach it from the body and to elevate it to the spiritual world.'[3] The Soul is to strip off all its own lower nature, as well as to cleanse itself from external stains ; what remains when this is done will be 'the image of Spirit.'[4] ' Retire into thyself and examine thyself. If thou dost not yet find beauty there, do like the sculptor who chisels, planes, polishes, till he has adorned his statue with all the attributes of beauty. So do thou chisel away from thy Soul what is superfluous, straighten that which is crooked, purify and enlighten what is dark, and do not cease working at thy statue, until virtue shines before thine eyes with its divine splendour, and thou seest temperance seated in thy bosom with its holy purity.'[5]

This ' purification ' is mainly a matter of constant self-discipline, and especially discipline of the thoughts. Plotinus gives no rules for the ascetic life, and no precepts

---

[1] This whole scheme of virtues is borrowed by Thomas Aquinas, who cites Plotinus.

[2] See especially *De Musica*, 6, 13-16.

[3] 3. 6. 5.   [4] 5. 3. 9.   [5] 1 6. 9.

which point to severe austerities. Outward action for him means so little, except as the necessary expression and 'accompaniment' of inward states, that he could not, without great inconsistency, attach importance to such exercises. He would have us live so simply that our bodily wants are no interruption to our mental and spiritual interests ; but beyond this he does not care to go. Platonism, the tendency of which is to make the intellect passionate and the passions cold, has not much need of asceticism of the severer type. The ascetics of antiquity were not the Platonists but the Cynics, whose object was to make themselves wholly independent of externals. Plotinus was, however, the inheritor of an old tradition about self-discipline (ἄσκησις) ; and it may be interesting to describe briefly what that tradition was.

We need not hunt for traces, in civilised Greece, of the most rudimentary form of asceticism—the abstinence from foods which are supposed to be *tabu*. This is barbarous superstition, though it may contain other ideas in germ. These other ideas are, speaking generally, two : the consciousness of sin, calling for propitiatory expiation, and the notion that 'the corruptible body presseth down the soul.' As early as the sixth and seventh centuries B.C. Greece had its fasting saints and seers, and abstinence from food before initiation into the mysteries was probably a, very ancient custom. The ' Orphic rule ' was adopted by communities formed for living the higher life, as early as the sixth century, and was specially popular in Magna Græcia. The disciples of ' Orpheus ' were strict vegetarians, counting even eggs forbidden ; some vegetables, especially beans, were also condemned ; and close contact with birth and death—the mysterious beginning and end of life—was a defilement.[1] This was

---

[1] Cf. Euripides, *Frag.* 475, v. 16–19.

πάλλευκα δ' ἔχων εἵματα φεύγω
γένεσίν τε βροτῶν καὶ νεκροθήκης
οὐ χριμπτόμενος, τήν τ' ἐμψύχων
βρῶσιν ἐδεστῶν πεφύλαγμαι.

See also Plato, *Laws*, 782.

no mere survival of *tabu*, nor was it primarily a way of mortifying the flesh. The Greeks, and the Romans too, were not great flesh-eaters ; beef was left to athletes in training. The main reason for abstaining from a meat-diet was the idea that it is a species of cannibalism. The unity of all life was an important part of the mystical tradition, which acknowledges no breaks in the great chain of existence. For this reason Empedocles, according to Aristotle,[1] taught that to kill for food things that have souls is forbidden by that universal law which pervades the whole earth and the firmament above.[2] A vegetarian diet became the rule among philosophers who were influenced by Pythagoreanism, which was an Orphic revival.[3] Porphyry, for instance, was a rigid abstainer from meat.

The other way of asceticism consisted in abstinence from marriage. The cult of celibacy appeared in Christianity as soon as it touched the Hellenistic world ;[4] its beginnings can be traced even in the New Testament. Galen and other Pagan writers show that the practice of lifelong continence by the Christians made a great impression on their neighbours ; it was considered a proof of such self-control as could be expected only from philosophers. Plotinus was himself an ascetic in this as in other ways. But his attitude towards human love is not the same as that of the Christian ascetics. The cause of sexual love, he says, is the desire of the Soul for the beautiful, and its instinctive feeling of kinship with the beautiful. There are secret sympathies in nature which draw us to what is like ourselves ; and just as nature owes its origin to the beautiful in the spiritual world, which makes the Soul desire to create after that

---

[1] *Rhet.* a 13. 2.

[2] Rohde, *Psyche*, 2. 126, says : 'The things from which they [the Orphists] kept themselves pure were those which represented in the symbolism of religion, rather than involved in actual practice, dependance upon the world of death and impermanence.' This is, I think, to underrate the moral reasons which made them vegetarians.

[3] Complete vegetarianism, however, was a comparatively late counsel of perfection. Zöckler, *Askese*, p. 105.

[4] The Essenes in Palestine also practised celibacy.

pattern, so the human Soul not only loves the beautiful in the visible world, but desires to create it—to ' beget in the beautiful.' Thus there is something laudable in the impulse which leads to sexual desire. But although our love of spiritual beauty inspires the love which we feel for visible objects, these visible objects do not really possess spiritual beauty. And so it is an error to suppose that the longing of the Soul can be satisfied by union with visible objects of love. This error is the cause of carnal desires, from which it is better for the philosopher to abstain.[1] True beauty should be sought in beautiful actions, and in beautiful thoughts. But earthly loves, according to all Platonists, may be the beginning of the ascent to the spiritual world. The lover has at any rate received his call to the philosophic life. This gentle idealism is preferable to the harsh dualism of flesh and spirit, from which Christian asceticism has not always been free. There is no hint in Plotinus that earthly beauty is a snare of the devil, or that there is something contaminating to the saint in the mere presence of the other sex. We may suspect that when persons hold this view, the reason is, if they are women, that Cupid has left them alone, and, if they are men, that Cupid will not leave them alone. The reason for chastity, in the Platonists, is not that we ought to be ashamed of the natural instincts, but that sensual indulgence impedes the ascent of the Soul from the material to the spiritual world, riveting the chains which bind it to Matter, and preventing it from seeing and contemplating supersensuous beauty.[2] That earthly love in its completest form—the mutual love of husband and wife—may be a sacrament of heavenly love, was a truth hidden from the eyes of Catholic, Gnostic, and Neoplatonic ascetics alike.[3]

[1] See 1. 2. 5, with Porphyry's comments, Ἀφορμαί 34. Plotinus allows only ' natural' desires, and these are not to be ' uncontrolled by the will ' (ἀπροαίρετα).

[2] A disciple of Iamblichus (*De Mysteriis*, 4. 11) says that prayers are not heard if the suppliant is ' impure ' in this sense.

[3] Benn rightly says that the story of Crates is the only romance in Greek philosophy. ' A young lady of noble family, named Hipparchia,

One object of asceticism is to ' keep under ' the body by diminishing its energy and activities. Suso, for example, asks : ' How can a man gain a perfect understanding of the spiritual life, if he preserves his forces and natural vigour intact ?   It would indeed be a miracle. I have never seen such a case.' [1] Plotinus would not have assented to this. ' Use your body ' (he says) ' as a musician uses his lyre : when it is worn out, you can still sing without accompaniment.' And again, ' the good man will give to the body all that he sees to be useful and possible, though he himself remains a member of another order.'[2] Health, he says, makes us feel more *free* in the enjoyment of the good ; though hardly any bodily ills need seriously impede this. But he does say that some experience of ill-health is better for the spiritual life than a very robust constitution ; and this is probably true.   There are some people who seem too rudely healthy to be spiritually minded. But deliberate injury to the bodily health is a very different thing. Many of the exercises practised by the mystics of the cloister were admirably designed to produce nervous excitement, hypnotic trance, and exhaustion. These in their turn produced the ' mystical phenomena ' which they valued so highly, but which in truth consisted mainly of hallucinations, or of stupor induced by extreme mental and bodily fatigue.   There is no trace of this in Plotinus.   His attitude is exactly that of Shakespeare's 146th sonnet :—

fell desperately in love with him, refused several most eligible suitors, and threatened to kill herself unless she was given to him in marriage. Her parents in despair sent for Crates. Marriage, for a philosopher, was against the principles of his sect, and he at first joined them in endeavouring to dissuade her. Finding his remonstrances unavailing, he at last flung at her feet the staff and wallet which constituted his whole worldly possessions, exclaiming, ' Here is the bridegroom, and that is the dower. Think of this matter well, for you cannot be my partner unless you follow the same calling with me.'   Hipparchia consented, and henceforth, heedless of taunts, conformed her life in every respect to the Cynic pattern ' (*Greek Philosophers*, p. 331).

[1] Sermons, transl. by Thiriot, 2. 358.
[2] 1. 4. 16.

Poor soul, the centre of my sinful earth,
My sinful earth these rebel powers array,
Why dost thou pine within and suffer dearth,
Painting thy outward walls so courtly gay ?
Why so large cost, having so short a lease,
Dost thou upon thy fading mansion spend ?
Shall worms, inheritors of this excess,
Eat up thy charge ? is this thy body's end ?
Then, soul, live thou upon thy servant's loss,
And let that pine to aggravate thy store :
Buy terms divine in selling hours of dross ;
Within be fed, without be rich no more :
    So shalt thou feed on death, that feeds on men,
    And death once dead, there's no more dying then.

And yet we cannot wholly approve of Plotinus' attitude towards our humble companion, ' my brother the ass,' as St. Francis calls his body.   The philosopher himself is reported to have said that he was ashamed of his body, as a reason for refusing to have his portrait painted. There is nothing in the Enneads, on this subject, so wholesome as the following beautiful passage from Krause. ' Spirit and body are in man equally original, equally living, equally divine ; they claim to be maintained in the same purity and holiness, and to be equally loved and developed.   The spirit of man wishes and requires of his body that it shall helpfully and lovingly co-operate with him in all his spiritual needs, that it shall enlarge his field of view, exercise his art, and unite him through speech with other men ; and kindly Nature does not disappoint this expectation, for the spirit is dear and precious to her, and she heaps love and good things upon it.   But the body should be just as dear and precious to the spirit. Let the spirit esteem the body like itself, and honour it as an equally great and rich product of the power and love of God.   Let it support, help, and delight the body in the organic process of its development to health, power, and beauty.   Let it form it into the mirror of a beautiful soul ; and let it consecrate and hallow it for the free service of the purposes of reason that are only worthy and good.' [1]

The conflict with evil is regarded by Plotinus rather as a process of emancipation, a journey through darkness into light, than as a struggle with a hostile spiritual power. Human wickedness is never absolute. ' Vice is still human, being mixed with something contrary to itself.' [2] This is akin to the mystical doctrine that even in the worst man there remains a spark of the Divine, which has never consented to evil and can never consent to it. Even Tertullian, it is interesting to find, has the same doctrine. In a fine passage of the *De Anima*[3] he says : ' The corruption of nature is another nature, having its own god and father, the author of corruption. And yet there remains the original good of the soul, which is divine and akin to it and in the true sense natural. For that which is from God is not so much extinguished as obscured. It can be obscured, because it is not God ; it cannot be extinguished, because it is from God. . . . In the worst there is something good, and in the best there is something of the worst.' Plotinus says that the bad man, ' deserting what the Soul ought to contemplate, receives in exchange ' for his true self ' another Form,' a spurious self. But this false Form is rather like a coating of mud concealing the real self. ' Hence all virtue is a cleansing' ($\kappa\acute{a}\theta a\rho\sigma\iota s$).[4] The doctrine of the ' other Form,' which the bad man gets in consequence of his base desires, may be illustrated from Hylton's *Scale of Perfection*. ' Now I shall tell thee how thou mayest enter into thyself to see the ground of sin and destroy it as much as thou canst. Draw in thy thoughts. And what shalt thou find ? A dark and ill-favoured image of thine own soul, which hath neither light of knowledge nor feeling of love for God. This is the image of sin, which

---

[1] Krause, *The Ideal of Humanity* (English translation by W. Hastie, D.D.), p. 31–2. This admirable philosopher has been far too much neglected both in England and in his own country.
[2] He opposes the Gnostic doctrine of ' total depravity.'
[3] Chap. 41.   [4] 1. 6. 5, 6.

St. Paul calleth a body of sin and death. It is like no bodily thing. It is no real thing, but darkness of conscience and a lack of the love of God and of light. Go as if thou wouldest beat down this dark image, and go through-stitch with it.' [1] The characteristic maxim of Plotinus, ' Never cease working at thy statue,' suggests a scheme of self-improvement more like that of Goethe than the Christian quest of holiness. There is little mention of repentance in our author : he urges us to make the best of a nature which is fundamentally good, though clogged with impediments of various kinds. The Neoplatonist does not make matters easy for himself ; but his world is one in which there are no negative values, no temperatures below zero. The last enemy is chaos and disintegration of the Soul, not its reintegration in the service of evil. And if the higher Soul is the man himself, the man himself never sins. Like Spirit, the higher Soul is ἀναμάρτητος. [2] This, however, is not allowed to paralyse the will to virtue ; for though the Soul itself is not within the time-process, in which evils occur, the process is within it, and concerns it. Plotinus is valuable also when he says [3] that most vice is caused by ' false opinions ' (ψευδεῖς δόξαι)—untrue valuations and ignorances of all kinds. Modern philanthropy would be more beneficent if we steadily combated ' false opinions ' whenever we met them, instead of assuming that good intentions cover all practical foolishness.

' Flight from the world,' as recommended by Neoplatonism, had the double motive of liberating the Soul from the cares and pleasures of this life, and of making it invulnerable against troubles coming from outside. The latter motive is very prominent in all the later Greek philosophy. The ' flight ' mainly consists in renun-

---

[1] Hylton, *Scale of Perfection*, Chap. 4 (abridged).
[2] The philosophical principle which underlies this is, ἐνέργεια οὐκ ἐστιν ἀλλοίωσις ; no activity, for better or worse, can change fundamental nature. This, a Christian might say, is the reason why a lost soul must always be miserable ; it can never be at home in hell.
[3] 3. 6. 2.

ciation of those things which the natural man regards as goods, and which from their nature, and from the fact that other men covet them, are most liable to be taken away from us. They include also some painful emotions not of a self-regarding nature, such as extreme compassion, which may ruffle the composure of the sage against his will. Only weak eyes, in Seneca's opinion, water at another's misfortunes. ' The end of all philosophy,' says Seneca again, ' is to teach us to despise life.' [1] According to Lucian's Demonax, happiness belongs only to the free man, and the free man is he who hopes nothing and fears nothing.' [2] The desire to be invulnerable is natural to most men, and it has been the avowed or unavowed motive of most practical philosophy. To the public eye, the Greek philosopher was a rather fortunate person who could do without a great many things which other people need and have to work for. Those philosophers who most disdainfully rejected pleasure as an end, made freedom from bodily and mental disturbance the test of proficiency and the reward of discipline. On this side, the influence of Stoicism is very strong in all the later Greek thought. Even suicide, the logical corollary of this system (since there are some troubles to which the sage cannot be indifferent), is not wholly condemned by Plotinus,[3] though he has the credit of dissuading Porphyry from taking his own life. The Stoics were well aware that a man has no right to cut himself off from the sorrows of his kind ; he must try to relieve them. But he is to preserve an emotional detachment ; or perhaps he would say that he wishes to show the same courage in bearing his neighbour's misfortunes as in

[1] *Letters*, 3. 5.   [2] Lucian, *Demonax*, 20.
[3] The authoritative passage on suicide for the school of Plato is *Phaedo*, p. 62, where Socrates says that a soldier must not desert his post. Plotinus argues that the suicide can hardly leave this life with a mind free and passionless ; if he had vanquished fear and passion he would, almost always, be content to live. But in 1. 4. 16 he says that the Soul is ' not prevented from leaving the body, and is always master to decide in regard to it.' Heinemann gives reasons for thinking that in 1. 9 we have not got the true text, but a paraphrase, possibly misleading, of a longer discussion.

bearing his own.   We remember La Rochefoucauld and smile.   Plotinus certainly errs in not emphasising the necessity of deep and wide human sympathy, for the growth of the Soul.   It follows really from his doctrine of Soul, which is in no way individualistic ; but he is a little too anxious to make his higher orders of Being comfortable.   The good man must enjoy an inner calm and happiness.   Greek and Roman ethics always seem to us moderns a little *hard*.   Greek civilisation was singularly pitiless ; the lot of the aged and the unfortunate was acknowledged to be cruel, but this knowledge raised no qualms of conscience.   The same pitilessness reappears in the culture of the Italian Renaissance ; it may have some obscure connexion with a flowering-time of the arts. Roman hardness was of a different kind, more like the hardness of the militarist clique in Germany ; the Stoical philosophy seemed to have been made for Romans.   The contrast between the Christian ideal of emancipation from self by perfect sympathy, and the Stoical ideal of emancipation by perfect inner detachment, is very significant.   It is perhaps for this reason that the later Platonism could do so little to regenerate society.   The philosopher saved himself ; his country he could not save. It is fair, however, to add that Plotinus repudiates the suggestion that the good man ought to desire injustice and poverty to exist, as giving a field for his virtues.   He may possibly have heard this said by some of his neighbours.[1]

The practical results of extreme moral idealism are shown in the attitude of Plotinus towards national misfortunes.   We are a little surprised to find so pious a man refusing to pity the victims of aggression who have trusted in heaven to protect them.   ' Those who by evil-doing have become irrational animals and wild beasts drag the ordinary sort with them and do them violence. The victims are better men than their oppressors, but are overcome by their inferiors in so far as they are themselves deficient ; for they are not themselves good, and have not

[1] 6. 8. 5.

prepared themselves for suffering. . . . Some are un-
armed, but it is the armed who rule, and it befits not God
himself to fight for the unwarlike. The law says that
those shall come safely out of war who fight bravely, not
those who pray. . . . The wicked rule through lack of
courage in the ruled ; and this is just.'[1] In the next
section he offers something very like a challenge to Christian ethics, and I think he has the Christians in his mind
throughout this discussion. ' That the wicked should
expect others to be their saviours at the sacrifice of themselves is not a lawful prayer to make : nor is it to be expected that divine Beings should lay aside their own lives
and rule the details of such men's lives, nor that good men,
who are living a life that is other and better than human
dominion, should devote themselves to the ruling of
wicked men.' The philosopher, it seems, will not be
much perturbed if his country is successfully attacked
by a powerful enemy. If the citizens are enslaved, that
does not matter to the Soul ; if they are killed, death is
only a changing of the actor's mask. If people must take
these things seriously, they ought to learn to fight better ;
God helps those who help themselves. This cool acceptance of monstrous acts of tyranny and injustice does not
commend itself to us just now, nor does it seem to accord
well with the doctrine that the Soul ' came down ' to give
order and reason to the outer world.

There is a very instructive parallel in Wordsworth's
Excursion. A ruined cottage conveyed to his heart

> ' So still an image of tranquillity,
> So calm and still, and looked so beautiful
> Amid the uneasy thoughts which filled my mind,
> That what we feel of sorrow and despair
> From ruin and from change, and all the grief
> The passing shows of Being leave behind,
> Appeared an idle dream that could not live
> Where meditation was.'

There speaks the Platonist. In later life he altered it
to—

[1] 3. 2. 8.

'Appeared an idle dream that could maintain
Nowhere dominion o'er the enlightened spirit,
Whose meditating sympathies repose
Upon the breast of faith.'

Purification (κάθαρσις) is in one sense a stage through which the soul must pass in order to reach a higher, in another it is a task that can never be completed while we live here.   In the former sense, it passes insensibly into the higher stage of Enlightenment.   We are often told that Greek philosophy, in and after Aristotle, spoke of the ' ethical ' virtues in connection with the lower stage, and of the ' intellectual ' virtues in connection with the higher. These words in their English dress have caused a great deal of misunderstanding.   The ' ethical ' virtues are not the constituents of all moral excellence ;   they are those virtues which we begin to practise mainly on authority, and which at last become matters of habit (ἦθος).   And the ' intellectual ' virtues are not those which require exceptional brain-power—if there are any such virtues ; they are for the most part the same as the ethical virtues, only now they are understood and willed with conscious reference to their ultimate ends.   The immediate ends are of course willed by the practical moralist ;   but these are not seen in their relation to universal laws until the stage of enlightenment is reached.

There is a sense in which virtue seems to be dehumanised by entering upon this higher level.   Its object of study or contemplation is now what is above man ;[1]   more especially it occupies itself with the nature of God.   Now here we do indeed come to a parting of the ways. Plotinus, like his great predecessors, honestly and heartily believed that the philosophic life is morally the highest.   He thought so, not because it happened to be his own trade ; he made it his own trade because he thought it the highest.   The life of active philanthropy, without reference to anything beyond the promotion of human comfort and the diminution of suffering, would have seemed to him to need further justification, as indeed it does.

[1] Bosanquet, *The Principle of Individuality and Value*, pp. 398–401.

What is it that we desire most for our fellow-men, and for
ourselves ; and why ? Altruistic Epicureanism would
not have appealed to him much more than egoistic ; and
the not infrequent modern phenomenon of the religious
or social worker who, though personally unselfish and
self-denying, is a hedonist in his schemes for improving
society, would have seemed to him to indicate mental
confusion. If happiness is identified with comfort and
pleasure, he does not even think it desirable ; if with
higher states of the mind, we may trust to being happy
as soon as we are inside the enchanted garden of the
spiritual world. The good life is an end in itself. If
any man seeks anything else in the good life, it is not the
good life that he is seeking—nor will he find it. But
this is not the Stoical pursuit of virtue for its own sake—
the rather harsh and bullying ethics of Kantians ancient
and modern. Experience has shown that as soon as
Stoicism ceases to be buttressed by pride—an unamiable
kind of pride, generally—its ethical sanctions lose their
cogency. There are too many unresolved contradictions
in Stoicism ; its moral centre is in personal dignity, the
consciousness of which is not universal, nor indefectible.
Some may doubt whether it is altogether desirable. For
the Platonist, the only true motive is the desire to ' become like to God,' an approximation which, it is needless
to say, can take place only in the region of will, love, and
knowledge. This, which is the Soul's highest good and
the realisation of its true nature, is its own reward ; from
it proceed, as if automatically, all good actions. But the
best life is impossible without the ' wisdom which is from
above ' ; and this demands a consecration and discipline
of the intellect not less than of the will. If the ultimate
good is to be something rather than to do something, the
philosophic life, in Plotinus' sense, is the best, and we
can understand what Blake meant when he said, ' The
fool shall not enter into heaven, be he never so holy.'

Thus for Plotinus all the virtues are in a sense a preparation for contemplation (θεωρία).[1] The object of contem-

plation is the Good, which, as we have seen, is one of his names for the Absolute. The chief test whether we are really pursuing the Good is that the Good cannot be desired for any reason outside itself. Heaven is in our Souls or nowhere.[1] If we associate pleasure with the Good as an essential aspect of it, we are not thinking of *the* Good, but only of *our* good.[2] There is nothing wrong in this ; we must set before us relative and partial goods while we are ourselves imperfect. Thus the good of Matter is Form, the good of the body is the Soul, the good of the Soul is virtue, and above virtue Spirit, the good of Spirit is the One, the 'first nature.' In Matter, Form produces order and beauty ; in the body, Soul produces life ; in the Soul, Spirit produces wisdom, virtue, and happiness ; and in Spirit 'the first light' produces a Divine light which transforms it, makes it see the Godhead, and share the ineffable felicity of the First Principle. Although Plotinus puts the life of Spirit 'above virtue,'[3] he is far from any Nietzschian idea of exalting his sage 'beyond good and evil.' He insists that it is by virtue that we resemble God, and that 'without genuine virtue God is but a name.'[4] He urges, against the Gnostics, that it is useless to bid men 'look towards God,' without telling them how they are to do it.[5] He does not deny the value of the Peripatetic conception of the end as 'good living' (εὐζωία), nor of the Stoic advice 'to accomplish one's own proper work,' nor even of the Epicurean 'good condition' (εὐπάθεια).[6] There is truth in all these ideals. The higher life, Spirit, and happiness, are identical—a good not extraneous to ourselves, but one which we already possess potentially. We *are* 'the activity of the spiritual principle.'[7]

We have said that for Plotinus all the virtues are in a sense a preparation for contemplation (θεωρία). The tendency of modern thought in the West is to view this conception of human life with impatience, and to insist

---

[1] 3. 4. 6.   [2] 6. 7. 25
[3] 1. 2. 3, ἡ ἀρετὴ ψυχῆς, νοῦ δὲ οὐκ ἐστιν.
[4] 2. 9. 15, ἄνευ ἀρετῆς ἀληθινῆς θεὸς λεγόμενος ὄνομά ἐστιν.
[5] 2. 9. 15.   [6] 1. 4. 1.   [7] 1. 4. 9.

that on the contrary all contemplation is useless unless
it is a preparation for action. The two ideals are not so
far apart as they appear ; or rather we should say that
a deeper consideration of the problem of conduct tends
to bring them together. We must as usual begin with an
attempt to understand the exact meaning, not of ' contemplation ' and ' action,' but of θεωρία and πρᾶξις.
Θεωρία in the Ionic philosophy meant ' curiosity ' ; a
traveller like Hecataeus or Herodotus might be said to
visit foreign lands θεωρίας ἕνεκα. In the mysteries the
word was applied to a dramatic or sacramental spectacle
such as the representation of a suffering God. Pythagoras
is said to have been the first to give it a new meaning,
as the contemplation, not of the sacrament, but of the
underlying truths which sacraments symbolise. He
found in the observation of the heavenly bodies a potent
aid to this kind of contemplation ; unlike Plato, who
speaks with contempt of star-gazing.[1] Plato in a well-
known passage describes the philosopher as the spectator
of all time and existence.[2] In Plotinus the true and perfect contemplation, the ' living contemplation,' is the
interplay of Spirit and the spiritual world.[3] But this
is no idle self-enjoyment. The quietness (ἡσυχία) of
Spirit is unimpeded activity ; its being is activity ; it
acts what it contemplates.[4] Contemplation is activity
which transcends the action which it directs. ' If the
creative force (λόγος) remains in itself while it creates,
it must be contemplation. Action itself must be different
from the λόγος which directs it ; the λόγος which is
associated with action (πρᾶξις) and oversees it, cannot
itself be action.' [5] Creation is contemplation ; for it is
the consummation (ἀποτέλεσμα) of contemplation, which
remains contemplation and does nothing else, but creates
by virtue of being contemplation. All things that exist are
a by-play of contemplation (πάρεργον θεωρίας) ; [6] because
though action is the necessary result of contemplation,

[1] Plato, *Republic*, 529.
[2] Plato, *Republic*, 486 ; and compare *Theaetetus*, 173.
[3] 3. 8. 8.   [4] 5. 3. 7 ; and cf. 3. 8. 3, ἡ ποίησις θεωρία ἐστίν.
[5] 3. 8. 3.   [6] 3. 8. 8.

contemplation does not exist for the sake of action, but for its own sake. Action is either a weakness of contemplation or its accompaniment, the former if it has no motive or object beyond itself, the latter if it results from some spiritual activity. This seems to me quite sound. Thoughtless and objectless action indicates a weakness of the Soul, which ought to control all our external life. Spinoza would say that contemplation is action inspired by reason, while all other action is ' passive,' reaction to external stimuli. The only proper ' action ' is purposive action, in which fortitude, high-mindedness and nobility are displayed.[1] But for Plotinus, contemplation is a rather less intellectual process than for Spinoza. It is an intuition which inevitably leads to appropriate action. I believe that this is truer to experience than is usually supposed. As Mr. Bosanquet says, ' The presence of adequate ideas which are inoperative in moral matters is vastly exaggerated.' [2] Ideas inadequately held, which do not pass into action, are not knowledge. The moral effort (so perhaps Plotinus would have us to believe) is in making our ideas adequate, in passing from dreams to thoughts, in converting visions into tasks, floating ideas into acts of will. When the thing to be done has quite clearly taken possession of our minds, it will be done, he tells us, with a sort of unconsciousness.

That this self-possession which he calls contemplation is difficult to win, Plotinus does not dispute. It requires the use of a faculty which all indeed possess, but which few use. Even so Spinoza concludes his Ethics with a passage which, except for difference of style, might have been written by Plotinus himself. ' The wise man is scarcely at all perturbed in spirit, but being conscious of himself and of God, and of things, by a certain eternal necessity, never ceases to be, but always possesses true

---

[1] Spinoza, *Ethics*, 3. 1. 59.
[2] Bosanquet, *Principle of Individuality and Value*, p. 348. So Mill says, ' Speculative philosophy, which to the superficial appears a thing so remote from the business of life and the outward interests of men, is in reality the thing on earth which most influences them, and in the long run overbears every other influence save those which it must itself obey.'

acquiescence of his spirit. If the way which I have pointed out as leading to this result seems exceedingly hard, it may nevertheless be discovered. Needs must it be hard, since it is so seldom found. How would it be possible, if salvation were ready to our hand, and could without great labour be found, that it should be by almost all men neglected ? But all things excellent are as difficult as they are rare.' Now this confession of difficulty should be enough to give pause to those who think that the praise of contemplation is a denial of Kingsley's advice to ' do noble things, not dream them, all day long.' For dreaming is very easy work. ' *Traümen ist leicht, denken ist schwer.*' The clear disciplined thinking which Plotinus called dialectic is not merely an organon of abstract speculation. It ' gives us reality at the same time as the idea of it.' And the outgoing movement which produces good actions is the natural and necessary activity of contemplation. This doctrine has never been better stated than by Ruysbroek.[1] ' Pure love frees a man from himself and his acts. If we would know this in ourselves, we must yield to the Divine, the innermost sanctuary of ourselves. . . . Hence comes the impulse and urgency towards active righteousness and virtue, for *Love cannot be idle*. The Spirit of God, moving within the powers of the man, urges them outwards in just and wise activity. . . . Christ was the greatest contemplative that ever lived, yet He was ever at the service of men, and never did His ineffable and perpetual contemplation diminish His activity, or His exterior activity.' Those only need quarrel with the Neoplatonic doctrine of contemplation who do not allow that clear thinking should precede right action.[2]

[1] Ruysbroek, *Flowers of a Mystic Garden*. Quoted by Herman, *Meaning and Value of Mysticism*, p. 88.

[2] Charles Péguy says excellently : ' Ce sont les mystiques qui sont même pratiques et ce sont les politiques qui ne le sont pas. C'est nous qui sommes pratiques, qui faisons quelque chose, et c'est eux qui ne le sont pas, qui ne font rien. C'est nous qui amassons et c'est eux qui pillent. C'est nous qui bâtissons, c'est nous qui fondons, et c'est eux qui démolissent. C'est nous qui nourrissons et c'est eux qui parasitent. C'est nous qui faisons les œuvres et les hommes, les peuples et les races. Et c'est eux qui ruinent.'

The Soul when joined to the body is inclined to evil as well as good.[1] The choice must be made. But are we in any sense free agents ?[2] We have an impression that we are free ; but how do we come by it ? We feel that we have a certain liberty, just when our freedom of action is threatened by fate or by violence. Finding with a sort of surprise that in such cases we are forced to act against our real will, we realise the general possibility of resisting external pressure and asserting our freedom. What we call our freedom, then, is simply the power of obeying our true nature. But what is our true nature ? Man is a complex being. Free-will certainly does not belong to our desires, or to our passions, or to sensation, or to imagination ; these things are too often our masters. We are not completely free agents so long as our desires are prompted by finite needs.[3] And the union of the Soul with the body makes us dependent on the general order of the world, over which we have no control. But though we are complex, we are also, as persons, each of us a whole.[4] It is the chief characteristic of psychical and spiritual life, that the whole is present in each part. We are therefore not merely cogs in a great machine ; we are the machine itself, and the mind which directs it. But this is only fully true of the personality which has realised its own inner nature ; the man of ordinary experience ' shares in Being and is a kind of Being, but is not master of his own Being.'[5] The imperfect man is pulled and pushed by forces which are external to himself, just because he is himself still external to his true Being. If we could see the course of events as they really are, we should find that the chain of causation is inviolable, but that ' we ourselves are causative principles.'[6] What is free in us is that spontaneous movement of the Spirit which has no external cause ;[7]

[1] πέφυκε γὰρ ἐπ' ἄμφω, 1. 2. 4.
[2] εἴ τι ἐφ' ἡμῖν ὂν τυγχάνει, 6. 8. 1.   [3] 6. 8. 4.
[4] ὅσον δὲ αὐτοί, οἰκεῖον ὅλον, 2. 2. 2 ; an important saying.
[5] 6. 8. 12.
[6] ἀρχαὶ δὲ καὶ ἄνθρωποι. κινοῦνται γοῦν πρὸς τὰ καλὰ οἰκείᾳ φύσει καὶ ἀρχὴ αὕτη αὐτεξούσιος, 3. 2. 10.
[7] 6. 8. 1–6.

it is the will of the higher Soul to return to its own Principle. The element of freedom in our practical activities
is this underlying motive, the spiritual activity of the
Soul. When the Soul becomes Spirit, its will is free ; the
good will, in attaining its desire, becomes spiritual
perception, and Spirit is free in its own right.[1] This resembles Spinoza's definition of freedom : ' We call that
free which exists in virtue of the necessities of our nature,
and which is determined by ourselves alone.'

Plotinus distinguishes invariable sequence from causation, and points out that rigid determination excludes
the very idea of causation.[2] If ' one Soul,' oper-
ating through all things, determines every detail, as
every leaf of a plant is implicit in its root, this
' exaggerated determinism ' ($\tau\grave{o}$ $\sigma\phi o\delta\rho\grave{o}\nu$ $\tau\hat{\eta}s$ $\grave{a}\nu\acute{a}\gamma\kappa\eta s$)
destroys the very idea of causation and necessary se-
quence, for ' all will then be one.' We shall then be no
longer ourselves, nor will any action be ours ; we shall be
mere automata, with no will or reasoning faculty. But
we must maintain our individuality ($\delta\epsilon\hat{\iota}$ $\check{\epsilon}\kappa\alpha\sigma\tau o\nu$ $\check{\epsilon}\kappa\alpha\sigma\tau o\nu$
$\epsilon\hat{\iota}\nu\alpha\iota$),[3] and we must not throw the responsibility for
our errors upon ' the All.' In another place [4] he says that
' providence is not everything ' ; otherwise there would
be no room for human wisdom, skill, and righteousness ;
indeed there would be nothing for providence to provide
for. The world does not consist only of mechanical
sequences ; it contains also real causation. Each in-
dividual soul is a little ' first cause ' ($\pi\rho\omega\tau o\upsilon\rho\gamma\grave{o}s$ $\alpha\grave{\iota}\tau\acute{\iota}\alpha$) ;
and the universal Soul is above the contradiction of
necessity and freedom. ' Necessity and freedom do not
contradict each other ; necessity includes freedom.' [5]

As for the wicked, their misdeeds proceed necessarily
from their character. Our character is our destiny ; but
our character is also our choice ; we must remember that
we have lived other lives before our present existence.[6]

---

[1] $\mathring{\eta}$ $\delta\grave{\epsilon}$ $\beta o\acute{\upsilon}\lambda\eta\sigma\iota s$ $\mathring{\eta}$ $\nu\acute{o}\eta\sigma\iota s$, 6. 8. 6.   [2] 3. 1. 4.
[3] 3. 1. 4 and 7.   [4] 3. 2. 9.
[5] $o\mathring{\upsilon}$ $\delta\iota\alpha\phi\omega\nu\epsilon\hat{\iota}$ $\grave{a}\lambda\lambda\acute{\eta}\lambda o\iota s$ . . $\mathring{\eta}$ $\tau\epsilon$ $\grave{a}\nu\acute{a}\gamma\kappa\eta$ $\kappa\alpha\grave{\iota}$ $\tau\grave{o}$ $\grave{\epsilon}\kappa o\acute{\upsilon}\sigma\iota o\nu$, $\grave{\epsilon}\pi\epsilon\acute{\iota}\pi\epsilon\rho$ $\check{\epsilon}\chi\epsilon\iota$ $\tau\grave{o}$
$\grave{\epsilon}\kappa o\acute{\upsilon}\sigma\iota o\nu$ $\mathring{\eta}$ $\grave{a}\nu\acute{a}\gamma\kappa\eta$, 4. 8. 5.   [6] 3. 3. 4.

It is not correct to say, with Mr. Whittaker,[1] that Plotinus is 'without the least hesitation a determinist.' He is quite convinced that mechanical necessity cannot explain psychical or spiritual life, and in these higher spheres he denies that necessity and free-will are incompatible. Virtue is not so much free as identical with freedom ; it is the unobstructed activity of the higher Soul. But though he endeavours to show the justice of holding men responsible for their actions, and of divine and human punishments, he nowhere clears up the difficulty about the original choice of a character which inevitably produces evil actions. Temptation, he says, is a gradual perversion of a living being which has the power of self-determined movement (κίνησις αὐτεξούσιος).[2] The inability to lead the divine and happy life is a moral inability.[3] The necessity is within us.[4] He says in effect that it takes all sorts to make a world, and that we must expect to meet with all degrees of goodness and badness. If we knew all, we might see that badness even conduces to the perfection of the whole.[5]

The conception of Chance (τύχη), in the modern sense, hardly enters into this philosophy.[6] Anaximenes had shrewdly remarked that chance is only our name for the incalculable.[7] Plato in the Tenth Book of the *Laws* names Nature, Chance, and Art as the three causes of events ; but he leaves no room for the operations of chance, except perhaps in the chaos which has not yet received Forms. In Aristotle [8] chance and spontaneity are merely defects (στερήσεις) ; but he also says that events which have an efficient though not a final cause may be said to be due to chance. This gives the word a legitimate use. In any other sense the word should perhaps be excluded from

---

[1] *The Neoplatonists*, p. 76.

[2] 3. 2. 4.   [3] 3. 2. 10, αὐτοὶ ἁμαρτάνουσιν.

[4] ib. τὸ τῆς ἀνάγκης οὐκ ἔξωθεν.   [5] 3. 2. 5 ; 3. 3. 5.

[6] Wendland shows that the conception of Chance filled a large place in Hellenistic philosophy. But Proclus practically turns Chance into Providence. *De Malorum Subst.* 44. 8–13. ' Let no one think that τύχη is ἀλόγιστος αἰτία καὶ ἀόριστος, instead of, as it is, θεία ἢ δαιμονία δύναμις'. I think Plotinus would have agreed.

[7] Stobæus, *Ecl.* 2, 346.

[8] Ritchie, *Philosophical Studies*, p. 202.

philosophy, which has no room either for uncaused events or for the conception of a whimsical fate. However, the pragmatists seem bent on rehabilitating this discredited deity.[1]

The dispute about free-will is usually a futile quarrel between those who attribute freedom to a man apart from his character, and those who attribute freedom to character apart from the man. Necessity is merely the nature of things; and what we call mechanism is itself a form of the struggle for life. The laws of mechanism are, as Lotze says,[2] 'only the will of the universal Soul,' and it is not surprising that nature, so guided, should have the appearance of an unbroken chain. It is not necessary to hold, with Renouvier, that phenomena are discontinuous, but we do deny that one phenomenon 'causes' another. What we call free will seems to depend on the fact of consciousness, and the presence of an ideal. In other words, he who asserts free will asserts the reality of final causes.

The general character of the Neoplatonic ethics will be clear from what has been said. The fundamental contrast, for all Greek philosophy and especially for Platonism, is not between egoism and altruism, but between a false and a true standard of values. The Soul, whether from its own choice and love of adventure, or by the will of the higher powers, has exchanged the peace of eternity for the unrest of time, and is or should be engaged on the return journey to its heavenly home. 'Our beginnings must be our ends'; [3] we must strive to realise 'the best part of our nature, that which in the spiritual world we already are.' The great moral danger is that we should forget ourselves and God. 'When the Soul has once tasted the pleasures of self-will, it indulges its opportunities of independence, and is carried so far away from its Principle that it forgets whence it came. Such Souls are like children brought up in a foreign country, who forget who they are and who are their

---

[1] Professor Pringle-Pattison has some good remarks on this. *The Idea of God*, pp. 185-6.

[2] *Microcosmus*, Vol. 1, p. 396 (English Tr.).   [3] 3. 9. 2.

parents. They have learnt to honour everything rather than themselves, to lavish their reverence and affection upon external things, and to break, as far as they can, the links that bound them to the Divine. Believing themselves to be lower than the things of the world, they regard themselves as mean and transitory beings, and the thought of the nature and power of the Deity is driven out of their minds.'[1] This self-contempt, which is the cause why so many are content to lead unworthy and useless lives, isolates us also from our fellows, whom we respect no more than we respect ourselves. A kind of moral atomism becomes our philosophy. We lose all sense of human solidarity, and become like faces turned away from each other, though they are attached to one head. If one of us could turn round, he would see at once God, himself, and the world. And he would soon find that the separate self is a figment ; there is no dividing-line between himself and the world. The ' external ' world is that part of the higher self of which he has not yet been able to take possession. ' All Souls are all things ; each of them is characterised by the faculty which it chiefly uses ; some unite themselves to the spiritual world, others to the discursive reason, others to desire. Souls, while they contemplate diverse objects, are and become that which they contemplate.'[2] The ascent cannot be made all at once ; the lower stages are rungs to climb by.[3] The end is unification ; ' goodness is unification and unification is goodness.'[4] Sympathy is thus based on the recognition of an actual fact, our membership one of another. Philosophy reveals this relationship, just as science reveals our physical kinships and affinities. But this membership is in truth not of the physical or psychical but of the spiritual order. Neoplatonic morality thus remains throughout theocentric. Souls are members of a choir which sing in time and tune so long as they look at their conductor, but go

[1] 5. 1. 1. [2] 4. 3. 8. [3] 5. 3. 9.
[4] Proclus, *Inst. Theol.* 13.

wrong when their attention is diverted to other things.[1]
Philanthropy, therefore, is not the end of true morality,
but its necessary consequence. It is natural to love our
neighbours as ourselves, when once we have understood
that in God our neighbours are ourselves. The higher
part of the self, including our ' reason ' (τὸ λογικόν)
is not divided among individuals ; sympathy, then, is
the natural result of a real identity.[2]

The highest stage hardly belongs to ethics : it is dealt
with in the preceding chapter. But the noble doctrine
that ' there is progress even in heaven '[3] must be again
quoted in this connexion. Plotinus is as emphatic as the
New Testament that we must put on the new man ;[4]
though this is otherwise expressed by saying that ' we
see ourselves as Spirit.' *Love* becomes more and more
important as we ascend further. Love is ' an activity
of the Soul desiring the Good.'[5] Plotinus follows Plato
in using mythical language about Love. There are
different ' Loves '—dæmonic Spirits—belonging to different grades in the hierarchy of existence. The Universal
soul has a Love ' which is its eye, and is born of the desire
which it has ' for the One.[6] There is a still higher Love
which is wholly detached from material things. Love
is not a relation between externals, but between Spirit
and Spirit. It is unity in duality, the reconciliation of
these opposites, known in experience. Human Love is
the sacrament of the union of Souls Yonder. It is
immortal ; almost immortality itself. We need not be
surprised that the Neoplatonists use ἔρως where the
Christians used ἀγάπη. For Plato and all his followers
the love of physical beauty is a legitimate first stage in
the ascent to the love of the divine Ideas. Plotinus says
that three classes of men have their feet on the ladder—

---

[1] 6. 9. 8., quoted above, p. 137.
[2] See the whole chapter, 4. 9 : Εἰ πᾶσαι αἱ ψυχαὶ μία.
[3] 1. 3. 1, κἀκεῖ βαδιστέον τὴν ἄνω πορείαν.
[4] 5. 3. 4, [δεῖ] παντελῶς ἄλλον γενέσθαι. Cf. Plato, *Phaedo*, 64, on the mystic death.
[5] 3. 5. 4.   3. 5. 3.

the philosopher, the friend of the Muses, and the lover.[1]
The intellect, æsthetic sensibility, and love are the three
' anagogic ' faculties.   He knows that they are apt to
flow over into each other.

It remains to notice that Plotinus attaches importance
to a calm cheerfulness of temper.   ' The good man is
always serene, calm, and satisfied ; if he is really a
good man, none of the things which are called evils can
move him.' [2]   Here again we see the influence of the
Stoics.

The defects of Plotinian ethics are in part common to
the school, and in part common to the age.   The following passage, true in the main, is marred by its last
sentence.[3]   ' Men complain of poverty and of the unequal
distribution of wealth, in ignorance that the wise man
does not desire equality in such things, nor thinks that
the rich has any advantage over the poor, or the prince
over the subject.   He leaves these opinions to the vulgar,
and knows that there are two sorts of life, that of virtuous
people, who can rise to the highest degree of life, that of
the spiritual world ; and that of vulgar and earthly
persons, which is itself double ; for sometimes they
dream of virtue and participate in it to some small extent,
and sometimes they form only a vile crowd, and are
only machines, destined to minister to the first needs of
virtuous men.'   Plotinus here uses the haughty tone
of an intellectual aristocrat, and assumes without
hesitation that the thinker has a right not only to
his leisure, but to be supported by the labour of those
who cannot share his virtues.   But we must remember
that a Neoplatonic saint would live so as to be a very
light burden on the community, and that it is well worth
while for a State to encourage a few persons to devote
themselves to such a life as Plotinus lived.   The only

---

[1] I. 3. I, φιλόσοφος, μουσικὸς, ἐρωτικὸς ἀνακτέοι.   But compare also the
important statement in 4. 3. 8, that there are three upward paths—
ἐνέργεια, γνῶσις, and ὄρεξις—practical, intellectual, and affective
activity.

[2] I. 4. 12.   [3] 2. 9. 9.

error (if it is made) is in supposing that humble occupations are a bar to the highest life.   The notion that the
dignity of work is determined by the subjects with which
it is concerned, and not by the manner in which it is
executed, is a mischievous error which Greek thought
never outgrew,[1] and which still survives in the learned
professions.   The effects of it were far-reaching, and had
not a little to do with the decay of Greek culture.   Early
Christianity was, in principle at least, free from this
fault, but it was, on the whole, blind to the joy of productive activity, which Plotinus recognises in his doctrine
of the Soul as creator, and to the value of industry in
secular things as a service of God, a side of ethics which
was not developed till the Reformation.   There is a
beautiful passage of Lotze which is entirely in accordance
with the principles of Neoplatonism, and which Plotinus
might have uttered if he had lived in a happier period
than the third century.   ' As in the great fabric of the
universe the creative Spirit imposed upon itself unchangeable laws by which it moves the world of phenomena,
diffusing the fullness of the highest good throughout
innumerable forms and events, and distilling it again
from them into the bliss of consciousness and enjoyment ;
so must man, acknowledging the same laws, develop
given existence into a knowledge of its value, and the
value of his ideals into a series of external forms proceeding from himself.   To this labour we are called ; and the
most prominent intellects in all ages have devoted themselves to the perfecting of the outward relations of life,
the subjugation of nature, the advancement of the useful
arts, the improvement of social institutions, though they
knew that the true bliss of existence lies in those quiet
moments of solitary communion with God when all
human daily toil, all culture and civilisation, the gravity

---

[1] Mr. Zimmern, in his brilliant and delightful book, *The Greek
Commonwealth*, indignantly denies that the craftsman was not respected in free Greece.   But surely the Athenian 'scholar and gentle-
man' spoke of the βάναυσοι very much as our grandparents spoke of
'the lower orders.'

and the burden of noisy life, shrink into a mere preliminary exercise of powers.'[1]

Another defect is the moral isolation of the Neoplatonic saint. In the most typical Christian contemplatives we find that sorrow for the sins of others, and pity for the world, often fill their hearts. Take as an example the short record of Margaret Kempe, an obscure precursor of Julian of Norwich. ' If she saw a man had a wound, or a beast ; or if a man beat a child before her, or smote a horse or another beast with a whip, she thought she saw our Lord beaten or wounded. If she saw any creature being punished or sharply chastised, she would weep for her own sin and compassion of that creature.' So Thomas Traherne exclaims : ' O Christ, I see thy crown of thorns in every eye, thy bleeding, naked, wounded body in every soul ; thy death liveth in every memory ; thy crucified Person is embalmed in every affection ; thy pierced feet are bathed in everyone's tears ; and it is my privilege to enter with thee into every soul.'[2] The ideas of corporate penitence and atoning sympathy are not to be found in Plotinus. He does not seem to realise that ' apathy,' which implies an external attitude towards sin, sorrow, and failure, closes one of the chief lines of communication by which the Soul may pass out of its isolation and identify itself with a larger life. A modern writer would add that it is a fatal bar to understanding and solving any social or moral problem. The call to seek and save that which was lost, the moral knight-errantry which ' rides abroad redressing human wrongs,' the settled purpose to confront ' the world '—that is to say, human society as it organises itself apart from God, a network of co-operative guilt with limited liability, with another association of active ' fellow-workers with God '—this call is but faintly heard by philosophers of this type, and they leave such work to others.

[1] Lotze, *Microcosmus*, Book III. Chap. 5.
[2] Quoted by Herman, *Meaning and Value of Mysticism*, pp. 91, 100.

The dependence of Souls *on each other* for the achievement of their perfection is a truth which Christianity taught and Neoplatonism neglected. ' In every individual spirit,' says Krause, ' particular faculties predominate for the glorification of the whole, and all other faculties are then found in diminishing strength and capacity as they are removed from those which are the ruling elements in its individuality. The individual spirit can only attain perfection through free social intercourse on all sides with the spiritual world. What it cannot bring forth by its own activity it receives spontaneously from others, who communicate it out of the fullness of their own being. This ever new stimulus and nourishment of the proper life of the spirit, and the potential universality of all spiritual formation, thus lie in the social intercourse of spirits with each other.' Christianity promises to make men free ; it never promises to make them independent. The self-sufficiency ($a\vec{v}\tau\acute{a}\rho\kappa\epsilon\iota a$) of St. Paul is an independence in relation to external conditions, but not in the same degree in relation to his fellow-men. We need each other ; and therefore we can never be quite so invulnerable as ancient philosophy hoped to make us. Human solidarity is a guarantee of pure freedom in the eternal world ; in the world of soul-making it is a bond of union, but still a bond. Therefore we must both give and take, without grudging and without pride ; we must find our complement in others, and in our turn must help to bear their burdens. Even Buddhism learned this truth better than Neoplatonism. Buddha himself said that he would not enter Nirvana till he could bring all others with him. The sense of organic unity with our fellows ought to make it intolerable for us to reach the One alone. Perhaps it is even impossible to do so.

But we must not end this section with words of censure. Plotinus himself was lovable and beloved, and he could not have used his great gifts to better advantage for posterity. The under-valuation of human sin and suffering which comes from an intense preoccupation with the eternal world is not a common defect, and it is a defect which is not far from heroic virtue.   It is only in a lower type of mystics that it is dangerous—in that class of aspirants to heavenly wisdom who make the tragic mistake of imagining that they *are* what they only dream about, and who in consequence miss that creative activity in the outer world without which the Soul cannot gain its freedom or perform its task.

Religion

The philosophy of Plotinus is a religious philosophy throughout, because for him reality is the truly existing realisation of the ideal.   Bosanquet's words are eminently true of Plotinus.   ' In so far as the religious experience comes to include the vision of all that has value, united in a type of perfection, metaphysic comes to be little more than the theoretical interpretation of it alone.'   There is no separation between the speculative and ethical sides of his system.   If it is true that all practice leads up to contemplation, it is equally true that contemplation is itself the highest kind of action, and necessarily expresses itself in moral conduct.   But for him the practice of the presence of God, in which religion consists, is very loosely connected with the myths and cultus of the popular faith. Plotinus himself felt no need of these aids to piety.   He even surprised his disciples by his indifference to public worship, and almost shocked them by the answer he gave to one who questioned him on the subject.   ' It is for the gods,' he said, ' to come to me, not for me to go to them.' Like most mystics, he saw no reason for ' esteeming one day above another,' and one place above another.   And it was part of his faith that the Soul must prepare itself for a divine visitation, but not demand it or try to force it. The words, ' I will hearken what the Lord God shall say concerning me,' express his attitude in devotion.   In this neglect of the externals of religion he differed from his greatest successor, Proclus, who was initiated into nearly all the mysteries,[1] and spent much of his time in devotional exercises ; but he was in agreement with the mystical tradition.   In the Hermetic writings, the whole duty of man is declared to be ' to know God and injure no man ' ; and the only religious practice (θρησκεία) which belongs to true religion is ' not to be a bad man.' [2]   As for the myths, the Neoplatonic doctrine is thought out wholly on the line of the philosophical tradition ; the myths are completely plastic in the hands of the allegorising metaphysician.[3]   His treatment of the gods is rather like Hegel's treatment of the Christian Trinity.[4]   The older philosophers sometimes looked upon the popular religion as a rival or an obstacle ; Plotinus twists it about in the most arbitrary manner to serve as an allegorical presentment of his system.[5]   His real gods were not Zeus, Athene, and Apollo, but the One, Spirit, and the Soul of the World.   These are often said to be the Neoplatonic Trinity ; and though the suggested parallel with Christian theology is misleading, it is true that Plotinus explicitly deifies these three principles.   The One, as has been said, is much the same as the Godhead of Eckhart and other mystics.   Of Spirit he says,[6] ' We have then to conceive of one nature—Spirit, all that truly exists, and Truth. If so, it is a great God.   Yes, this nature is God—a second

---

[1] Iamblichus (*Vita Pyth.* 3. 14) says the same of Pythagoras, and Julian (*Orat.* 7) advises μεμνῆσθαι πάντα τὰ μυστήρια. References to the mysteries are frequent in Plotinus, and some scholars, especially Picavet, have suggested that Neoplatonism as a religion had a regular sacramental side.   But this was probably left to the taste of the individual, at any rate until Athens, with Eleusis close at hand, became the headquarters of the school.

[2] See the quotations in Zeller, p. 252 ; and for the last passage here quoted compare the almost identical precept in the Epistle of James. 1. 27.   Porphyry has the fine saying that ' the best sacrifice to the gods is a pure spirit and a passionless soul.'

[3] Whittaker, *The Neoplatonists*, p. 100.

[4] e.g. Apollo is ' unity in difference.'   Schopenhauer goes further than Hegel.   ' If I wished to try to resolve the deepest mystery of Christianity, that of the Trinity, in the fundamental concepts of my philosophy, I might say that the Holy Spirit is the resolute negation of will ; the man in whom this is manifested is the Son.   He is identical with the will which affirms life and hence produces the phenomenon of the visible world, that is to say the Father ' (*The World as Will and Idea*, Vol. 3).

[5] Cf. 3. 5. 8, 9 ; 4. 3. 14 ; 5. 1. 7 ; 5. 8. 12.   [6] 5. 5. 3.

God.' (The triad in this sentence is equivalent to νοῦς—
νοητά—νόησις.) And elsewhere [1] he gives us in an
ascending scale ' the best men, good dæmons, the gods
who dwell on earth and who contemplate the spiritual
world, and above all the ruler of the whole universe, the
all-blessed Soul ; thence we should sing the praise of the
gods of the spiritual world, and over all the great king of
that world '—i.e. Νοῦς.

Nevertheless Plotinus leaves room for the gods of the
popular worship. Like Aristotle, he holds that the universe contains beings more divine than man—' dæmons,'
and ' gods ' who are dæmons of a superior order. But
he calls in his theory about the compenetration of all
spiritual substances to fuse his ' gods ' into one God,
who none the less ' remains multiple.' The following
passage is instructive : ' Suppose that the world, remaining in all its parts what it is and not confounded, is conceived of in our thought as a whole, as far as possible.
. . . Imagine a transparent sphere placed outside the
spectator, in which one can see all that it contains, first
the sun and the other stars, then the sea, the land, and
all living creatures. When you thus represent in thought
a transparent sphere containing all things that are in
movement or repose, or sometimes one and sometimes
the other, keep the form of the sphere, but suppress the
ideas of mass and extension, and banish all notions derived
from Matter. Then invoke the God who made the world
of which you have formed an image, and implore him to
descend. Let him come bringing his own world with him,
with all gods that are in it, he being one and all, and each
of them being all, coming together into one ; and being
distinguished in their powers, but all one in their single
great power ; or rather the one [God] is all [the gods].
For he suffers no diminution by the birth of all the gods
who are in him. All exist together, and if each is distinct
from the others, they have no local separation, nor any
sensible form. . . . This [the sphere of the Divine] is
universal power, extending to infinity, and infinite in its

[1] 2. 9. 9.

powers; and so great is he that his parts are also infinite'[1]

Plato had maintained strongly that religion must be mythological in its earlier stages. Education must begin with what is untrue in form, though it may represent the truth as nearly as possible, under inadequate symbols.[2] He lays down certain standards (τύποι θεολογίας) whereby we may distinguish 'true' myths from false. God is good and the cause only of good; He is true and incapable of change or deceit. 'True myths' ascribe these qualities to God; false myths contradict them. So Plato does not disapprove of the 'medicinal lie,' which has been used to justify all religious obscurantism. But he would banish all who try to misrepresent the character of God and the moral law in the interest of a priestly caste or a corporation.

Aristotle, who entirely rejects the ideas of communion with God and of anything like a covenant between God and man, holds that ' the rest of the tradition [about the gods] has been added later in mythical form with a view to persuasion of the multitude, and to its legal and utilitarian expediency.'[3] He attributes no scientific or philosophical value to mythology. Nevertheless he is anxious to show that popular theology and the worship of the sun and stars have some value and justification. Hence perhaps his curious theory of concentric circles, which is puzzling to his readers, who cannot be sure how far it is meant to be taken literally. Plotinus and Dante have both borrowed from him here; and in both the same difficulty is felt.[4]

It is interesting that Origen finds it possible to pour scorn on the philosophers who, though they boast of their knowledge of God and Divine things obtained from philosophy, yet run after images and temples and famous mysteries; whereas the Christian knows that the whole universe is God's temple, and can pray as well in one

---

[1] 5. 8. 9.   [2] Plato, Republic, p. 376 sq.
[3] Aristotle, Metaphysics, 1074b. Cf. Webb, Problems in the Relations of God and Man, p. 225.
[4] Wallace, Lectures and Essays, p. 35.

place as another, shutting the eyes of sense and raising upwards the eyes of the soul. ' Passing in thought beyond the heavens, he offers his prayers to God.' It is plain that neither Origen nor Plotinus would have seen anything but nonsense in Herrmann's dictum that ' mysticism is Catholic (as opposed to Protestant) piety.' Iamblichus and Proclus might have admitted a partial truth in it.

' The gods of the spiritual world are all one, or rather one is all.' [1] A second class of divine beings are the sun and stars.[2] This world is ' the third god.' [3] The earth is conscious and can hear our prayers, though not as we hear sounds ; [4] and the same is true of the stars.[5] But all their motions are determined by ' natural necessity,' not by thought.[6] The influence which, in his opinion, the heavenly bodies have on human affairs is not the result of caprice or predilection, nor can it be deflected by any sorceries ; it is part of the chain of sympathies which runs through all nature. Prophecy is thus rationalised as scientific prevision, based on the study of analogy.[7] The vulgar astrology, then so widely practised, receives no countenance from Plotinus. The stars may indicate coming events ; they cannot cause them.[8] But he is even more indignant with the Gnostics (and no doubt also with the orthodox Christians), for denying the divinity of the sun and stars, which seem to him far higher in the scale than human beings.

The dæmons, or lower order of Divine beings, are confined to those spheres of existence which are below the spiritual world. If the ideal Dæmon (ὁ αὐτοδαίμων) is in the spiritual world, we had better call him a god.[9] ' The nature of the universe is a mixture, and if we

---

[1] 5. 8. 9. So Damascius says, ' All the gods are one God.'
[2] 3. 5. 6. θεοὶ δεύτεροι μετ᾽ ἐκείνους καὶ κατ᾽ ἐκείνους τοὺς νοητοὺς ἐξηρτημένοι ἐκείνων. For the great influence of worship of the heavenly bodies at this time see Cumont, *Oriental Religions and Roman Paganism*, p. 162 sq. ; Gilbert Murray, *Hibbert Journal*, Oct. 1910 ; Dill, *Roman Society*, p. 585 sq.
[3] 3. 5. 16.   [4] 4. 4. 20.   [5] 4. 4. 30.   [6] 3. 5. 6.
[7] 3. 6 ; referred to by Berkeley, *Siris*, § 252.
[8] 3. 1. 5.   [9] 3. 5. 6.

separate from it the separable soul, what is left is not great. If we include the separable soul, the nature of the universe is a god ; if we omit this, it is, as Plato says, a great dæmon, and its affections are dæmonic.'[1] The dæmons then are powers proceeding from the Soul as a dweller on the earth ; their power is confined to the region ' below the moon.'[2] They are everlasting (ἀΐδιοι), and can behold the spiritual world above them ; but they have bodies of ' spiritual Matter,' and can clothe themselves in fiery or airy integuments ; they can feel and remember, and hear petitions.[3]

If this rather crude spiritism appears unworthy of Plotinus, we have to remember that he inherited a long tradition on the subject, which he could hardly cast aside. The belief in dæmons carries us back to the primitive animism which preceded the Olympian mythology. Almost all the philosophers dealt tenderly with this deeply-rooted faith. The Pythagoreans especially cherished the belief ; they regarded the dæmons as representing the Souls of the dead. The air is full of them ; they are often visible ; and they send dreams and warnings to men, nay, even to animals. They are a kind of guardian-angels while we live,[4] and flit about like ghosts when we are dead. When Heracleitus said that ' each man's character is his dæmon,' he meant that our fate is determined by our inner qualities, and not by any external power. There are bad dæmons as well as good ; these are the disembodied Souls of wicked men. Socrates, as is well known, believed that he heard a warning voice from time to time, restraining him from doing what he was about to do, and this was called ' the dæmon of

---

[1] 2. 3. 9, μεμιγμένη ἡ τοῦδε τοῦ παντὸς φύσις, καὶ εἴ τις τὴν ψυχὴν τὴν χωριστὴν αὐτοῦ χωρίσειε, τὸ λοιπὸν οὐ μέγα. θεὸς μὲν οὖν ἐκείνης συναριθμουμένης, τὸ δὲ λοιπὸν δαίμων, φησί, μέγας καὶ τὰ πάθη τὰ ἐν αὐτῷ δαιμόνια. Cf. Plato, Symp. 122 ; Tim. 89.

[2] 3. 5. 6. ' Every being above the moon is a god.'

[3] 3. 5. 6 ; 4. 4. 43.

[4] Marcus Aurelius, 5. 27, ὁ δαίμων, ὃν ἑκάστῳ προστάτην καὶ ἡγεμόνα ὁ Ζεὺς ἔδωκεν. See the excellent discussion of the subject in Rohde, Psyche, Vol. 2, pp. 316–318.

Socrates.' Plato, speaking mythically, makes the dæmons the sons of gods by nymphs or some other mothers.[1] Every man has a dæmon who attends him during life and after death, watching over his charge like a shepherd. The dæmon is the intermediary between gods and men ; he carries our prayers to the gods, and transmits to us the wishes of Heaven.   Love is ' a great dæmon.' [2]   In the *Timaeus*, however, he seems to identify the dæmon in each man with his higher Soul.   The Stoics firmly believed in dæmons, who in our life-time share our good and evil fortune, and after our death float about the lower air. Each man's Soul may be called the dæmon born with him.   Plutarch says that the Souls of good men, ' when set free from rebirth and at rest from the body,' may become dæmons.[3]

Under the Empire, there was a fusion between the Greek ' dæmon ' and the Roman ' genius,' which also hovered on the borderland of divinity.   Tibullus writes :—

> ' At tu, Natalis (= Genius), quoniam deus omnia sentis,
>   Adnue ; quid refert clamne palamne roget ? ' [4]

In a more familiar passage, Horace describes the genius as

> ' Natale comes qui temperat astrum,
> Naturae deus humanae, mortalis in unum
> Quodque caput.' [5]

So Apuleius says that the genius is ' is deus qui est animus suus cuique, quamquam sit immortalis, tamen quodam modo cum homine gignitur.' [6]   But the Romans paid honour also to the ' genius ' of an institution, such as a legion, or even a permanent tax.   I do not think that the Greek dæmon was ever placed in charge of an institution.   On the other hand, the belief in evil dæmons grew ;

---

[1] *Apol.* 27.
[2] Plato, *Phaedo*, 107 ; *Polit.* 271 ; *Symp.* 202.
[3] Plutarch, *Romulus*, 28.   Glover, *Hibbert Journal*, Oct., 1912.
[4] Tibullus, 4. 5. 20.
[5] Horace, Ep. 2. 2. 183.
[6] Apuleius, *De Deo Socr.* 15.   Warde Fowler, *Roman Ideas of Deity*, p. 19.

Plutarch tries to explain moral temptation in this way. 'A typical utterance, from this point of view, is that which was attributed to Charondas in the spurious proems of his *Laws*: "If a man is tempted by an evil spirit, he should pray in the temples that the evil spirit may be averted." '[1] There is nothing of this kind in Plotinus, who is far less inclined to moral dualism than Plutarch. The whole belief in intermediate beings is part of the current religion of the time, and has no inner connexion with the philosophy which we are considering.[2]

The kindred subject of magic and sorcery is dealt with in a curious manner by Plotinus. The spiritual man is above all such dangers, for his conversation is in heaven, where no evil influences can penetrate. He who contemplates the eternal verities is one with the object of his contemplation; and no one can be bewitched by himself.[3] The higher soul is also exempt. It is only the irrational soul, which, by allowing itself to be entangled among the temptations of covetousness, self-indulgence, ambition, or fear, becomes liable to injuries from magical arts. Magic can influence our external activities; for example, it can cause diseases, and even death. This power belongs to the law of sympathies which runs through nature;[4] the dæmons have power within their own sphere, which extends to the 'irrational' part of nature. Porphyry, however, tells us that when a certain Olympius, from Alexandria, tried to bewitch Plotinus, his sorceries recoiled from his own pate, and after suffering excruciating pains he was obliged to desist! In the same section of his biography Porphyry says that an Egyptian priest, wishing to give proof of his powers during a visit to Rome, begged Plotinus to come and see him evoke the dæmon of Plotinus himself. Instead of

[1] Farnell, *The Higher Aspects of Greek Religion*, p. 116.
[2] Porphyry, however, believes in evil spirits, and he is followed by the later Neoplatonists. See an excellent note by Bouillet, Vol. 2, p. 533. [3] 4. 4. 43.
[4] 4. 4. 41–43. He speaks of σύνταξις μία, σύμπνοια μία, in all nature. The stars are amenable to magic, 4. 4. 35. See further references in Cumont, p. 273.

the dæmon there appeared a god, which caused the enchanter to congratulate Plotinus on having a being of the higher rank to watch over him.[1] It is not likely that the philosopher was himself the authority for this story, any more than that Iamblichus encouraged the belief that he floated in the air when he said his prayers. It was a superstitious and unscientific age ; and Neoplatonism was not well protected on this side. Indeed, by admitting the reality of witchcraft, it helped to elevate superstition into a dogma.[2]

Prayer, in the wider sense of any ' elevation of the mind towards God,' was of course the very life of religion for the Neoplatonists.[3] But the efficacy of petitionary prayer was a problem for them, both because of their belief in the regularity of natural law, and because it was not easy for them to admit that the higher principle can be affected in any way by influences from beneath. Plotinus would have us approach the higher spiritual powers by contemplation and meditation, without proffering any requests ; it is the lower spirits that are amenable to petitions, this kind of prayer being in fact a branch of sympathetic magic. All the attractions and repulsions that pervade nature are for him a kind of magic (γοητεία or μαγεία) ; ' the true magic is the friendship and strife that exist in the great All.'[4] Love, with all its far-reaching influence in the world, is the first wizard and enchanter. Only contemplation is above enchantments (ἀγοήτευτος). Magic in this sense is only an empirical knowledge of the subtle laws of attraction in nature ; prayer works no miracles, but only sets in motion obscure natural forces. But Plotinus attaches small value to this kind of praying. The only prayers that seem to him worthy of the name are the unspoken

---

[1] Cf. 3. 4. 6, δαίμων τούτῳ [τῷ σπουδαίῳ] θεός.

[2] Porphyry did not really encourage theurgy, and Augustine thought he was a little ashamed of his theosophical friends. Cf. Chaignet (Vol. 5, p. 62), who argues that theurgy is no integral part of Neoplatonism. Proclus, however, was credited with miracles.

[3] Porphyry, Ad Marcell. 24, ἡ ἐπιστροφὴ πρὸς τὸν θεὸν μόνη σωτηρία. The word ' salvation ' became as familiar to Neoplatonists as to Christians.   [4] 4. 4. 40.

yearnings of the Soul for a closer walk with God. Of this ' prayer of quiet ' he speaks finely in 5. 1. 6. The desire which all creatures feel to rise towards the source of their being is itself prayer ; so that Proclus can say, in a striking sentence, that ' all things pray, except the Supreme (the One).' The Oriental mystic Kabir expresses the same thought. ' Waving its row of lamps the universe sings in worship day and night. There the sound of the unseen bells is heard ; there the Lord of all sitteth on his throne.' It is plain that Plotinus would have entirely agreed with George Meredith's words : ' He who rises from his knees a better man, his prayer has been granted.' The whole object of prayer is to become one with the Being to whom prayer is addressed, and so to win the blessed life. ' Even here below a wise life is the most truly grand and beautiful thing. And yet here we see but dimly ; yonder the vision is clear. For it gives to the seer the faculty of seeing, and the power for the higher life, the power by living more intensely to see better and to become what he sees.'[1]

So the whole of religion is summed up in the vision of God. It is the experimental verification of the act of faith in which religion begins, by virtue of ' the consciousness inherent in the finite-infinite being, so far as his full nature affirms itself, that he is one with something which cannot be shaken or destroyed, and the value of which is the source and standard of values.'[2] This is the substance of the Neoplatonist's creed. What Mr. Bosanquet calls the finite-infinite nature of the finite spirit is a truth revealed to our consciousness with increasing clearness as we advance morally and intellectually. Plotinus repeatedly appeals to the religious experience of his readers ;[3] he knows that he cannot carry us with him further than we have the power to see for ourselves. For

---

[1] 6. 6. 18, καὶ ἐνταῦθα φρόνιμος ζωὴ τὸ σεμνὸν καὶ τὸ καλὸν κατ' ἀλήθειαν ἐστί, καίτοι ἀμυδρῶς ὁρᾶται ἐκεῖ δὲ καθαρῶς ὁρᾶται. δίδωσι γὰρ τῷ ὁρῶντι ὅρασιν καὶ δύναμιν εἰς τὸ μᾶλλον ζῆν καὶ μᾶλλον εὐτόνως ζῶντα ὁρᾶν καὶ γενέσθαι ὃ ὁρᾷ.

[2] Bosanquet, *The Value and Destiny of the Individual*, p. 241.

[3] e.g. 6. 8. 19.

it is as the greater Self that we come to know God, not
as a separate anthropomorphic Being over against ourselves. Our struggle to reach Him is at the same time a
struggle for self-liberation. We lose our Soul in order
to find it again in God. There is no barrier between the
human and divine natures. The human Soul has only
to strip itself of those outer integuments which are no
part of its true nature, in order to expand freely by means
of the ' organic filaments ' which unite it with all spiritual
being. This expansion is at the same time an intensi-
fying of life, an ' awakening ' from the dream of sensuous
existence. Our environment, which we make while it
makes us, changes all the time. Our perception becomes
spiritual intuition ; the air we breathe becomes the
atmosphere of eternity, not of time. The problem of
immortality is changed for us in such a way that it
ceases to be a vague and chimerical hope and becomes
an experience—*sentimus et experimur nos aeternos esse*,
as Spinoza says. The question of the survival in time
of the empirical *ego* loses its interest, since the empirical
ego is no longer the centre, much less the circumference,
of our thoughts. The Soul that never dies is not something that belongs to us, but something to which we
belong. We shall belong to it after we are dead, as we
belonged to it before we were born. Its history is our
history, and its super-historical existence is our immortality. The life of this great Soul to which we belong
has two aspects—contemplation and creation. Its gaze
is turned steadily upon the eternal archetypes of all that
is good and true and beautiful in the universe. It adores
God under these three attributes, by which He is known
to man. The inner religious life consists of continual
acts of recollection, when we ' turn away our eyes lest
they behold vanity,' and resolutely try to realise the
glories of the unseen world which encompasses us. The
other activity of the Soul, creation of good, true, and
beautiful things and actions in the world of space and
time, follows so naturally and necessarily from a right

direction of the thought and will and affections, that it is not worth while to bring forward other motives for leading an active and useful life. The true contemplative cannot be selfish or indolent.   He makes the world better, both consciously and unconsciously, by the very fact that his conversation is in heaven. It is other-worldliness that alone can transform the world.

If any man is disposed to take Plotinus as his guide, not only in search for truth, but in the life of devotion, he will naturally ask to what Being his prayers should be addressed, and his acts of worship offered. We have seen that the sphere of the Divine (τὰ θεῖα) includes not only the One, but Spirit and the Universal Soul. In spite of the unity which forbids any notion of separate existence in the eternal world, there are distinctions between the three Divine Hypostases which make the question legitimate and inevitable. I have already suggested that when our thoughts are turned towards anything that we hope for in space and time, we shall most naturally address ourselves to the Universal Soul, which upholds the course of this world and directs it, and seems to be itself engaged in the great conflict between good and evil. When we are praying for spiritual progress and a clearer knowledge of God, or when we are longing for the bliss of heaven and the rest that remaineth for the people of God, it is to the Great Spirit, the King, as Plotinus calls him, that we shall turn. Lastly, if ever we are rapt into ecstasy, and pass a few minutes in the mystical trance, we shall hope that we are holding communion with the One—the Godhead who ' dwelleth in the light that no man can approach unto.' No stress need be laid, for purposes of devotion, on the Neoplatonic doctrine of the three Divine hypostases. But it seems to me that we do in fact envisage God under these three aspects in our prayers and meditations, and that without much violence we might even classify theologians and religious thinkers under these three heads. Some would have us worship the Soul of humanity, or the Soul of the world ; others the Lord of the eternal and spiritual realm , others the ineffable Godhead. It is one of the strong points of Plotinus that he finds room for all three, and shows how we may pass from one mode of worship to another.

A brief comparison between Neoplatonism and Christianity is necessary for an understanding of the former, though this book is not written as a contribution to Christian apologetics. I will first summarise the opinions of Rudolf Eucken, in his valuable book entitled *Lebensanschauungen Grosser Denker*. ' That which unites Plotinus with Hellenism must separate him from Christianity. In criticising the Christian Gnostics, he blames them first for overvaluing humanity. For him mankind is a mere part of the world, the whole of which is penetrated by the Divine power. He blames them for despising and despiritualising the world, which contains spiritual beings far higher than the common run of men. He blames them for unpractical activity. Those who are too proud to fight must acquiesce in the victory of the bad cause. Whether these criticisms apply to Christendom as well as to the Gnostics, we need not here discuss ; in any case Plotinus follows the Hellenic tradition in asserting the co-ordination of humanity with the All, the soul-life and even the deification of natural forces, the expectation of happiness from active conduct, the high estimation of thought and knowledge as the Divine spark in man. Plotinus is really further removed from Christianity than these statements express, but he is also more akin to it than the collision between the two allows to appear. In both we find an uncompromising inwardness and a drawing of all life towards God, and in both rather by a renunciation of the world than by co-operation with it. But Plotinus finds this inwardness in an impersonal spirituality, Christianity in a development of the personal life. In the former all salvation comes from the power of thought, in the latter from sincerity of heart. Such a fundamental difference implies a different answer to the most important problems of life. In Plotinus we find an abandonment of the first world, a fading of time in the light of eternity, a repose in view of the Whole. In Christianity we find an entrance of the eternal into time, a world-historical movement, a power working against the irrationality of the actual. In the former we have a disappearance of man before the endlessness of the All; in the latter, a transposition of man and humanity into the central point of the All. In the former, an isolation of the thinker on the heights of contemplation of the world; in the latter a close welding together of individuals in full community of life and sorrow.' He ends by finding a contradiction in Neoplatonism between the doctrine of inwardness and the fundamental impersonality of the world of which man is a part.

Baron von Hügel also finds a radical inconsistency between Plotinus the metaphysician and Plotinus the saint, a criticism which has often been made in the case of Spinoza. I have already quoted (p. 147) the words in which the Baron brings the charge that 'in Plotinus' philosophy God is exiled from his world and his world from him,' while at the same time he attaches special value to his 'constant, vivid sense of the spaceless, timeless character of God; of God's distinct reality and otherness, and yet of his immense nearness; of the real contact between the real God and the real soul, and of the precedence and excess of this contact before and beyond all theories concerning this, the actual ultimate cause of the soul's life and healing. Indeed, reality of all kinds here rightly appears as ever exceeding our intuition of it, and our intuitions as ever exceeding our discursive reasonings and analyses.'[1]

There is much in these estimates that deserves respectful attention. Eucken's enumeration of differences is very illuminating. But in my judgment this writer overstates the intellectualism of Plotinus, while Baron von

[1] Von Hügel, *Eternal Life*, p. 85 sq.

Hügel follows too closely those French critics (such as Vacherot), who regard the method of abstraction—of ' peeling the onion '—as the characteristic instrument of Plotinian dialectic. As I have insisted more than once in this book, we cannot understand Plotinus unless we realise that the spiritual world, with its fullness of rich content, is for him the real world, and the ultimate home of the Soul. This is quite consistently the conclusion of the dialectic, and I can see no contradiction between the philosophy and the religion of Neoplatonism. Nor does it seem to me that these two sides of the Plotinian teaching have shown any tendency to fall apart in his disciples. The whole system is still coherent, as he left it, a strong argument that it is not vitiated by inner contradictions.

The criticism of Augustine remains, in my opinion, the most profound that has proceeded from any Christian thinker. We have to remember that Augustine was converted to Platonism before he was converted to Christianity ; that by ' the Platonists ' he meant Plotinus and his school ; and that he became a Christian because he found something in Christianity which he did not find in Plotinus. What that was, he tells us very clearly. ' In the books of the Platonists, which I read in a Latin translation, I found, not indeed in so many words, but in substance and fortified by many arguments, that " In the beginning was the Logos, and the Logos was with God, and the Logos was God ; and the same was in the beginning with God ; and that all things were made by him, and without him was nothing made that was made ; in him was life, and the life was the light of men ; and the light shineth in darkness and the darkness comprehended it not." Further, that the soul of man, though it bears witness to the light, is not itself that light, but God, the Logos of God, is the true light that lighteth every man that cometh into the world. And that " he was in the world, and the world was made by him, and the world knew him not." But that " he came unto his own, and his own received him not ; but as many as received him, to them gave he power to become sons of God, even to them that believe on his name "—this I could not find there. Also I found there that God the Logos was born not of flesh, nor of blood, nor of the will of a husband, nor of the will of the flesh, but of God.[1] But that " the Logos was made flesh and dwelt among us," this I found not there. I could discover in these books, though expressed in other and varying phrases, that " the Son was in the form of the Father, and thought it not robbery to be equal with God," because by nature he was the same substance. But that " he emptied himself, taking upon him the form of a servant, being made in the likeness of men ; and being found in fashion as a man he humbled himself and became obedient unto death, even the death of the Cross ; wherefore also God exalted him, etc. ; this those books do not contain. For that before all times and above all times, thy only-begotten Son abideth unchangeable and coeternal with thee, and that of his fullness all souls receive, that they may be blessed, and that by participation in the eternal wisdom they are renewed, that they may be wise, that is there. But that in due time he died for the ungodly, that thou sparedst not thine only Son but deliveredst him up for us all, this is not there.'[2]

The religious philosophy to which Augustine was converted, and in which he found satisfaction, was the Platonism of Plotinus with the doctrine of the Incarnation added to it. It matters not for our present purpose that his sympathies were afterwards progressively alienated from the ancient culture, so that even the *Confessions* does not accurately represent the state of mind in which he first accepted Christianity.[3] What

---

[1] Augustine clearly read, in John I. 13, ὃς ἐγεννήθη for οἳ ἐγεννή-θησαν. I agree with Loisy that this reading has better attestation than the plural, which is accepted in our texts.

[2] Augustine, *Confessions*, 7. 10.

[3] This is proved conclusively by the short treatises which he wrote in the years immediately after his conversion.

we have to note is that ' the Logos made flesh, that I
found not there,' was the decisive consideration which
made him a Christian. From a doctrine of the Incarnation follows, as he saw, the love of God for the world,
the pity and care of God for the weak and erring, the
supreme self-sacrifice of God to seek and save that which
was lost. We are here concerned with the Incarnation,
not as an isolated historical event, but as the revelation
of the highest law of the spiritual world ; that God not
only draws all life towards himself, as a magnet attracts
iron, and not only ' moves the world as the object of its
love,' in Aristotle's famous words, but voluntarily
' comes down ' to redeem it. If this is true, there is an
end of the theory that the Soul would have done better
not to have entered the body ; for the same moral and
spiritual necessity which caused the supreme manifestation of the Divine in the flesh, must also send Souls into
the world to do their part in ransoming the creation from
the bondage of corruption. This doctrine, so far from
being in contradiction with the philosophy which is the
subject of this book, seems to me to complete it. It
gives an adequate motive for the ' descent of the Soul,'
which obviously perplexed Plotinus ; it exalts Love as
the highest and most characteristic Divine principle,
the motive of creation and of redemption alike ; it enables
us to see the social as well as individual ' purification '
wrought by suffering, and entirely forbids that moral
isolation which has seemed to us a weak point in Plotinian
ethics. But there is one act of surrender which this
doctrine demands from us, and this few or no Greek
philosophers were willing to make. The Christian is
neither independent nor invulnerable. He needs his
fellows, as they need him ; and he must be content ' to fill
up, for his part, what is lacking in the afflictions of Christ
for his Body's sake.' It seems sometimes as if the
Greek thinkers, with all their contempt for pleasure and
pain, shrank in the last resort from grasping the nettle
of suffering firmly. Nor is there any religion or philos-

ophy except Christianity, which has really drawn the sting of the world's evil.

A concluding paragraph may be desirable on the attempts made by Christian Platonists to equate the doctrine of the Trinity with the three Divine hypostases of Neoplatonism. I have already said that the attempt was a failure; but it was very natural that it should be made; just as in later times the Hegelians attempted the same thing, with no better success. Hegelianism would seem logically to place the Holy Spirit above the Father and the Son; Platonism, if it identifies the Logos-Christ with Νοῦς, and the Holy Spirit with the universal Soul, cannot maintain that the three Persons are co-equal. Numenius may have influenced Christian thought in this matter, before the rise of the Neoplatonic school. His three Gods, as Proclus says, are the Father, the Creator (or instrument in creation) and the World. According to Eusebius, he boasted that he had gone back to the fountain-head in reviving this doctrine of ' three Gods.' The fountain-head is not so much the *Timaeus*, in which the Demiurge forms the World-Soul according to the pattern of the Ideas, as the Second Epistle of Plato, which Plotinus also uses as an authority. But in Numenius the Second and Third Gods (he does not call them Persons, ὑποστάσεις) are not quite distinct; ' the Second and Third Gods are one.'[1] It is interesting to find Origen[2] saying that ' the Stoics call the World as a whole the First God, the Platonists the Second, and some of them the Third.' This hesitation illustrates the great vagueness of Christian speculative thought about the Holy Spirit, down to the fourth century. Clement also refers to the Second Epistle of Plato, and tries to explain the Trinity Platonically.[3] Justin Martyr had done the same before him.[4] Theodoret[5] says explicitly, ' Plotinus

---

[1] Euseb., *Praep. Ev.* 11. 18, 1 and 24.
[2] Origen, *Contra Celsum*, 5. 7.
[3] Clement, *Strom.* 4. 25; 5. 14; 7. 7.
[4] Justin, *Apol.* 1. 60.
[5] Theodoret, 4. 750.

and Numenius, developing the thought of Plato, say that he has spoken of three transcendent principles. The immortal principles are the One, Spirit (νοῦς), and the universal Soul. We call the One, or the Good, the Father; Spirit, we call the Son or the Logos; the Platonic Soul our divines call the Holy Spirit.' Many other examples might be cited from patristic literature. Plotinus certainly calls his three Divine principles 'hypostases'; but he never thinks of calling them persons.[1] And the Cappadocian Fathers, Basil and the two Gregorys, are determined to maintain the unity of the Godhead against prevalent tendencies to tritheism. This they uphold by making the Father the one fountain of Godhead, and by their doctrine of co-inherence (περι-χώρησις), which forbids any sharp distinction of attributes in the Trinity. They thus try to escape the subordina-tionism of Origen, which naturally results from a close following of Platonic methods of thought. Nevertheless, the metaphor of emanation is used to express the relation of the Third Person to the First. It is perhaps difficult for a religious philosopher to distinguish between the 'begetting' of the Son and the 'procession' of the Spirit. Christian Platonists like Eckhart consistently teach that the Son is continually and eternally 'begotten' by the Father, a doctrine which takes the relation between the First and Second Person finally out of the region of anthropomorphic symbolism, and seeks to explain it as Plotinus would have explained it.

Æsthetics

Throughout this enquiry we have been hampered by difficulties of nomenclature. 'Æsthetics' is not a good name for the philosophy of τὸ καλόν, the beautiful, noble, and honourable. Αἴσθησις is, as we have seen, Plotinus'

---

[1] ὑπόστασις and *persona* are by no means identical. Cf. Augus-tine, *De Trinitate*, 5. 9: 'Ita ut plerique nostri qui haec Græco tractant eloquio dicere consueverint μίαν οὐσίαν, τρεῖς ὑποστάσεις, quod est, Latine unam essentiam, tres substantias.'

name for sensuous perception. But the beautiful, in this philosophy, can only be known by the highest faculty, which apprehends supra-sensuous reality. The word ' æsthete' has also undignified associations in modern English. We must therefore remember, all through this section, that τὸ καλόν includes all that is worthy of love and admiration, and that beautiful objects, as perceived by our senses, are only an adumbration of a Divine attribute which belongs to the spiritual order. It is impossible to separate æsthetics, thus understood, from ethics and religion. Even in the dialectic, love is the guide of the intellect, and opens to it the last door of which love alone has the key.

The doctrine of the Beautiful is expounded formally in one chapter of the Enneads (1. 6), an admirably clear statement which we shall do well to follow.

The Beautiful affects chiefly the sense of sight ; but also, in music, the sense of hearing. In a higher region, actions, sciences, and virtues are beautiful. Some beautiful things ' share in ' beauty ; others, like virtue, are beautiful in themselves. The Stoics say that beauty consists in proportion, and in harmonious colour.[1] If this were true, beauty would reside only in the whole, not in the parts, and simple colours, like gold, would not be beautiful, nor would single notes, however sweet, be beautiful. Still less can this canon be applied to intellectual, moral, and spiritual beauty. There may be inner harmony and proportion in bad things, though they conflict with the harmony of the whole. And since measure and proportion are quantitative ideas, they are inapplicable to spiritual realities.[2] Beauty is a property in things which the Soul recognises as akin to its own essence, while the ugly is that which it feels to be alien and antipathetic. Beautiful things remind the Soul of its own spiritual nature ; they do so because they partici-

---

[1] Cf. Cic. Tusc. 4. 13.

[2] This is not quite true. Plotinus says elsewhere that the ' political virtues ' teach us measure and proportion.

pate in form (μετοχῇ εἴδους), which comes from the spiritual world. The absence of such form constitutes ugliness; the absolutely ugly is that which is entirely devoid of 'Divine meaning' (θεῖος λόγος). The form co-ordinates and combines the parts which are to make a unity, and this unity is beautiful, as are also its parts. They become beautiful by sharing in the creative power (κοινωνίᾳ λόγου) which comes to them from the gods.

When we pass from visible and audible beauty to the beauty which the Soul perceives without the help of the senses, we must remember that we can only perceive what is akin to ourselves—there is such a thing as soul-blindness. Incorporeal things are beautiful when they make us love them. But what constitutes their beauty? Negatively, it is the absence of impure admixture. An ugly character is soiled by base passions; it is like a body caked with mud; in order to restore its natural grace it must be scraped and cleansed. This is why it has been said[1] that all the virtues are a purification. The purified soul becomes a form, a meaning, wholly spiritual and incorporeal. The true beauty of the Soul is to be made like to God. The good and the beautiful are the same, and the ugly and the bad are the same. The Soul becomes beautiful through Spirit; other things, such as actions and studies, are beautiful through Soul which gives them form. The Soul too gives to bodies all the beauty which they are able to receive.

It remains, Plotinus says, to mount to the Good towards which every Soul aspires. 'If anyone has seen it, he knows what I say; he knows how beautiful it is. We must approach its presence stripped of all earthly encumbrances, as the initiated enter the sanctuary naked. With what love we must yearn to see the source of all existence, of all life and thought! He who has not yet seen it desires it as the Good; he who has seen it admires it as the Beautiful. He is struck at once with amazement and pleasure; he is seized with a painless stupefaction,

---

[1] Plato, *Phaedo*, 69.

he loves with a true love and a mighty longing which laughs at other loves and disdains other beauties. If we could behold him who gives all beings their perfection, if we could rest in the contemplation of him and become like him, what other beauty could we need ? Being the supreme beauty, he makes those who love him beautiful and lovable. This is the great end, the supreme aim, of Souls ; it is the want of this vision that makes men unhappy. He who desires to see the vision must shut his eyes to terrestrial things, not allowing himself to run after corporeal beauties, lest he share the fate of Narcissus, and immerse his soul in deep and muddy pools, abhorred of Spirit. And yet we may train ourselves by contemplating noble things here on earth, especially noble deeds, always pressing on to higher things, and remembering above all that as the eye could not behold the sun unless it were sunlike itself, so the Soul can only see beauty by becoming beautiful itself.'

There are a few other passages which throw light on the doctrine of the Beautiful. The relation of the Beautiful to the Absolute, the Good, is discussed in 6. 7. 32, a passage which has been already considered in the chapter on the Absolute.[1] I have there shown that Beauty is really given the same dignity as Truth and Goodness in this system. In another place,[2] Reality (οὐσία) is identified with Beauty. The everlasting (τὸ ἀΐδιον) is said to be ' akin to the Beautiful.' [3]

Plotinus makes a distinct advance in æsthetic theory in refusing to make symmetry the essence of the Beautiful. This had been one of the errors of Greek art-criticism. Plotinus does not anticipate the profound saying of Bacon, ' There is no excellent beauty that hath not some strangeness in the proportion ' ; but he insists that beauty is essentially the direct expression of reason or meaning, in sense, by æsthetic semblance. The forms of beauty are the mode in which the creative activity of the universal Soul stamps the image of itself on Matter. Like all other

[1] p. 124.   [2] 5. 8. 9.   [3] 3. 5. 1.

creative activity, the production of beauty is not directly willed. So Krause says, ' If Spirit freely rules the form of what is individual according to the Idea, beauty arises of itself as by a beneficent necessity ' (p. 72).   The question why such and such forms express spiritual beauty is not much discussed ; the answer ' because they are symmetrical ' has been dismissed.   The soul recognises in certain forms a meaning which it understands and loves ; the sensuous forms have a natural affinity to certain ideas.   Plotinus believed that beautiful forms in this world have a real resemblance to their prototypes in the spiritual world.   Earth is a good copy of heaven ; earthly beauty, we must remember, is the creation of Soul, not a property of matter.   But the beauty which we find in objects is not put into them by the individual observer.   All beauty is the work of Soul, but not of the individual Soul which admires it.   The individual Soul can only appreciate what is akin to itself ; but it is not the perceiving mind of the individual which gives to inert matter a meaning by impressing ' form ' upon it. That would be to make the individual Soul the creator of the world, which Plotinus says we must not do.   And yet the individual Soul is never wholly separated from the universal Soul ; and we must further remember that no perception, not even the perception of external objects, is mere apprehension.   Something is always done or made in the act of perception.   The Soul, in contemplating Beauty, is identifying itself with the formative activity of its own higher principle.

In the Eighth Chapter of the Fifth Ennead he says that ' everything is beautiful in its own true Being ' ; the beauty of true Being is the beauty of the archetype.   The same passage develops the notion of the supreme holiness and beauty of *light*.   ' Everything shines yonder.' [1]   Much more important is the argument by which Plotinus finds

---

[1] Compare with the Prologue of the Fourth Gospel 1. 6. 3, φῶς ἀσώματον καὶ λόγος καὶ εἶδος ὄν; and with the Biblical ' in thy light shall we see light,' 5. 3. 17, δι' οὗ γὰρ ἐφωτίσθη, τοῦτό ἐστιν ὃ δεῖ θεάσασθαι.

room for Art in the realm of the beautiful. The artist realises the beautiful in proportion as his work is *real*. The true artist does not copy nature. Here he agrees with Philostratus, who in an epoch-making passage says that great works of art are produced not by imitation (the Aristotelian μίμησις), but by imagination (φαντασία), ' a wiser creator than imitation ; for imitation copies what it has seen, imagination what it has not seen.' The true artist fixes his eyes on the archetypal Logoi, and tries to draw inspiration from the spiritual power which created the forms of bodily beauty. Art is not only genuinely creative ; it is among the highest and most permanent forms of creation. Some spiritual values are revealed only in art. The artist has more freedom than is possible to mechanical skill or to outward action. Art, therefore, is a mode of contemplation, which creates because it must. This is a real advance upon Plato and Aristotle. Plotinus does not, like Schopenhauer, arrange the arts in an ascending scale—sculpture, painting, poetry, music ; music being the highest because it works with the most ethereal medium ; but this is genuine Platonism. There are said to be some musicians who prefer reading the score to hearing it played. If such men exist, they are ultra-Platonists.

What would Plotinus have said to Hegel's [1] opinion that we have left behind the stage of culture in which art is the highest means by which we apprehend the Divine ? We can no longer adore images, and art no longer satisfies our religious instincts. Perhaps this change is not so universal as Hegel thought ; but Plotinus would have seen nothing unexpected in it. By emphasising the beauty of noble *actions*, Plotinus agrees with Kant and Lotze that beauty consists, partly at least, in harmony with a *purpose*. Lotze even suggests that it arises in the conflict between what is and what ought to be ; but this is not Platonic. It is unquestionable that our age does not naturally express itself in beautiful

[1] Hegel, *Works*, Vol. 10, Part 1.

forms. The self-consciousness of modern architecture
illustrates well the doctrine of Plotinus that we spoil our
creations by thinking too much about them. But it
would be rash to assume that a time will never come
when we shall again create beautiful things without
knowing why they are beautiful. The ugliness of our
civilisation can hardly be set down to the fact that we
have advanced beyond the artistic mode of self-expression.

Plotinus is not very happy in his treatment of ugliness.
Ugliness is not, as he supposes, absence of form ; it is
false form. The ugliest thing in nature, a human face
distorted by vile passions, revolts us because the evil
principle seems there to have set its mark on what was
meant to bear the image of God. Plotinus tells us that
all virtue is purification ; but he never admits that there
can be ' defilement of the flesh *and spirit*,' though all real
ugliness consists not in the incrustation of incorporeal
purity by something alien to itself, but in indications that
the Soul itself has been stained and perverted. There is
nothing repulsive in the sight of a marble statue half-
covered with mud, or in a fine picture blackened with dirt
and smoke ; yet this is the type of ugliness which Plotinus
gives us in his theory of evil. While we sympathise with
his determination to make no compromise with metaphysical dualism, we cannot help feeling that his opti-
mistic view of the world causes him to ' heal slightly ' the
wounds of humanity, in æsthetics as in morals.

But there is deep truth in this philosophy of the
Beautiful. We cannot see real beauty while we are
wrapped up in our petty personal interests. These are
the muddy vesture of decay, of which we must rid ourselves. Art is the wide world's memory of things, and
beauty is the universal and spiritual making itself known
sensuously, as Hegel says. Æsthetic pleasure is in truth
the pleasure of recognition and consequent liberation.
The soul sees the reflection of its own best self ; and
forthwith enters into a larger life. This is effected by
recognising some of its hidden sympathies in nature.

Very much of the pleasure which we find in poetry and painting arises from brilliant *translations* of an idea from one language to another, showing links between diverse orders of being, symbols of the unseen which are no arbitrary types, or evidences of the fundamental truth about creation, that the universal Soul made the world in the likeness of its own principle, Spirit. Ultimately all is the self-revelation of the One and the Good.

Among later writers on æsthetics, Schiller, Schelling, Hegel, Schopenhauer, and Hartmann are all indebted to Plotinus. So is Goethe, who regards the unity of the True, the Beautiful, and the Good as the absolute ground of all Being. Shaftesbury, at the end of the seventeenth century, was a kindred spirit. He finds that there are three orders or degrees of beauty—' first, the dead forms, which have no forming power, no action, or intelligence. Next, the forms which form ; that is, which have intelligence, action, and operation. Thirdly, that order of beauty which forms not only such as we call mere forms, but even the forms which form. For we ourselves are notable architects in Matter, and can show lifeless bodies brought into form, and fashioned by our own hands ; but that which fashions even minds themselves contains in itself all the beauties fashioned by those minds, and is consequently the principle, source, and fountain of all beauty. Therefore whatever beauty appears in our second order of forms, or whatever is derived or produced from thence, all this is eminently, principally, and originally in this last order of supreme and sovereign beauty. Thus architecture, music, and all which is of human invention, resolves itself into this last order.' [1]

It is not easy to find much similarity to Plotinus in the æsthetic theory of Croce, which is just now attracting much attention. He holds that beauty does not belong to things ; it is not a psychic fact, it belongs to man's

[1] Shaftesbury, *Moralists*, Part 3, Sect. 2.

activity, to spiritual energy. Æsthetic activity is imaginative and concrete intuition, as opposed to the logical and general conception. It belongs to the Will, and its manifestations are Soul-states—passion, sentiment, personality. ' These are found in every art and determine its lyrical character.' Art is expression. Croce insists rightly that we cannot appreciate a work of art without, in a sense, reproducing the work of the artist in ourselves.

LECTURE XXII

CONCLUDING REFLECTIONS

I HAVE admitted that throughout these lectures I have studied Plotinus as a disciple, though not an uncritical one. I hold that this is the right attitude towards a great thinker; and if an ancient philosopher is not a great thinker, I do not think it is worth while to spend several years in studying him. I should not care to write a book about a philosopher whose system seemed to me entirely out of date, or vitiated by fundamental errors. Such books are not uncommon; but they seldom really elucidate the thought of the author who is so criticised, and the tone of superiority which they assume is unbecoming. A great writer has a message for other times as well as for his own; but in order to bring this out it is by no means incumbent on his modern expositor to observe the same proportions, or the same emphasis, as his author; nor need he be afraid of using modern terms and trains of thought to develop speculations which his author handles only as a pioneer. I know, for example, that the doctrine of reality as a kingdom of values, on which I have laid stress, is not explicit in Plotinus; and that on the other side the Platonic and Aristotelian categories occupy much more space in the Enneads than in my book about them. But I have tried throughout to deal with Neoplatonism as a living and not as a dead philosophy, and to consider what value it has for us in the twentieth century. My own convictions are, of course, derived from many other sources besides the later Greek philosophy, and I may have sometimes read them into my author. But I still think that his real contribution to the never-ending debate about ultimate truth and reality is more likely to be brought out by the method of respectful discipleship than by the criticism of those who have been content to classify the Enneads among other specimens of extinct philosophies, and to place their author, as they hope, on his right shelf in their collection of fossils.

I said in my introductory lecture that I hoped we might find in Plotinus some message of comfort in our present distress. The greater part of my book was written long before the war, and the materials were put together without any direct reference to contemporary problems. It was indeed a pleasure to me to escape from politics and controversies into a purer air. When I began my task, our civilisation was plethoric, congested, dyspeptic. The complacent and sometimes blatant self-confidence of the Victorian Age had given place to wide-spread and growing discontent. The great accumulations of a hundred prosperous years seemed to be only apples of Sodom. Universal covetousness had outstripped the means of gratifying it ; the possessors of wealth were frightened, the less fortunate majority were sour and bitter. The ideas on which the great industrial structure was based were becoming discredited. The thinly veiled materialism of nineteenth century science was tottering under blows dealt from every side, with the result that a coherent though very unsatisfactory philosophy of life had lost its grip, and left nothing in its place but a sentimental irrationalism and scepticism, powerless against the inroads of superstition and the waves of popular emotion. The Government of the country had fallen into a state of the most pitiable imbecility, cowering before every turbulent faction, and attempting to buy off every threat of organised lawlessness. In the midst of great outward prosperity, the symptoms of national disintegration had never been so menacing. Certain idols of the market-place commanded the lip-service of the politician and the journalist ;

but of robust faith and clear vision there was little or none. I now lay down my pen amid more tragic scenes. Civilisation lies prostrate, as a maniac who after burning her house and murdering her children is bleeding to death from self-inflicted wounds, her wealth and credit destroyed, her hopes of reasonable and orderly progress shattered. The parallel between the decay of our social order, the beginning of which I think we are now witnessing, and the economic ruin of the Roman empire in the third, fourth, and fifth centuries seems now even closer than when I wrote my introductory lecture.[1] In particular, the fate of the *curiales*,. the middle class, in the Roman empire is likely to repeat itself in this country. That unfortunate bourgeoisie was saddled with nearly the whole weight of a continually increasing taxation. At last, as Sir Samuel Dill tells us,[2] 'the curial's personal freedom was curtailed on every side. If he travelled abroad, that was an injury to his city ; if he absented himself for five years, his property was confiscated. He could not dispose of his property, which the State regarded as security for the discharge of his financial obligations. The curial in one law is denied the asylum of the Church, along with insolvent debtors and fugitive slaves. When he is recalled from some refuge to which he has escaped, his worst punishment is to be replaced in his original rank. . . . Many fled to a hermitage, others hid themselves among miners and lime-burners.'[3] The money wrung from the taxpayers went partly for wars and the army, partly to a host of officials, and partly in doles to the rabble of the great cities. A fiscal tyranny hardly less galling may be in store for the class

<hr>

[1] Those who think this forecast too unfavourable may be briefly reminded (1) that we have mortgaged our economic future beyond the possibility of redemption ; (2) that fraudulent bankruptcy is no remedy where the social organism rests on credit ; (3) that the conditions which made recovery possible after 1815—cheap labour, thrifty administration, and freedom from foreign competition—are conspicuously absent.

[2] *Roman Society in the Last Century of the Western Empire*, p. 214.

[3] The parallel was drawn out, before the war, by Mr. Flinders Petrie, in his little book called *Janus in Modern Life*.

to which most of us here belong. It will therefore be our wisdom to see what philosophy can do for us in helping us to bear the inevitable.

If we consider, in the light of Platonism, the causes which, at a week's notice, turned Europe into a co-operative suicide club, we are driven to look for some super-individual psychical force, and it is tempting to think of the old hypothesis of an evil World-Soul. On this plausible theory, the race-spirit is an irreclaimable savage dressed in the costume of civilisation, who has remained morally and intellectually [1] on the level of the Stone Age. His acquisitions have been purely external ; his nature has not been changed. Civilised man, we may remind ourselves, when at peace usually devotes that part of his time which is at his own disposal to playing at those occupations which are the serious business of the savage. His games are mock battles ; his sports mock hunting ; his sacred music (a cynic might say) recalls the howls by which the savage tries to attract the attention of his god. But from time to time he grows tired of shams, and craves for the real thing, hot and strong. So Driesch in his Gifford lectures says that 'mankind is always advancing, but man always remains the same.' A biologist might remind us that since there is no natural selection in favour of morally superior types, there is no reason to expect any real progress in the human species.

Now it is quite true that the thought-habits of a hundred thousand years are not likely to have been very much modified by a few centuries of civilisation, interrupted as they have been by the almost unmitigated barbarism of the Dark Ages between Justinian and the twelfth century. But all pessimistic estimates of human nature based on survivals of savage instincts are condemned by the doctrine which Plotinus asserts as strongly

---

[1] It is well established that the brain-capacity of the Neanderthal race, in spite of their ape-like appearance, was as great as that of modern Europeans, while the Cro-Magnon skulls are considerably above the average of any existing race.

as Aristotle, that the ' nature ' of everything is the best
that it can grow into ; and that the best of human
nature is divine.   We have to remember that outbreaks
of moral savagery in civilised humanity are neither
normal not habitual nor the result of a bad will.   They
no longer appear without stimulation ; they are not
consciously willed ; they are now a disease.   On the
other hand, the noble qualities of heroism and self-
sacrifice, which have never been more conspicuous than
in the course of this tragedy, are consciously willed ;
they are essential parts of our human character as it is.
Our complex nature, no doubt, contains elements which
link us to pre-human ancestors ; the transformations of
the embryo before birth, which seem to recapitulate the
whole course of biological evolution, are a proof of that ;
but does it not also contain anticipations of a higher
state than we have yet reached, but which we have a
right to claim as human because we find it manifested in
human beings ?   The ascent of the soul to God, which is
made by thousands in the short span of a single life, may
be an earnest of what humanity shall one day achieve.
Nor is it quite correct to deny all progress within the
historical period.   There are, after all, horrors described
in the Old Testament, in Greek history, in Roman history,
in medieval history, which only the Bolsheviks have
rivalled, and which indicate a degree of depravity which
we may perhaps hope that civilised humanity has out-
grown.   And if there has been perceptible progress in the
last two thousand years, the improvement may be considerable in the next ten thousand, a small fraction,
probably, of the whole life of the species.   The Soul of
the race is no demon, but a child with great possibilities.[1]
It is capable of what it has already achieved in the
noblest human lives, and the character which it has
accepted as the perfect realisation of the human ideal is
the character of Christ.

[1] I have said in the course of these lectures that there is no law of
progress.   But there is no law which forbids progress.

We should also greatly misapprehend the causes of this tragedy if we sought them merely in atavistic instincts. Hobbes enumerates the causes of war as ' competition, distrust, and glory.' We should supplement these with the help of Plato's diagnosis, that a warlike atmosphere indicates disease within the State. In this case a military monarchy, with an admirable scientific organisation for peace as well as war, found itself threatened by intestine troubles. A successful war seemed to its rulers to be the only prophylactic against a democratic revolution, and to be the less of two evils. We know what Plato thought of the rule of the ' stinged drones,' the demagogues ; and we may perhaps understand him— and the Germans—better ten years hence. Our opponents would probably have preferred to keep the advantages of military organisation without another great war. But there is a fatal logic about militarism. A man may build himself a throne of bayonets, but he cannot sit on it ; and he cannot avow that the bayonets are meant to keep his own subjects quiet. So the instrument has to be used ; an occasion for war has to be found ; and the nation has to be sedulously indoctrinated with fanatical patriotism, and hatred or contempt for the alien. Fear and distrust are also artificially stimulated ; and this is easily done. As Bentham said very truly about his own countrymen : ' The dread of being duped by other nations—the notion that foreign heads are more able, though at the same time foreign hearts are less honest than our own, has always been one of our prevailing weaknesses.' Patriotism, once kindled into a flame, has the tremendous power of all spiritual ideas. In our time it connects itself with the idea of *nationality*, producing not only great self-devotion, but inordinate pride, and *esprit de corps* pushed to insanity. The true moral is that ideas are terrible things ; they are stronger than private interest, stronger than reason, stronger than pity, stronger than conscience. In the future we shall see a great conflict between the idea of nationalism and that of internationalism, which divides men differently, by classes, or religions, or types of culture. We shall hear again such tirades as this of Lamartine :

> ' Nations ! Mot pompeux pour dire barbarie !
> L'amour s'arrête t'il où s'arrêtent vos pas ?
> Déchirez ces drapeaux, une autre voix vous crie :
> L'égoisme et la haine ont seuls une patrie ;
> La Fraternité n'en a pas.'

But we shall be sadly deceived if we suppose that internationalism, any more than nationalism, means peace and goodwill.

There is no ground for pessimism about the future of the race, if we take very long views ; and there is every reason to hope that as individuals we are not debarred from the highest life. ' Living one's own life in truth is living the life of all the race,' says Tagore. But we shall need all that religion and philosophy can do for us in the troublous time which certainly awaits us. The Stoic and Pythagorean disciplines will again come into their own. In ancient times a considerable austerity of life was expected from the philosopher, and one of the chief attractions of philosophy was that it made its votary indifferent to most of the things which other men desire. For us, too, to get rid of the superfluous will be the only road to freedom. But it should be a Greek austerity, a beautiful, well-ordered and healthy life, not like the squalor (Cynic, not Neoplatonic) of the Emperor Julian and the Christian monks. The cult of the simple life is difficult only when it is left to a few eccentrics. When it is professed and followed by a whole class, it is easy. It should be based, as it was in antiquity, on a separation of real from factitious wants. As soon as we cease to be afraid of fashion (of δόξα, as the Greeks said), we can cut down superfluities right and left without being any the poorer in comfort or in happiness. The cheerful acceptance, by the richer classes in this country, of the loss of the luxuries and comforts to which they are accustomed, is a good omen for the future. It does not detract from the nobility of their conduct to say that they have found these sacrifices easier to bear than they expected. Our motive must not be the selfish one of making ourselves invulnerable. We have a precious tradition to preserve at all costs—the deposit of truth committed to the Hebrews, the Greeks, and the Romans, which is now threatened by a collapse of authority which may end in barbarism. What the Church did in the Dark Ages, the combined forces of Christianity and humanism must do now. We need a class withdrawn from the competitive life. The struggle for existence, when individual, sharpens a man's faculties and develops his intelligence ; the collective struggle tends to make a man a mere cog in a machine and narrows him to a poorer life. And yet individual competition is only an inchoate stage towards group-competition ; the right to combine is the logical development of *laissez faire ;* the strike, and war, are its fruits. Unrestricted competition, it appears, must end in civil and international war. Group-competition sinks from inanition in the absence of external danger, and the group organised for competition decays rapidly when this stimulus is withdrawn ; on the other hand, when the competition is acute and effective, the competitors destroy each other, or the victor becomes parasitic on the vanquished and at last disappears. Hence the only final integration is a spiritual one, for spiritual movements are non-competitive, and on this plane only is there real community of interests. Moral progress is only possible by the resistance of individuals to herd-instincts, and the resistance itself is a movement of the race-spirit ; there are no really independent thinkers. It is a struggle for self-adaptation to a changing environment. Our task is very much the same as that which was laid on Plotinus and his successors in their day. They also had a precious tradition to preserve ; and, as happens so often in human life, they won their victory through apparent defeat. They resisted Christianity, and were beaten ; but the Church carried off so much of their honey to its own hive that Porphyry himself would have been half satisfied if he had seen the event. For us, the whole heritage of the past is at stake together ; we cannot preserve Platonism without Christianity, nor Christianity without Platonism, nor civilisation without both.

Neoplatonism differs from popular Christianity in that it offers us a religion the truth of which is not contingent on any particular events, whether past or future. It floats free of nearly all the ' religious difficulties ' which have troubled the minds of believers since the age of science began. It is dependent on no miracles, on no unique revelation through any historical person, on no narratives about the beginning of the world, on no prophecies of its end. No scientific or historical discovery can refute it, and it requires no apologetic except the testimony of spiritual experience. There is a Christian philosophy of which the same might be said. There are Christians who believe in the divinity of Christ because they have known Him as an indwelling Divine Spirit ; who believe that He rose because they have felt that He has risen ; who believe that He will judge the world because He is already the judge of their own lives. Such independence of particular historical events, some of which are supported by insufficient evidence, gives great strength and confidence to the believer. But it does not satisfy those who crave for miracle as a bridge between the eternal and temporal worlds, and who are not happy unless they can intercalate ' acts of God ' into what seems to them the soulless mechanism of nature Christianity, however, is essentially a struggle for an independent spiritual life, and it can only exert its true influence in the world when it realises that spiritual things are spiritually discerned, and when it stands on its own foundations, without those extraneous supports which begin by strengthening a religion and end by strangling it.

In most other respects the two systems are closely allied. Neoplatonism, like Christianity, gives us a clear and definite standard of values, absolute and eternal. What this standard is has, I hope, been sufficiently shown by quotations in these lectures. It may be objected that Plotinus gives us only principles and outlines, without imparting much help in concrete problems, such as the choice of a profession, the use of money, and the political duties of a citizen. The same criticism might be, and has been, brought against the ethics of the New Testament. But the man who studies Plotinus as a moral guide will not often be at a loss except in problems which it is not the province of religion or philosophy to solve. The vitally important thing is that we should believe in Goodness, Truth, and Beauty as Divine and absolute principles, the source and goal of the whole cosmic process, and not as imaginings of the human mind, or ideal values which have no existence.[1]

Closely connected with this faith in absolute values is that conception of eternal life which has been discussed, perhaps at disproportionate length, in these lectures. I know that some of my hearers and readers will probably think that I have been too ready to separate immortality from the quality of duration, and to sink individuality in the all-embracing life of soul and spirit. As regards the first, I agree that our accepted methods of moral valuation assume that duration has a meaning and value for the life of spirit. We prefer what we call the higher goods partly because we find that they are the most durable ; and the idea of teleology is inseparable from that of value. Persistence, as I have said, seems to be the time-form of eternity, and progress the time-expression of the Divine goodness. With regard to our individuality,

---

[1] Mr. Clutton Brock's new book (1918), *Studies in Christianity*, is excellent on this subject. He shows that for a Christian ' absolute value ' and ' love ' are the same thing.

Plotinus would not object to the statement that Spirit is individual in each of us, because it is potentially *all* in each of us. To deny the individuality of Spirit would be to believe in νοητά without νοῦς ; and we are often warned in the Enneads against supposing that the Great Spirit, or the Universal Soul, is split up among individual spirits or souls. The ' offspring ' of Spirit is not fragmentary spirit-life, but souls living in worlds half-realised. In ethics, the sense of guilt is the awful guardian of our personal identity, but the sense of forgiveness is the blessed assurance that we are sharers in a higher personality than the self that sins. The great difficulty, how to account for individuation, is lessened when we think of the individual focus as potentially all-embracing. We are limited, not so much because we are distinct individuals as because we are half-baked souls. The perfect man. would not be less perfect because he lived in a particular century and country. A broad mind is not cramped by a narrow sphere. We should not be wiser if we lived in a dozen scattered bodies. It seems to me that when Bradley finds finite centres ' inexplicable,' and when he is driven to say that ' the plurality of souls is appearance and their existence is not genuine,' his difficulty is caused by his theory that the Absolute ' divides itself into centres,' which is surely impossible.[1] The notion that all individuals are (as it were) shaken up together in a bag, the Absolute, thus neutralising each other's defects, seems very crude. Plotinus, I venture to think, navigates successfully the narrow channel between these rocks and the opposite error of pluralism. The soul needs real *otherness* ; else there could be no love, and no worship ; but it needs also real identity, and for the same reason.

Neoplatonism respects science, and every other activity of human reason. Its idealism is rational and sane throughout. The supremacy of the reason is a favourite theme of the Cambridge Platonists of the seventeenth

---

[1] cf. Pringle-Pattison, *The Idea of God*, p. 287, who comments on the similar treatment of the problem by Lotze and Bosanquet.

century, who had drunk deep of the Neoplatonic spirit.
' Sir, I oppose not rational to spiritual,' writes Whichcote
to Tuckney, ' for spiritual is most rational.'   And again,
' Reason is the Divine governor of man's life ; it is the
very voice of God.' [1]   The difference between this reverence for man's intellectual endowments, which always
characterises true Platonism, and the sentimental,
superstitious emotionalism of popular ' mysticism ' is
much more than a difference of temperament.   It is
because he is in rebellion against nature and its laws, or
because he is too ignorant or indolent to think, that the
emotionalist flies to the supernatural and the occult.
Very different is the Platonic spirit, which breathes in
such acts of devotion as this of Wordsworth :

> ' Wisdom and Spirit of the Universe !
> Thou Soul, that art the eternity of thought !
> And givest to forms and images a breath
> And everlasting motion ! not in vain,
> By day or starlight, thus from my first dawn
> Of childhood didst thou intertwine for me
> The passions that build up our human soul,
> Not with the mean and vulgar works of man,
> But with high objects, with enduring things,
> With life and nature, purifying thus
> The elements of feeling and of thought,
> And sanctifying by such discipline
> Both pain and fear.'

But while reverencing the natural order as the *modus
operandi* of the Universal Soul, Neoplatonism asserts consistently that the world as seen by the spiritual man is a
very different world from that which is seen by the carnal
man.   Spiritual things are spiritually discerned ; and
the whole world, to him who can see it as it is, is irradiated
by Spirit.   A sober trust in religious experience, when
that experience has been earned, is an essential factor in
Platonic faith.   Our vision is clarified by the conquest of
fleshly lusts, by steady concentration of the thoughts,
will, and affections on things that are good and true and
lovely ; by disinterestedness, which thinks of no reward,

[1] See my *Christian Mysticism*, p. 20.

and by that progressive unification of our nature which in the Gospels is called the single eye. ' It is everywhere the whole mind,' says Lotze, ' at once thinking, feeling, and passing moral judgments, which out of the full completeness of its nature produces in us these unspoken first principles.' Julian of Norwich says the same thing in simpler and nobler words : ' Our faith cometh of the natural love of the soul, and of the clear light of our reason, and of the steadfast mind which we have of God in our first making.'[1] There are three avenues to the knowledge of God and of the world and of ourselves— purposive action, reasoning thought, and loving affection, a threefold cord which is not quickly broken. To quote Wordsworth again :

> ' We live by admiration, hope, and love,
>   And even as these are well and wisely fixed,
>   In dignity of being we ascend.'

So the whole of Platonism, on its religious side, may be summed up in the beatitude, ' Blessed are the pure in heart, for they shall see God.' For, in the words of Smith, the Cambridge Platonist, ' Such as men themselves are, such will God appear to them to be.'

If we see things as they are, we shall live as we ought ; and if we live as we ought, we shall see things as they are. This is not a vicious circle, but the interplay of contemplation and action, of θεωρία and πρᾶξις, in which wisdom consists. Action is the ritual of contemplation, as the dialectic is its creed. The conduct of life rests on an act of faith, which begins as an experiment, and ends as an experience. Platonism affirms, no doubt, a very deep optimism ; it claims that the venture of faith is more than justified ; but has anyone who has tried it left on record that the experiment has failed ?

Nevertheless, it is the extreme optimism of the Neoplatonic creed which gives us pause. Are there not certain stubborn facts in life, facts more than ever

---

[1] See my *Personal Idealism and Mysticism*, p. 4.

apparent just now, for which it fails to account ? Would a perfectly good and wise man see the world we live in as it is and pronounce that ' it is very good ' ? Would he not, in proportion to the clearness of his vision of what the world ought to be, be filled with grief, pity, and indignation at what it is ? The brave man may conquer his own fears, and make light of his own misfortunes ; but ought he, like the Stoic sage, to practise benevolence without pity, acquiescence in inevitable evil without revolt, and to love the Lord without hating the thing that is evil ?

Plato recognised that we cannot get rid of moral evil without pain. But how slight is the emphasis, and how little he grasps the law of vicarious suffering ! The Cross is 'foolishness to the Greeks,' as St. Paul says. And yet the place which Plotinus gives to Love should have carried him all the way. If the vision of the Godhead is reserved for the ' spirit in love,' it follows from the principles of this philosophy that God is love ; for we can only see what we are. But if God is love, He must ' declare His almighty power most chiefly in showing mercy and pity ' ; He must reveal Himself most fully in the supreme activity of love, that is, self-sacrifice. If this is admitted, it follows that the most inalienable and distinctive attribute of Divinity is no longer deathlessness, or unlimited power, or freedom from inner perturbation ; it is sympathy, and willingness to suffer for others. If this is the character of the Deity, it must be our ideal, for, as Plotinus says, ' our aim is not to be without sin, but to be what God is.' Suffering must be either accepted or shirked by every man in a world where 'truth's for ever on the scaffold, wrong for ever on the throne.'[1] We have seen that other religions besides Christianity worshipped a suffering and even a dying God ; but the Neoplatonist would, I fear, have shrunk from such a doctrine with horror, or dismissed it with contempt. It would have seemed to undo all the work of deliverance which his philosophy had built up for him, and to plunge him

[1] Lowell.

back into the slough of despond, the morass of pleasures and pains. How can a perfectly good man, much more a God, feel pain and grief ? Is he unable to control these emotions, or is he dissatisfied with the inevitable operations of nature, which the sage accepts as preordained ? Can a Divine creator be dissatisfied with his own work, and submit to martyrdom in order to undo the evil which his own laws have indirectly caused ?

And yet until we accept the doctrine that vicarious suffering, that scandal of the moral world on the theory of individualism, is Divine, the sting of the world's evil remains undrawn. ' Vicarious suffering,' I have said elsewhere,[1] ' which on the individualist theory seems so monstrous and unjust as to throw a shadow on the character of God, is easy to understand if we give up our individualism. It is a necessity. For the sinner cannot suffer for his own healing, precisely because he is a sinner. The trouble which he brings on himself cannot heal his wounds. Redemption must be vicarious ; it must be wrought by the suffering of the just for the unjust.' Irenæus says that Christ, ' for His immense love towards us, was made what we are, that He might make us what He is.' Plotinus, as we have seen, insists that no man may deliver his brother, and there is, of course, a sense in which this is true ; but it seems to me that he fails to apply his doctrine of the unity and solidarity of soul-life exactly where it might be most fruitful.

Love and suffering cut the deepest channels in our souls, and reveal the most precious of God's secrets. Even in national life we can see that the characteristic utterances of ages of prosperity—the Augustan Ages of history— are less penetrating and of less universal significance than those which have been wrung from nations in agony. The uses of chastisement have been often celebrated. Plato in the *Gorgias* argues that it is a misfortune to escape punishment, when we have deserved it ; Augustine says, ' *Nulla poena, quanta poena !* ' But the journey

[1] *Personal Idealism and Mysticism*, p. 178.

which brings at last both wisdom and salvation is not a
sad one. ' Hard and rugged is the path of virtue,' says
Hesiod, ' at first ; but when one comes to the top, it is
easy, though it be hard.'

The philosophy which holds that we are independent
and impervious monads, *solida pollentia simplicitate*,
makes it so utterly impossible to find justice in the world,
that some of our pluralists have fallen back on the old
theory of a limited, struggling God, who does his best to
overcome insuperable obstacles. This dualism corresponds to the attitude of the pure moralist, who is occupied in combating evil without trying to account for it ;
but it is intolerable both for philosophy and for religion.
Platonism and Christianity prefer to reject individualism.
No injustice is done in the real world, because the individual who is the subject of claims is an abstraction, and
the real self, the soul, is willing, for a time, to bear the
sins and sorrows of others. In the language of Christianity, the good man is willing to ' fill up, for his part,
what was lacking in the afflictions of Christ for his Body's
sake, the Church.' And the sacrifice is effectual ; the
redemption is won. Evil, which can never be overcome
by evil, can be overcome by good. The Christian doctrine that if one soul has triumphed completely in this
combat, all share in the victory, is quite intelligible on
Neoplatonic principles, in spite of the sentence in the
Enneads which seems to glance at the doctrine in a
hostile manner.[1] It is not intelligible to a modern
individualist, nor can it be defended by changing it, as
Western theology has often done, into a forensic trans-
action.

Humanity needs martyrs. Plotinus says that it does
not much matter if the good are killed by the bad, for it
only means that the actors change their masks ; the
good man does not really die. But this is a kind of

---

[1] Compare the remarkable lines of Sophocles :

ἀρκεῖν γὰρ οἶμαι κἀντὶ μυρίων μίαν
ψυχὴν τάδ' ἐκτίνουσαν, ἢν εὔνους παρῇ.—*O. C.* 498.

docetism.   It cheapens the sacrifice, which only the heroic victim has the right to do.   Our dying soldiers may say and feel,

> ' Nil igitur mors est ad nos, neque pertinet hilum ' ;

but *we* must not say it for them.[1]   The evils wrought by sin in the world are not imaginary.   We are only justified in hoping that they are the symptoms by which the disease may work itself out.   The disease is the selfishness, stupidity, and moral ugliness which obstruct the manifestation in the world of the Divine attributes of goodness, wisdom, and beauty.   The symptoms are the suffering through which these evils are recognised as evil.   The fact of suffering is not an evil but a good, since it is the chief means of progress, of which it implies the possibility. A common error in our day is horror at the symptoms and neglect of the disease.

There were many before the war who wished to be Christians without the Cross ; there are still some, but they are fewer.   The soldier and the soldier's family have learnt the lesson without difficulty ; those who have used the war to increase their own wages or profits have yet to learn it.   The jealous determination not to put into the common stock a pennyworth more than we are allowed to take out of it has embittered modern life more than any economic inequalities.

Human happiness depends on the ratio between the *human costs* of living and the return which we get for them ; and human costs are very different from work and wages.   They are determined by our standard of values.   Who are the happiest people, so far as we can judge ?   I should say, the real Christians, whose affections are set on things above ; whose citizenship is in heaven ; whose thoughts are occupied with things that are pure, noble, and of good report ; who believe that all things work together for good to those who love God ;

---

[1] Plotinus himself says that the indifference of the soldier to death is a proof that the Soul knows itself to be indestructible.   This, I think, is true.

and whose labour is costless to themselves, because it is a labour of love. Next to these, the happiest are those whose lives are devoted to some great super-personal interest, such as science, art, literature, or philosophy. And thirdly, those who, without any clear vision, follow duty as the ' stern daughter of the voice of God,' and strive to ' live ever in their great Taskmaster's eye.' And who are the most unhappy ? The selfish, especially the envious, the grasping, and the fearful. These are the men whose work, whether well paid or ill, costs them most ; and no social readjustments can satisfy them, because such desires are, as Plato says, insatiable and incapable of being gratified. Envy especially is a passion to which no pleasure is attached. Unhappy also are they who worship the various idols of the market-place, the fetishes of herd-morality. In proportion as their devotion is sincere, they must feel the bitterness of disappointment ; where it is insincere, they become, Plotinus might say, like the parrots and monkeys whom they imitate.

Neglect of these truths has thrown our whole view of life out of perspective, and it is more distorted now than in times which it is fashionable to despise. The Puritan idea was that productive work is the best service of God, the task for which we were sent into the world, to prepare ourselves for the repose of eternity. By attributing a sacramental virtue to secular labour they made a real ethical advance ; for this is what we miss in Platonism and Catholicism. But Puritanism was incapable of intelligent self-criticism ; and in practice it led to a vast accumulation of money and commodities without any wisdom in using them. Protestant civilisation has in consequence been ugly and tasteless, and all classes alike have been weighed down by the supposed necessity of satisfying wants which in reality had no existence. In defect of any rational standard of good, a merely quantitative valuation took its place. The success of a nation was measured by its statistics of trade and population, the

success of a man by the number of pounds sterling that
he was ' worth.' Our litanies were tables of figures ; the
word ' expansion ' stirred in us a luscious sense of pride.
But though the Puritan ethics were unintelligent, they
were not entirely out of touch with the laws of nature,
like some of the fetishes which we now delight to honour.
There has never been a time when the ruinous error that
we can revoke the laws of nature by ignoring them has
been more prevalent than in modern social politics.
' Science,' it has been wisely said,[1] ' is not the handmaid
but the purgatory of religion '—and of politics. A bad
philosophy leaves us in such a cruel world that we dare
not look the facts in the face. This is the origin of
sentimentalism, ultimately the most merciless of all
moods. The dethronement of these modern idols is one of
the greatest services which a sound philosophy can render
to humanity.

But how shall we bring our criticism of life to bear on
the chaotic mass of prejudice, sentimentalism, and
cupidity which goes by the name of public opinion ?
Plotinus will tell us that if we want to help others, we
must testify that which we have *seen*. No one needs
more than the Platonist to ' make his life a true poem,'
for in his philosophy moral effort and moral experience
supply the materials for spiritual intuition and creation.
The ' civic virtues,' as we have seen, must be practised, but
as a kind of symbol or sacrament of the eternal order. The
philosopher, Plato thinks, will not willingly take part in the
politics of his city, but will live as a citizen of ' his own
country, of which a type is laid up in heaven.' Opinions
may differ as to how far Plato's good man can mix in
politics at the present time ; but unless the philosopher
thinks often and earnestly how he may help to build a city
of God on earth, he is likely to miss his way to the heavenly
city. It would be a worthy and fruitful task to try to
work out some of the problems of human society in the

[1] By the late A. C. Turner, Fellow of Trinity, Cambridge, on the
Roll of Honour in this war.

light of Christian Platonism.   The difficulty of finding a
decent form of civil government has hitherto baffled
human ingenuity.   This unsolved problem has been and
still is the deepest tragedy of history.   Nation after nation
fails to answer the riddle of the Sphinx, and is hurled
down or torn in pieces.   The strength and weakness of
military monarchies have been summarised in this
lecture ; and we must add the probability that the
monarch may be a fool or a knave.   Readers of the
Republic will know where to look for a true character
of democracy.   Theocracy, which in theory should be
the best of all governments, is in practice one of the
worst, since, except in brief periods of spiritual exaltation, the priesthood has no physical force behind it, and
must rely on superstition and bigotry, which accordingly
have to be stimulated by keeping the nation in ignorance
and intellectual servitude.   The problem of the reformer
is complicated by the fact that we must accept the heavy
burdens of the past.   The wisest man can only achieve
an application of the living past to the living present.
Plotinus, as we have seen, expresses no preference for
one form of government over another.   His remedy for
all social evils is to suppress the lusts that war in our
members, and to correct our standard of values, remembering that we make our own world, by the reaction of
our Soul upon its environment, and of the environment
upon our Soul.   Many of our discontents are externalised
soul-aches.   By brooding over them we hurt our Souls
and immerse them in ' Matter.'   A restoration of internal
and external peace is possible only when we rise to the
vision of the real, the spiritual world.   When we consider
the achievements of any nation which even for fifty
years has grasped a fringe of the mantle of God, we shall
not think that Christ, or Plato, is bidding us to lose
substance for shadow.   The Soul of the race mocks at
the triumphs of Sennacherib and Attila.   They, and
Cleon, are only remembered because their victims have
thought it worth while to hold them up to infamy. Human

societies are happy in proportion as they have their treasure in that class of goods which are not lessened by being shared. As Proclus says, ' Goods that are indivisible are those which many may possess at once, and no one is worse off in respect of them because another has them. Divisible goods are those in which one man's gain is another man's loss.' [1] This is after all the truth which the philosopher and the minister of religion must preach incessantly ; for *numquam nimis dicitur quod numquam satis discitur.* Neither those who bow before the Crucified nor those who venerate the hero of the *Phaedo* can have any dealings with the men who wish to make the Christian Church the jackal of any dominant political party. Such movements are always with us. They fill chapters in the history of ecclesiasticism, but they have no connexion with either religion or philosophy.

Is there any marked difference in the upward path, as traced by the Platonic mystic, and other schemes which have gained wide acceptance ? The essence of Neoplatonic mysticism is the belief that the Soul, which lives here in self-contradiction, must break in succession every form in which it tends to crystallise. This is where it differs most from Catholicism, as generally taught. Catholicism promises peace as the immediate result of submission and obedience, and even Catholics of Newman's calibre have recorded that their spiritual journeys were ' of course ' over, and their mental histories at an end, when they came to rest in the Catholic fold.[2] But for the mystic there is no halting-place, no rest from striving to see what he cannot yet see, and to become what as yet he is not. To stop short anywhere is to leave the quest unfinished. Cases of arrested development are the rule, not the exception. The world arrests most of us ;

[1] Proclus, *in Alcib.*, p. 439.
[2] I do not, of course, mean that the Catholic ' counts himself to have apprehended ' before his probation is over. But the search for truth is not put before him as an abiding motive. I do not think that he has, *qua* Catholic, much sympathy with Clement, who held that if the saint were offered the choice between the possession of truth and the search for it, he would without hesitation choose the latter.

the Church others. Some are now arrested by ' the social state,' which (says Tarde) ' is, like the hypnotic state, only a form of dream.' So a supra-social philosophy is often called unsocial ; Plotinus, like other mystics, has incurred this censure. To the Platonists, all earthly forms of association are at best adumbrations of a true society ; he cannot give himself entirely to any of them. He must expect to outgrow many early enthusiasms before the end of his course. For this life is a ' *schola animarum*,' as Origen said ; and we are learners to the end. The future is hidden from us ; but through the darkness the light of heaven burns steadily before us ; and we know that ' yonder,' amid the eternal ideas of Truth, Goodness, and Beauty, is our birth-place and our final home.

> ' Si nôtre vie est moins qu'une journée
> En l'éternel ; si l'an qui fait le tour
> Chasse nos jours sans espoir de retour ;
> Si périssable est toute chose née ;
> Que songes-tu, mon âme emprisonnée ?
> Pourquoi te plaît l'obscur de notre jour,
> Si, pour voler en un plus clair séjour,
> Tu as au dos l'aile bien empennée ?
> Là est le bien que tout esprit désire,
> Là le repos où tout le monde aspire,
> Là est l'amour, là le plaisir encore !
> Là, ô mon âme, au plus haut ciel guidée
> Tu y pourras reconnaître l'idée
> De la beauté qu'en ce monde j'adore.' [1]

[1] Du Bellay.

ADDENDA

VOL. I

Page 76. Proclus quotes with approval the saying of Iamblichus, that the whole theoretical philosophy of Plato is to be found in the *Timaeus* and *Parmenides*.

Page 86. The word metempsychosis, though it does not accurately describe the Neoplatonic doctrine of rebirth, is not, as is sometimes asserted, a modern coinage. It occurs first (I think) in Proclus, in his commentary on Plato's Republic (Vol. II, p. 340, Kroll's edition).

Page 145. In one isolated passage (in *Timaeum*, 147) Proclus throws out an interesting suggestion to account for some of the ugliness and evil of the world. He says that ' the *laughter* of the gods gives substance to the contents of the world.' It is the myth of Ares and Aphrodite surprised by Hephæstus which suggests this theory to him ; but I have often thought that we may be wrong in not admitting a sense of humour in the Creator. The absence of this sense is accounted a defect in a human character ; and there are some animals, such as the mandrill, the hippopotamus, and the skunk, which surely can only have been made for a joke. We may have the same suspicion about some members of our own species. If this is so, the laughing philosophers may be nearer the truth than their always solemn rivals, and we may allow ourselves to smile at some misadventures which worry the pure moralist.

Page 152. Can we divide the imperfections of our view of the world into two classes—(1) those which proceed from error, failure, ignorance in ourselves, (2) those which proceed from the fact that as self-conscious units we are *involved* in the process of working out a Divine idea ? We should not even wish to reach the goal without traversing the course, and while so employed we are subject to psychic, not noëtic conditions. Thus we must accept time, space, and evil as realities for us, though we know that they are not so for Spirit. The fact that for us Soul is tethered, as it were, to a particular human life shows that the Universal Soul is not conscious in us. Our individual souls are teleological units, each working out some creative thought. ' We,' are that creative thought objectified. (The self-conscious ' I ' is much less than this.) This limitation then must be accepted as necessary in this life ; we look to a more ' glorious liberty ' when our task is done.

Page 174. Teleology really needs no proof ; it is almost a necessity of thought, an universal postulate. It is the time-form of value, and without valuation there can be no thinking. We should ask ourselves why ' All's well that ends well ' is an accepted proverb, and ' All's well that begins well ' an absurdity. Why do we say, ' Respice finem,' and ' Call no man happy before he dies ' ? It is not because time acquires more value as it goes on ; it is because every process has a meaning, and the whole is stultified by final failure.

Page 177. On continuity or evolution. Damascius, one of the later disciples of Plotinus, has an exceedingly interesting passage on this subject (*De Principiis* §112), in which he says that all movement is discontinuous, and progresses ' by leaps ' (κατὰ ἅλματα). This sounds like an anticipation of the modern doctrine (De Vries, &c.) of evolution by mutations, not by almost imperceptible modifications ; and still more, perhaps, like the yet more modern Quantum theory ; but it has a metaphysical importance, as asserting that even the slightest real change breaks continuity. It disposes of mechanical causation. So Leibnitz says, ' Le principe de continuité est chez moi ' ; it is psychic or spiritual. Materialism, if consistent with itself, is atomism ; the essence of it (including all monad-ism) is disconnexion. So Mr. Bertrand Russell has said that ' all monism must be pantheistic, all monadism atheistic.' Atomism, no less than materialism, was an object of Plotinus' polemic. It is inconsistent not only with any spiritual philosophy, but with any doctrine of evolution. Darwinism, properly understood, does not naturalise man ; it spirtualises nature ; it is a doctrine of final causes. ' Origins ' and ' Finalism ' are obviously the same road viewed from the two ends. Nineteenth-century naturalism was a revolt against the *ignava ratio* of supernaturalism. But neo-vitalism is in danger of re-introducing the dualism ; or perhaps it shows that we have not yet explained the dualism in experience, out of which it grows. Driesch, for example, sets life and mechanism against each other, and speaks of ' temporary suspensions,' which are too much like miracles. Tyndall, in his famous address (1874) was accused of materialistic atheism because he found in Matter ' the promise and potency of all life.' But this is objectionable only if we identify Matter with ponderable stuff.

Page 210. Our ideals are the Logoi which shape our lives from within.

Page 216. Krause, like Plotinus, holds that the fellowship of higher and lower is immediate and direct ; between beings on the same plane it is mediate and in-direct. We know each other only through God.

Page 228. I ought to have said that some ancient thinkers appear to have given a more exalted place to φαντασία. Proclus, on Plato's *Republic* (p. 107), says that ' some of the ancients identify φαντασία with νοῦς, while others distinguish them, but say that there is no ἀφάνταστος νόησις.' I confess that this statement surprises me, and I do not know who the ' some ' were. Proclus says that there is a double νοῦς, one ' that which we are ' ; the other ' that which we put on.' The latter is ' the imaginative νοῦς,' before which ' the dæmons who preside over nature ' place myths and ritual and religious symbols of all kinds, in which the imaginative νοῦς finds delight. The myths are not true in the literal sense, but they keep the Soul in contact with truth. So the imagination is a veritable revealer of Divine things. He adds the very remarkable complaint that when the ancient mysteries and myths were believed in, ' all the space round the earth was full of all kinds of goods, which the gods give to men, whereas now, without them, all is lifeless and cut off from the light of heaven.' Proclus craved for something like the Catholicism which we know. ' Epaississez-moi la religion,' said Madame de Sévigné, ' dans la crainte qu'elle s'évapore.' Elsewhere Proclus says that imagination is νοῦς τις παθητικός, hindered in its internal activity by the fall into Matter.

Page 234. The passage on δόξα, at the end of Book 5 of Plato's *Republic*, is often ridiculed, but it is one of the keys of Platonism. ' Opinion ' has as its subject-matter neither full reality nor the completely unreal, but a field partly real and partly unreal. Degrees of reality are absurd only if we divorce reality from value, which cannot be done.

Page 245. ' *My* Soul.' Dr. L. P. Jacks, in his brilliant essay called ' The Universe as Philosopher,' says very truly that we seem unable even to think except in terms of proprietorship. It is very different in the East. For us, riches are not so much the cause of our forgetting God, as the form under which we try to remember Him. God is the proprietor of the world. So too a man ' has ' a Soul, an experience, a personality. ' Who is the owner of these job-lots ? ' He is behind the scenes, not to be found. Why again does a man talk of ' my religion,' ' my philosophy,' but never of ' my science ' ? The possessive case is an obsession with Western thinkers.

Page 253. The harmony achieved by the Will is for ever finite and incomplete. Will is the principle of becoming, become self-conscious.

VOL. II

Page 38. Professor Taylor has suggested to me that 'understanding' would be the best equivalent for νόησις. Coleridge, as is well known, chose the word to render *Verstand*, a lower faculty than *Vernunft* ; but it might be restored to its proper dignity.

Page 87. The reference is to a fanciful derivation (from the *Cratylus*) of Κρόνος from κόρος and νοῦς.

Page 103. Mr. Bosanquet's words, that reliance on the future has become a disease, may be illustrated by a passage in Carlyle's ' Past and Present ' (Book 3, chapter 14). ' Ils s'en appelaient à . . .' ' A la posterité ? ' ' Ah, Monsieur, non, mille fois non l They appealed to the Eternal God ; not to posterity at all l C'était différent.'

Page 105. Dialectic is the logic of religion which always leads us beyond our premisses. And compare Bradley, *Logic*, Book 3, Part 1, chap. 2. ' The idea that this is a sort of experiment with conceptions in vacuo is a caricature. . . . The opposition between the real, in that fragmentary character in which the mind possesses it, and the true reality felt within the mind, is the moving cause of the unrest which sets up the dialectic process. . . . The process goes on till the mind, therein implicit, finds a product which answers its unconscious idea ; and here, having become in its own entirety a datum to itself, it rests in the activity which is self-conscious in its object.'

Page 113. Bradley's ' absolute experience ' corresponds closely to Plotinus' ἀθρόα ἐπιβολή.

Page 146. The ' Spirit in love ' is not in a state of passive emotion. Proclus says, ὁ μὲν θεῖος ἔρως ἐνέργειά ἐστιν, just as Spinoza says, ' Mentis amor intellectualis erga Deum actio est.'

Page 170. The idealist who is not something of an ascetic is generally a dilettante or a self-deceiver.

Page 192. It appears sometimes as if Plotinus were oblivious of those social organisms which come between the individual and the universal Soul. Proclus cannot be charged with this defect. In his treatise *De Decem Dubitationibus*, which only survives in a medieval Latin translation, he says : ' Omnis civitas et omne genus unum quodque animal est maiori modo quam hominum unus quisque, et immortalius et sanctius.'

Page 198. The later Neoplatonists believed in an order of ' angels,' superior to the dæmons, who operate on the plane of νοῦς, as the dæmons on that of ψυχή. The angels are specially commissioned to liberate the Soul from Matter. Proclus even argues that Plato knew of the angels, so that the belief in them is not derived from ' barbarous ' (i.e. Christian) sources. See references in the index to Kroll's edition of Proclus on the *Republic*. There are several passages in Proclus where πνεύματα and δαίμονες seem to be identical.

Page 214. The *Sublime* is the symbol of abstract Will ; it suggests to us contending forces held in check by mighty power. This impression is often conveyed by inorganic masses, which are prevented from being merely beautiful by an element of τὸ ἄπειρον.

Page 216. The later Neoplatonists rebelled against Plato's disparagement of art and poetry. Proclus says that Plato is himself as true a poet as Hómer, and that he would certainly have been turned out of his own Republic.

Page 227. I agree with the concluding words of Dr. A. J. Hubbard's thoughtful book, *The Fate of Empires*. ' That which is temporal is never an end in itself, but becomes only the means of expressing the cosmocentric purpose of our lives. Thus a true and stable civilisation can never be more than a by-product of religion. It is to be attained by those alone by whom it is not sought : and we see that in the long run the world belongs to the unworldly ; that in the end empire is to those to whom empire is nothing ; and we remember with a sense of awe the most astonishing of the Beatitudes : Blessed are the meek, for they shall inherit the earth.' Dr. Hubbard's main thesis is the view which is also taken by Mr. Whittaker (*The Neoplatonists*, p. 269), that in human history ' the choice has been between Egyptian or Byzantine [or Chinese] fixity on the one hand, and movement through upheavals and submergences on the other.'

Page 237. I am more and more convinced that Christianity as a religious philosophy is a development from the later Platonism, which contains Aristotelian and Stoical elements. Calvinism is simply baptised Stoicism, and accordingly it has a place, though not very securely, within Christianity. Mr. E. V. Arnold, in his able book *Roman Stoicism*, emphasises (I think rather too much) the Stoical element, especially in St. Paul. But it is difficult to separate Latin Stoicism and Latin Platonism. The adoption of the Stoical πνεῦμα for νοῦς by the Christians is certainly significant. The creed of many modern scientists has affinities to Stoicism and Calvinism. Other philosophies, such as Epicureanism, Indian pantheism, Persian dualism, modern pluralism, agnosticism, seem to me to resist any attempt to Christianise them. It would clarify our ideas about Christianity if we recognised that it is based on a definite view of the world, which is not universally accepted, but which forms the basis not only of a religion but of the greatest of all philosophies. We should then be able to discriminate between the vital part of Christianity and the superstructure which belongs to the history of ecclesiasticism rather than of religion. The all-important modification of Platonism which we owe to Christ Himself has, I hope, been emphasised sufficiently in these lectures.

INDEX